Transitional Justice

and the Rule of Law

in New Democracies

Kwan S. Kim and David F. Ruccio, eds.
Debt and Development in Latin America (1985)

Scott Mainwaring and Alexander Wilde, eds.
The Progressive Church in Latin America (1989)

Bruce Nichols and Gil Loescher, eds.
The Moral Nation: Humanitarianism and U.S. Foreign Policy Today (1989)

Edward L. Cleary, O.P., ed.
Born of the Poor: The Latin American Church since Medellín (1990)

Roberto DaMatta
Carnivals, Rogues, and Heroes: An Interpretation of the Brazilian Dilemma (1991)

Antonio Kandir
The Dynamics of Inflation (1991)

Luis E. González
Political Structures and Democracy in Uruguay (1991)

Scott Mainwaring, Guillermo O'Donnell, and J. Samuel Valenzuela, eds.
Issues in Democratic Consolidation: The New South American Democracies in Comparative Perspective (1992)

Roberto Bouzas and Jaime Ros, eds.
Economic Integration in the Western Hemisphere (1994)

Mark P. Jones
Electoral Laws and the Survival of Presidential Democracies (1995)

Dimitri Sotiropolous
Populism and Bureaucracy: The Case of Greece under PASOK, 1981–1989 (1996)

Peter Lester Reich
Mexico's Hidden Revolution: The Catholic Church in Law and Politics since 1925 (1996)

Michael Fleet and Brian Smith, eds.
The Catholic Church and Democracy in Chile and Peru (1997)

A. James McAdams
Transitional Justice and the Rule of Law in New Democracies (1997)

Transitional Justice and the Rule of Law in New Democracies

EDITED BY

A. JAMES McADAMS

To Dan

In memory of great times at Notre Dame

Tim

Notre Dame
April 13, 11

UNIVERSITY OF NOTRE DAME PRESS

NOTRE DAME AND LONDON

© Copyright 1997 by
University of Notre Dame Press
Notre Dame, IN 46556
All rights reserved.
Manufactured in the United States of America
Book design by Will H. Powers
Set in Palatino and Syntax type by Stanton Publication Services, Inc.,
St. Paul, Minnesota.

Library of Congress Cataloging-in-Publication Data
Transitional justice and the rule of law in new democracies / edited
    by A. James McAdams.
        p.   cm. — (A title from the Helen Kellogg Institute for
    International Studies).
    Includes bibliographical references and index.
    ISBN 0-268-04202-0 (cloth : alk. paper). — ISBN 0-268-04203-9
    (paper : alk. paper)
    1. Rule of law.   2. Crimes against humanity.   3. Justice.
    I. McAdams, A. James.   II. Series.
    K3171.T73   1997
    340'.11—dc21   97-5313
                                                                        CIP

∞ The paper used in this publication meets the minimum requirements of
the American National Standard for Information Sciences—Permanence
of Paper for Printed Library Materials, ANSI Z39.48-1984.

Dedicated to Rev. William M. Lewers, C.S.C.,
who knows what it means to do justice,
love tenderly,
and walk humbly with God.

Contents

Preface

IT IS NOT SURPRISING that new democracies have frequently become engulfed in controversy when they have sought to bring their former dictators to trial. Due to long-standing legacies of oppression and injustice, passions are deeply rooted, and the stakes of any decision are high for perpetrators and victims alike. Moreover, it says something about the uncertain legal terrain on which these regimes have acted over the last few decades that we are still far from reaching a consensus about either the utility or the advisability of using national courts as instruments to right the wrongs of the past.

On the one hand, it is easy to sympathize with the compelling arguments that have been made on moral grounds in support of accountability trials. A half century after the convening of the international tribunals at Nuremberg and Tokyo, the advocates of trials contend, states can no longer afford to be indifferent to the plight of the victims of despotic regimes. As Justice Robert Jackson elegantly stated in his oft-cited opening remarks for the prosecution at Nuremberg, "The privilege of opening the first trial in history for crimes against the peace of the world imposes a grave responsibility. The wrongs which we seek to condemn and punish have been so calculated, so malignant, and so devastating, that civilization cannot tolerate their being ignored, because it cannot survive their being repeated."[1] For the proponents of trials in new democracies, the situation is no different in the contemporary era. Those who have suffered unspeakable acts of torture and abuse, who have lost loved ones and associates, and who have had their lives torn apart by capricious and uncaring governments must be able to feel that their losses have been addressed and that their new leaders have taken seriously the necessity of restoring the moral order of a damaged world. This attention, it is felt, is owed to the victims simply by virtue of their humanity.

But in addition to providing legitimacy for their practitioners, accountability trials may have a very specific relevance to the needs of new democracies. Unlike the Nuremberg and Tokyo tribunals, which were imposed from without, the primary impetus for these trials comes from within, and it is frequently bound up with the task of democratization. This is in no small part due to the fact that those who are called to make the choice about pursuing criminal prosecutions are simultaneously engaged in the act of founding a new political order. For this reason, the supporters of trials contend, the decision to act upon past abuses will amount to more than simply finalizing the break with authoritarianism. Assuming they are properly conducted, these proceedings should provide tangible evidence of the guiding principles—equality, fairness, and the rule of law—that are meant to define the new order of things. What better way can there exist of demonstrating that radically different legal and political norms are in effect than by showing that the García Mezas, Erich Honeckers, and Chun Doo Hwans of the old world are no longer immune to prosecution for their offenses, and that they will be held accountable to the same standards of behavior as any other citizens?

Furthermore, the proponents of transitional justice argue, the seriousness with which these states act upon the crimes and abuses of their former leaders today will go a long way toward winning popular credibility tomorrow and instilling confidence in democratic norms and values. In this vein, scholars frequently cite the failure of West German authorities to pursue prominent war criminals and remove former Nazi officials from key judicial and administrative positions in the 1950s and 1960s as an example of underestimating the consequences of inaction. In the Federal Republic, this neglect of the obligation to seek retribution for past crimes promoted widespread cynicism among the German population about its government's commitment to making a full break with authoritarianism, and from the perspective of some observers, it ultimately contributed to the violent rejection of German democracy by many young people after 1968.

On the other hand, it is equally easy to appreciate the arguments

that have been made against involving the courts in the quest for retrospective justice. Like the Allied tribunals at Nuremberg, which
seemed at times (e.g., in the case of "crimes against humanity") to
stretch established legal standards in order to justify the prosecution
of the leaders of Nazi Germany, new democracies often find themselves on uncertain jurisprudential ground in seeking to bring their
former dictators to justice. In their rush to judgment, the critics of
such proceedings contend, these states run the risk of abusing a cardinal principle of the rule of law, *nullem crimen nulla poena sine lege.*
That is, individuals should only be held accountable to laws that
were in effect at the time they acted. Should states lose sight of this
principle and subject the accused to ambiguous and ill-defined legal
standards, the law will lose its uniquely democratic quality of applying consistently and fairly to everyone. Bringing this problem into
even sharper focus is the fact that in many new democracies, such as
Poland in the early 1990s, electoral politics and naked political ambi-
tions have often gotten the upper hand in crusades to "root out the
dictators" and punish the leaders of old. In these instances, democratic regimes have allowed themselves to become caught up in
processes that have little, if anything, to do with the realization of justice per se. For the skeptics, the result of these campaigns has invariably been to cheapen the currency of democracy and weaken public
faith in government.

The critics of accountability trials also point out that new democracies face a concrete challenge that was never at issue at Nuremberg.
In the latter case, the Allied powers had one unquestionable advantage over domestic courts in their quest for justice. They were able to
impose their judgments upon a completely defeated enemy. In contrast, in many of the former states, from southern Europe in the 1970s
to Latin America and Africa in the 1980s and 1990s, emerging democratic regimes have enjoyed, at best, only a tenuous hold on political
power. All too often, these governments have inherited societies that
are fractured and divided as a result of the experience of authoritarian rule. In many instances, the same representatives of the old
regime whom they would most like to bring to trial—the leaders of
the military, for example—are watching and waiting in the wings for
the first democratic misstep that will allow them to rally their forces

for a return to power. Under these circumstances, even forceful advocates of trials have conceded that the fledgling democracy may have no choice but to temper its hopes of holding its former oppressors accountable for their misdeeds and concentrate instead on the immediate challenge of political survival. As human rights activist Aryeh Neier has observed, "Permitting the armed forces to make themselves immune to prosecution for dreadful crimes seems intolerable; yet it also seems irrational to insist that an elected civilian government should commit suicide by provoking its armed forces."[2] As a consequence of such situations, states as diverse as Spain, Chile, Brazil, and South Africa have opted on prudential grounds to confine their efforts to settle accounts with their predecessors to approaches to the past—political proclamations, truth commissions, reparations, and even amnesties—that seem more likely to lessen political and social divisions than to give rise to new tensions.

Clearly, powerful arguments can be made both for and against using the courts to redress past wrongs. Yet as the essays in this book suggest, this does not mean that new democracies are necessarily reduced to an either-or choice between undertaking criminal prosecutions with abandon or, conversely, turning a blind eye to the human rights abuses of their predecessors. Quite frequently, the decisive issue is not whether justice should be pursued but rather *how* it is to be sought. According to what legal standards should former dictators be held to account for their crimes? And under what circumstances might transitional justice be considered both possible and desirable in light of the aims of a new democracy?

For example, it would certainly be a grievous error for any democratic regime to give short shrift to due process in its desire to punish past dictators. Given the abuses inflicted upon the rule of law under authoritarianism, it is reasonable to expect that the legal practices of a democratic government will be beyond reproach. Nevertheless, it would also be incorrect to think that all new democracies are therefore bereft of the legal resources and precedents required to bring the perpetrators of egregious human rights violations to justice. In the mid-1980s and early 1990s, both Argentina and Germany, respectively, were provided with the opportunity to conduct Nuremberg-style accountability trials, in which they could have achieved speedy convictions on the basis of sweeping pronouncements about the immorality of the dictatorial regimes that preceded them. However, rather than take this option and risk providing their critics with evidence that they were interested only in imposing "victors' justice" upon their one-time adversaries, both states chose instead to base their prosecutions on preexisting, codified laws that would have been known to the accused at the time they committed their crimes. This approach resulted in fewer convictions, but arguably, it was well worth the sacrifice. Each of the governments was able to send its population a more valuable message about the benefits of the rule of law in a democratic society.

In addition, the democratizing regimes of the contemporary age are privileged to draw upon a substantial body of *international* legal precedents that was not available to the courts at Nuremberg. Human rights scholar Tina Rosenberg has captured this revealing difference in circumstances by pointing out that the new democracies of the 1980s and 1990s enjoy the blessing of having come late in history. "Paradoxically," she has written, "Nuremberg's weaknesses, not its strengths, have proven most enduring. Even Nuremberg's most vociferous supporters admit that the prosecutions had only the shakiest foundations in existing law; prosecutors at the International Military Tribunal and in later U.S. tribunals in Nuremberg and international tribunals in Tokyo improvised as they went along. But Nuremberg's principles have now been codified and accepted by most nations of the world and form the basis for much of current international and human rights law."[3]

We are still some distance away from achieving an effective international regime to enforce these principles. Still, there can be no doubt that the currency of international law has grown enormously over the past fifty years. On this basis, the parties to such international accords as the Geneva Conventions, the Genocide Convention, the International Covenant on Civil and Political Rights, and the UN Convention Against Torture would seem bound to abide by the norms contained within these agreements and are, therefore, obliged to take some kind of action against the violators of such standards. Of the cases under consideration in this volume, South Africa might appear at first glance to be an obvious exception to this rule, due to its long-standing isolation from the world community. But even in this instance, one should not rush to judgment. The South African government was not only a party to the Charter of the United Nations, but as we shall see later, the case can be made that its former leaders were also required to abide by customary international-law rules governing crimes against humanity and torture.

Finally, the chapters in this volume provide much cautionary evidence about the importance of avoiding seemingly easy solutions to the tough decisions that are involved in conducting or, conversely, eschewing accountability trials. There may be times when the most responsible way of dealing with a legacy of human rights abuse is, in fact, to pass over the crimes of a former dictatorship in silence, that is, to forget and if possible, to forgive past offenses in the interest of national reconciliation. By the same logic, the most sensible choice at other times may be to turn instead to less divisive means of wrestling with the past, such as those availed by truth commissions and other fact-finding agencies. However, one should always be circumspect about arguments that too readily dismiss calls for justice and accountability by appealing to an all-encompassing "political realism."

For one thing, reasonable individuals may differ about whether there is cause for a trade-off between demands for retribution and the requisites of political order. One person's fears that trials will promote political strife and instability in a given setting may be matched by another's equally well-grounded conviction that lasting peace will only be achieved by addressing the issue of accountability. Thus, some form of transitional justice could be perfectly compatible with a fledgling democracy's requirements for survival. By the same token the argument for realism can also become, whether intentionally or not, an unhealthy pretext for sidestepping the difficult moral choices that any democratic regime is called to make. Hence, what appears to one observer to be a measured act of sobriety may represent to another a fundamental misreading of actual political circumstances. As former Americas Watch director Juan Méndez noted in 1991 about the controversial 1989 and 1990 decisions of Argentina's president, Carlos Menem, to pardon the high-ranking officers behind his country's military dictatorship (including individuals who had already been convicted for their crimes), Menem may have thought he was acting in the interest of forgiveness and national reconciliation, but the former junta leaders had other ideas: "It would be easier to understand the reconciliation rationale if there were any sign that the military is genuinely contrite about its role during the 'dirty war,' and is ready to seek reconciliation with their victims. In fact, the opposite is true: the armed forces view the pardons as a step in the direction of full vindication for their victory in 'defeating subversion.'"[4]

The contributors to this book have different, and sometimes even sharply contrasting, views on when and how democratizing regimes should address the issue of transitional justice. This is to be expected, given the fact that the authors are dealing with such diverse countries and political settings. The experiences of these states with dictatorship are quite dissimilar, as even a cursory examination of the differences between the bureaucratic authoritarianism of many Latin American dictatorships and the complex history of Marxism-Leninism in Europe will reveal. Accordingly, the requisites of democratic consolidation in these states are likely to be dissimilar as well. Nevertheless, in two essential respects, the authors of the following chapters are of one mind. They all believe that the legacy of human rights abuse in these countries cannot be simply ignored. They are also convinced that the responses that the leaders of these states devise to this challenge will be directly relevant to the quality and sustainability of democracy.

This study originated as an interdisciplinary symposium on "Political Justice and the Transition to Democracy," which was held at the University of Notre Dame on April 28, 1995. The symposium was sponsored by the Helen Kellogg Institute of International Studies and the Center for Civil and Human Rights of the Notre Dame Law School and included three of the contributors to this volume (Carlos Acuña, Jorge Correa Sutil, and myself) and three others (Paulo Sergio Pinheiro and Oscar Viera of Brazil and the late Etienne Mureinik of South Africa). However, the book that has resulted from this meeting has gone far beyond its modest beginnings. In preparing this volume, I felt that it was essential to have a representative international sample of the many cases in the postwar period in which new democracies have sought, with varying degrees of success, to involve their courts in the quest for retrospective justice. To this end, I was extremely fortunate in being able to locate a remarkably devoted group of contributors from a wide variety of intellectual traditions, ranging from political science to international law. These scholars were not only willing to take the time to write original essays for this book, but they also shared my conviction that this was a project whose time had come. I am particularly grateful to them for their patience and diligence in adhering to my entreaties that we never lose sight of the central theme of this study: the complex relationship between the uses of the law to pursue transitional justice and the founding of new democracies. It is a tribute to them that we have lived up to this all-important task.

This book has been long in coming, and I have incurred many debts in the process of bringing it to fruition. Without the financial support of the Center for Civil and Human Rights, the Kellogg Institute, and the Institute for Scholarship in the Liberal Arts, the project would never have been possible in the first place. But as is always the case, the help and encouragement of specific individuals were what counted the most. Of my many scholarly colleagues at Notre Dame and our visiting fellows program at the Kellogg Institute, I am especially thankful to Michael Francis, Donald Kommers, Albert Le May, Scott Mainwaring, Garth Meintjes, Juan Méndez, Guillermo O'Donnell, Paulo Sergio Pinheiro, Timothy Scully, Jennifer Warlick, and John Yoder for their gracious support at many stages of this endeavor. On numerous occasions, Mainwaring and Meintjes provided crucial insights into the content and organization of the book. Additionally, I would like to thank Martha Sue Abbott, Bettye Bielejewski, Caroline Domingo, Dolores Fairley, Nancy Hahn, Tina Jankowski, Vonda Polega, and Joetta Schlabach. Without their patient and expert assistance, I would never have mustered the resources necessary to complete this project. I am grateful to Gabriela Ippolito, Marianne Hahn, Erin Joyce, Charlie Kenney, Marcelo Leiras, Eva Rzepniewski, Carol Stuart, and Elizabeth Yoder, who helped me with countless research and editorial tasks along the way. I am also indebted to Rebecca DeBoer, Jim Langford, Jeannette Morgenroth, and Carole Roos, all of the University of Notre Dame Press, for generously supporting this project from its inception and producing it in record time.

Finally, I extend a special word of thanks to Bill Lewers, to whom I dedicate this volume. Fr. Lewers' contributions to the life of the mind and the soul at Notre Dame have been enormous. His inspiration transformed the idea for this book into a reality.

A. JAMES MCADAMS
November 1, 1996

NOTES

1. Cited in Telford Taylor, *The Anatomy of the Nuremberg Trials: A Personal Memoir* (New York: Alfred A. Knopf, 1992), p. 167.

2. Aryeh Neier, "What Should be Done about the Guilty?" *The New York Review of Books*, February 1, 1990, p. 34. Yet Neier also insists that this concession to reality should *not* become an excuse for doing nothing. "[I]f the new civilian governments are to evolve into genuine democracies," he writes in the same paragraph, "it is essential that the rule of law should prevail and that the armed forces should be subordinated to democratic rule."

3. Tina Rosenberg, "Tipping the Scales of Justice," *World Policy Journal* (Fall 1995): 55.

4. Juan E. Méndez, *Truth and Partial Justice in Argentina: An Update* (New York: Human Rights Watch, 1991), p. 69.

Contributors

CHAPTER 1

Juan E. Méndez is Director of the Inter-American Institute on Human Rights in San José, Costa Rica. He is a past executive director of Americas Watch and was, until 1996, general counsel for Human Rights Watch. He is the author of numerous books, among them *Truth and Partial Justice in Argentina* (1987) and *Political Murder and Reform in Colombia* (1992).

CHAPTER 2

Nicos C. Alivizatos is a professor of constitutional law at the University of Athens, Greece, where he also teaches constitutional history. His publications include *Les institutions politiques de la Grèce à travers les crises, 1922-1974* (1979), *Introduction to the Constitutional History of Modern Greece* (1981), and *The Constitutional Status of the Armed Forces* (1987, 1992). **P. Nikiforos Diamandouros** is Director of the Greek National Centre for Social Research and Professor of Political Science and Public Administration at the University of Athens. In addition to many articles on authoritarianism and democracy in Greece, he has written *Hellenism and the First Greek War of Liberation* (1976) and *Cultural Dualism and Political Change in Postauthoritarian Greece* (1994), and coedited *The Politics of Democratic Consolidation* (1995).

CHAPTER 3

René Antonio Mayorga is senior researcher at CEBEM, La Paz, Bolivia. He has taught political science at numerous universities, including FLACSO, Mexico, the Free University of Berlin, and Saint Antony's College at Oxford. He is the author of many books, monographs, and articles on the state, democracy, and social movements, including the coauthored book, *La cuestión militar en cuestión: Democracia y fuerzas armadas* (1994).

CHAPTER 4

Carlos H. Acuña is a research scholar at the Center for the Study of State and Society (CEDES) and the Argentine National Council for Scientific and Technological Research (CONICET), Buenos Aires, Argentina. He teaches politics at the National University of Buenos Aires, among other institutions. He is the author of several books, including *La nueva matriz política Argentina* (1995), as well as coeditor of *Democracy, Markets, and Structural Reforms in Latin America* (1994) and *Latin American Political Economy* (1994). **Catalina Smulovitz** is also a research scholar at the Argentine National Council for Scientific and Technological Research. She teaches politics at the Universidad Di Tella, and has published numerous articles on political parties, constitutional reform, legislatures, and the military and human rights in Latin America's southern cone.

CHAPTER 5

Jorge Correa Sutil is a professor of law at the Universidad Diego Portales and a practicing attorney in Santiago, Chile. From 1990 to 1991 he was the executive secretary of the Chilean National Commission on Truth and Reconciliation. He is the author of many articles on judicial independence and human rights during the transition to democracy.

CHAPTER 6

Gábor Halmai is currently a professor of law and Director of the Center for Human Rights at Central European University, Budapest College, as well as a professor of law at the University of Györ. Between 1990 and 1996 he was chief counselor to the President of the Hungarian Constitutional Court of Hungary. He is the author of books (in Hungarian) on free speech and on freedom of association and in 1996 held a Fulbright fellowship at the University of Michigan. **Kim Lane Scheppele** is Professor of Law, Political Science and Sociology at the University of Pennsylvania and codirector of the Program on Gender and Culture at Central European University, Budapest College. Between 1994 and 1996 she was a researcher at the Constitutional Court in Hungary on grants from the National Science Foundation while also holding the Arthur F. Thurnau Associate Professorship in Political Science, Public Policy, and Law at the University of Michigan. She is the author of *Legal Secrets: Equality and Efficiency in the Common Law* (1988).

CHAPTER 7

Andrzej S. Walicki is the O'Neill Family Professor of History at the University of Notre Dame. He is the author of many books, including *A History of Russian Thought from the Enlightenment to Marxism* (1979), *Legal Philosophies of Russian Liberalism* (1987), *The Enlightenment and the Birth of Modern Nationhood* (1989), and *Marxism and the Leap to the Kingdom of Freedom* (1995).

CHAPTER 8

A. James McAdams is a faculty fellow at the Kellogg Institute of International Studies and a professor of government at the University of Notre Dame. He is the author of *East Germany and Detente* (1985) and *Germany Divided: From the Wall to Reunification* (1993, 1994), and coauthor of *Rebirth: A History of Europe since World War II* (1993).

CHAPTER 9

John Dugard is a professor of law at the University of Witwatersrand, South Africa. In 1995-1996 he was Director of the Research Centre for International Law and Arthur Goodhart Professor in Legal Science at Cambridge University, England. He is the author of several books, including *Human Rights and the South African Legal Order* (1978), *Recognition and the United Nations* (1987), and *International Law: A South African Perspective* (1994).

Transitional Justice

and the Rule of Law

in New Democracies

1

In Defense of Transitional Justice

Juan E. Méndez

REDRESSING THE WRONGS committed through human rights violations is not only a legal obligation and a moral imperative imposed on governments. It also makes good political sense in the transition from dictatorship to democracy. In fact, the pursuit of retrospective justice is an urgent task of democratization, as it highlights the fundamental character of the new order to be established, an order based on the rule of law and on respect for the dignity and worth of each human person. Yet it is also one of the hardest choices that any democracy has to make, if only because the effort to restore truth and justice where denial and impunity have reigned is frequently attacked as destabilizing and vindictive. In this context, the temptation is great to equate reconciliation with a forgive-and-forget policy. Nonetheless, democratic leaders have increasingly recognized that some crimes are of such a magnitude that the wounds they leave in society cannot and must not be simply swept under the rug. As the essays in this book exemplify, there are in fact many options between the indefensible choice of total oblivion and the improbable realization of complete justice. The hardest question of all is how to pursue the objectives of justice and of reconciliation without falling into tokenism and a false morality that only thinly disguises the perpetuation of impunity.

Since the 1970s, there has been a virtual tidal wave of new democracies emerging from countries with an authoritarian or totalitarian past. Beginning in Southern Europe (Greece, Spain), moving through

Latin America (Argentina, Chile, Brazil, Uruguay) and to Eastern Europe (Poland, East Germany, Hungary) and now in South Africa, new democratic leaderships have looked hopefully to the future. In defining a vision of this future for their populations, however, they have had to reckon with the legacy of human rights violations left by the recent authoritarian past. They all share in common this feature, even if each country chooses to adopt different measures to deal with the past.

In Spain and, at least to some extent, more recently in Poland, new democratic regimes have sought to foster a policy of drawing a "clean slate," that is, of seeking to bury the past and to forego any form of accountability for it. In both cases, one cannot deny that they have met with success, if success is measured exclusively in terms of the stability of the new order. However, it is unlikely, even in these instances, that demands for truth and justice will simply go away; if the wounds in society are fresh and the crimes particularly egregious, oblivion is not an option. In other cases, such as Chile, governments have chosen quite different means of dealing with the past, for example, the disclosure of the truth about human rights abuses and the insistence on a public acknowledgment of crimes and even an apology to the victims. While skeptics initially regarded such disclosures as dangerously destabilizing, these "truth commissions" have rapidly gained acceptance in some circles as a desirable symbolic break with the past. However, with that acceptance there sometimes arises a simplistic conception that "truth" is preferable to justice and that the reports of truth commissions are a desirable alternative to any sort of criminal prosecutions for human rights violations.

In fact, this attitude may reflect a deeper hostility to the idea of trials per se, and not merely the understandable recognition of the difficulties in conducting them. Certainly, there is no guarantee that trials are the best means of redressing past human rights violations, nor are they appropriate in all circumstances. Several of the chapters in this volume offer ample testimony to the way that such trials may be perverted to serve political ends. Thus, one has to assume for the sake of argument that all prosecutions for the crimes and abuses of former dictatorships are carried out under strict conditions of legitimacy and due respect for the rule of law. In the majority of cases we will consider in this volume, there are strong political, legal, and moral arguments to be made for the role of criminal trials in laying the foundations for a truly renovated democratic order.

The primary task is to recognize that there is a past to be reckoned with. The nature of the transition to democracy itself means that there is unfinished business with respect to how we put distance between the challenges of the present and the traumas of the recent past. Some argue that the best way to do so is to forget past crimes and abuses and look forward, presumably because nothing can be done about the lives that have been lost or the pain that has been suffered. In Brazil and Uruguay, elected authorities have managed to impose this vision despite considerable societal pressure to do otherwise; in Uruguay, the matter was actually settled, though very narrowly, by a national referendum in 1989, brought about under extremely adverse circumstances as a result of pressure from broad sectors of civil society that objected to the extension of impunity. Even in these countries, as well as in Argentina, the inherent force of the idea of accountability has resulted in magnificent efforts by civil society to document past violations and to rescue the memory of the victims from oblivion.[1] Then too, there is a variation on the forgive-and-forget attitude. Instead of holding that nothing should be done about the past, the proponents of this position maintain that there are no rules about what should be done and that the world must therefore trust elected leaders to know best what, if anything, should be done in each country under its specific circumstances.[2]

As I shall argue in this essay, these positions reflect a very short-sighted and mechanical view of the requirements of democratic stability, and they ignore the very real probability– clearly documentable in the case of Haiti—that impunity will only encourage new abuses in the near or distant future. Of course, in most cases other than Haiti, the deterrent effect on the future of either a policy of impunity or one of accountability is an unprovable proposition. There is really no way to predict the future behavior of relevant actors. For example, it is impossible to know whether torturers will be deterred from torturing anew as a result of a policy of leniency or, conversely, by a policy of punishment. For this reason, a policy of letting bygones be bygones is not wrong primarily because its view of stability looks suspiciously like yielding to thuggery and blackmail. Rather, I would argue that it is morally wrong because it fails to recognize the worth and dignity of each victim. It is also politically wrong because it sets the new political order on the weak foundation of privilege and the denial of the rule of law. Such a democracy may not be worthy of its name.

Fortunately, there seems to be a growing consensus that the past demands something from us in situations of transition. The more substantial debate is about what exactly is required, what the choices are, and how we should sort out the ethical, legal, and political consequences of these choices. In this regard, it is undeniable that the transitional setting presents important limitations on what can be done, constraints that are determined primarily by the residual power retained by the forces of the old order.[3] If, by definition, any transitional situation will include limits on what can be done about the past, it is important to determine what role criminal trials can play in restoring truth and justice and redressing wrongs, within a scheme that must include other forms of truth-telling and reparations as well. Before establishing the limits of the possible, however, it is worth clarifying what obligations a democratizing regime might have, both toward the victims and toward society as a whole, when confronting a legacy of serious and pervasive abuse.[4]

An Emerging Principle of International Law

As an affirmative obligation on the part of states to redress wrongs inflicted by human rights violations, accountability has legal, ethical, and political dimensions. It is fair to say that no single one of these aspects should be allowed to overshadow the other two. Therefore, just as it makes no sense to exaggerate the political obstacles, it is equally wrong to postulate an obligation to punish the perpetrators of past offenses without regard to the potential consequences for the future enjoyment of rights by all others. The lack of adequate regard for this need to address all aspects of the problem has sometimes made the victims of abuse sound shrill to their critics, making it that much easier to dismiss their demands. Yet these demands for accountability have firm legal, ethical, and even political foundations.

The international law of human rights recognizes that the state is obliged not only to refrain from committing certain acts against the individual but also to carry out duties of an affirmative nature. Specifically, the state must give each person the right to seek remedial action for all behavior constituting a violation of that person's rights under the relevant treaties. The content of this remedy may vary according to the seriousness of the harm induced and according to the importance of the rights violated. But it is commonly understood that the victim of a human rights violation deserves some remedy. In addition, it is recognized that some rights are so fundamental that they can never be abridged or derogated, not even in an emergency situation that "threatens the life of the Nation."[5] Since these rights cannot be formally suspended, their de facto suspension is also prohibited. Clearly, ex post facto laws, that is, laws that have the effect of legalizing behavior considered illegal at the time it was undertaken, would violate this nonderogable rights clause. More specific to our argument, amnesties, pardons, or prosecutorial decisions not to prosecute violations of these rights should also constitute an impermissible derogation after the fact, which is a fortiori forbidden in nonemergency situations as well.

This catalogue of nonderogable rights corresponds rather neatly with the violations of basic human rights that have come to be known as "crimes against humanity" since the end of World War II. Both in these cases and in the matter of crimes against humanity, the idea behind singling out a special category of crimes has been to generate the affirmative obligation to investigate, prosecute, and punish human rights abuses. This maxim applies, firstly, to the country having jurisdiction over these offenses, but it also applies to other members of the international community. Notably, when the same crimes have been committed in the context of armed conflict, they have been considered "grave breaches" of the laws and customs of war. In these instances, both the obligation to punish and the concept of universal jurisdiction have been universally recognized, even before World War II.[6] Similarly, in the postwar era, decisions by international tribunals and treaty bodies, reports by experts, and nonbinding resolutions by international lawmaking bodies have consistently backed the trend in treaty law to extend this obligation to punish the most egregious violations of fundamental rights.[7]

The Moral Connotations of an Obligation to Punish

If the legal underpinnings of accountability are increasingly well established, its moral foundations have been subject to much greater debate. Even if we accept the proposition that some duty is owed to the victims of human rights violations, many commentators have warned that imposing a duty to punish would be morally wrong if, in attempting to fulfill this maxim, authorities should put at risk the existence of democracy itself or prevent the possibility of a genuine reconciliation between old enemies. In this view, the only justification for trials and punishment is deterrence. If, under the circumstances of time and place, the object of deterring future crimes would be better served by leniency than by punishment, then the ethical choice would favor the former.

An opposing view holds that punishment is not only justified for some egregious crimes, it is also mandatory. For the proponents of this view, the moral justification of punishment is not deterrence, since it is impossible to predict the future behavior of any given political actors. Societies may hope that punishment will deter, but they cannot find any satisfactory justification for it in deterrence. Rather, they punish both to uphold the rule of law and to remain faithful to the principle that criminal law in a democracy protects the innocent and the powerless. In this sense, we must punish because it is imperative to let the victims of state-sponsored abuses know that their plight has not gone unheeded.[8] An important variation of this admittedly retributionist theory has been proposed in Latin America. It holds that societies must punish because, in the new democratic order they are building, the norms that prohibit torture, extralegal executions, and "disappearances" must be held in special regard. That special place for these norms requires that we signify intolerance for their breach by punishing any counternormative behavior.[9]

A corollary of this debate is the question of the right of the victims to insist on punishment as opposed to the will of the majority. Proponents of deterrence as the moral basis for trials agree that victims are owed recognition by the state, but they reject the notion that this right should become an effective veto power over whatever the democratic majority wants to do about forgiveness. In fact, modern penal systems do recognize a role for the victim in this process.[10] It is unnecessary to carry this question to the obscene extreme of using the argument of "victims' rights" to tie the hands of judges in mandatory sentencing or to remove prosecutors who have doubts about seeking the death penalty, as is done in the United States with alarming frequency. Victims do not have a right to a specific form of penalty; they have a right to see justice done. Blanket amnesties or pardons that prevent the process of pursuing justice from taking place at all are quite simply an abuse of majoritarianism, even if arrived at in full, open, and democratic debate. In a true democracy, the rights of minorities—even the seemingly miniscule category of victims of gross state abuse—simply cannot be forced to depend on the will of the majority.

There is no question that there are opponents of trials for past abuses in the camp of democratically-minded liberal thinkers who have much to contribute to shaping the contours of democracy in transitional societies. These individuals sometimes justify their positions by stating that, in times of transition, a logic of peace should substitute for what they consider to be the logic of war that prevailed in the confrontations of the pre-transitional period. Presumably, a logic of peace indicates that bygones should be allowed to be bygones, whereas a logic of war would require punishment for past wrongs.[11] Actually, this position is used to object not only to criminal trials but to all efforts to achieve a reckoning with the recent past; the position's advocates prefer, in fact, to draw a "thick line" that divides the past from the present.[12] This choice makes sense if the alternative—all too real in some Eastern European experiments with democracy after 1989—is to exploit the courts as a self-serving way of getting back at officials of the *ancien régime*, not for crimes they may have committed or the abuse of their power, but instead for their ideas. But this is not the only alternative. A policy of accountability based on respect for the victims and for the rule of law seeks only to punish crimes that are committed against humanity, not to twist the rule of law to satisfy vindictive sentiments (no matter how understandable they might be) against sycophants, cheerleaders, and collaborators whose actions may have been morally reprehensible but not necessarily criminal when they were committed. The Polish intellectual, Adam Michnik, has said that "murder is murder" and should therefore be punished. In this sense, the distance between the logic of peace and the logic of retribution is more apparent than real.[13]

Significantly, it is far from clear that a policy of prosecutions narrowly drawn to address egregious crimes would represent a logic of war. If anything, such a policy would help to impose civilized rules on an earlier violent conflict; moreover, these rules are not only nonviolent but eminently fair to all sides.[14] Actually, a logic of peace is perfectly consistent with the principle of accountability for egregious violations of the laws of war, as both the Geneva Conventions show and as the international community has realized with regard to the former Yugoslavia and Rwanda. Indeed, settling the problem of criminal liability for the very worst crimes is essential to peace, because it separates the responsibility of the individual who exploits the fears and anxieties of the population for shameless political gain from the collective guilt that is wrongly assigned to collectivities. The perception of collective guilt only fosters new cycles of retribution, and it is imperative that it be corrected.[15]

To the extent, however, that the "thick line" theory rejects any effort to investigate the past and to disclose to the public the misdeeds of former intelligence and police forces, this approach is also in conflict with the state's internationally binding obligation to preserve freedom of expression and the right to seek and impart information.[16] The public's right to know is a fundamental tenet of democracy, and it should not be sacrificed to the supposedly higher interest of reconciliation. On the contrary, ways and means must be sought to allow its exercise with appropriate regard for privacy and the rights of potentially implicated persons to due process. As we shall see below, a policy that respects the latter rights does not have to lead to the complete suppression of the facts, nor must it amount to the denial of memory.

Retrospective Justice and the Political Constraints of Transition

The fact that there are strong legal and moral arguments in favor of prosecuting former human rights abusers does not eliminate the enormous political difficulties that such a policy faces in the delicate balance of powers that characterizes most transitions. In addition to the problem of honest disagreements among democratic forces about how to deal with the past, previously authoritarian and antidemocratic sectors of the population are bound, almost by definition, to retain a quota of power and are likely to create new obstacles along the path of reform. An early test of their residual powers is, precisely, the attempt to protect their own representatives against any settling of accounts for past human rights violations. In this context, it makes no sense for a newly elected democratic regime to act as if these political constraints do not exist.

On the other hand, a realistic and sober appreciation of political realities does not automatically constitute an argument for inaction. The resistance that criminals might show to any form of accountability, and particularly their threats to destabilize the transition, cannot be allowed to determine government policy.[17] Yielding to these pressures only amounts to letting democracy be blackmailed and starts the transitional period on shaky ground. It signals to the public that odious privileges from the old order still apply, as long, that is, as the targets of criminal prosecution retain a modicum of power. In general, this sort of blackmail undermines democratic authority. It defers the subordination of all state powers to the freely elected government to some indefinite and, under these conditions, highly dubious future point. Politically, it makes no sense to assume that newly democratic powers must be weak by definition; this weakness becomes a self-fulfilling prophecy. The point, of course, is not to deny the harsh reality of political pressures on transitional governments. Rather, it is important to assess the threats before the new government realistically, to take into consideration as well the countervailing strength of democratic forces in society, and to add effectively to the latter by offering them moral and political support.

In Chile, Argentina, and Uruguay, the military establishments quickly made it clear that democracy had its limits, even if in the latter two countries, Pinochet's counterparts preferred their threats to be somewhat less blunt, if nonetheless quite real. In all three countries, democratic forces—including newly elected leaders—were immediately forced to make choices, and often these choices were stark: Would they stand for principle, or would they instead allow the new democracy to be blackmailed by its enemies? In Uruguay, President Sanguinetti opted for a "thick line" approach and became a champion of forgiving and forgetting. When a petition drive forced a referendum on this policy, he campaigned in favor of retaining his country's pseudo-amnesty law by openly telling voters that the choice was between justice and democracy—they could not have both. At the time of this writing, Sanguinetti is once again president of Uruguay after a period out of office, and much as before, he steadfastly refuses to allow any official effort to secure the truth about human rights cases that remain mired in secrecy. In Argentina, Raúl Alfonsín at first withstood the pressures around him, and he actively supported both truth-telling and criminal prosecutions, at least of the highest-ranking military commanders. However, he eventually succumbed to the pressure of failed military revolts and finally terminated all remaining prosecutions through two pseudo-amnesty laws. Alfonsín's successor, Carlos S. Menem, then pardoned those who could still be prosecuted and even applied this edict a year later to the commanders who had previously been convicted. In Chile, the new democracy accepted the legal and political effects of a shameful "self-amnesty" passed by Pinochet in 1978, opting for a complete and thorough truth-telling exercise instead of prosecution. To be sure, a few cases not covered by this amnesty have continued their slow march through the courts, and the country's democratic leaders deserve credit for resisting pressures to enact further amnesties or pardons. In fact, one major case even reached a final verdict in Chile. As a result, the notorious leader of Pinochet's intelligence service, General Manuel Contreras, is currently serving a six-year sentence for his role in the transnational murder of Orlando Letelier and Ronnie Moffitt.

If the outcome in each of these three examples is less than satisfactory, they at least demonstrate that it is by no means clear that the best response to pressures from the old regime is always to give ground on the principle of accountability. Pressures do not go away even after the military or other conservative forces get what they want. Moreover, there is a serious risk that by yielding, one contributes to the consolidation of an alternate power within the state, one that is not subject to democratic subordination and that is incon-

sistent with the idea of democracy itself. On the other hand, these examples also show that it is possible to withstand such pressure without necessarily risking instability, in part because the residual power
retained by the military may be weakened by the transition itself. In
all three of the above countries, democracy is now stable; however, it
is by no means clear that such stability was gained through concessions to antidemocratic forces. On the contrary, in different measures,
the efforts at settling accounts with the past seem to have contributed
to the creation of a growing public consciousness about the dangers
of authoritarianism. The democratic mood to be found in the public
opinion of all three countries is the single most important factor in
the present stability of democracy.

A realistic assessment of the possibilities of pursuing justice
would also give full regard to the institutional limitations established
by the politics of transition in each case. These institutional limitations may in fact tie the hands of a democratic government seeking to
redress past wrongs, but they do so only within the rule of law. For
example, since due process and fair-trial guarantees should be an absolute condition of legitimacy in any accountability scheme, it makes
no legal, moral, or political sense to insist on prosecution in the presence of amnesties that have obtained legal effect despite their immorality. Accepting such reasoning would violate the cardinal rule of
nullum crimen nulla poena sine lege, in the sense that defendants always have the right to the most benevolent law that can be applied to
them after the commission of a crime. The same point would be true
if we insisted on new prosecutions against the rule of double jeop-
ardy *(non bis in idem),* as long as the prior trial represented a good
faith effort at prosecution and not simply a pretext for impunity.
Even as we accept the notion that institutional limitations of this sort
are part of the hand that has been dealt to the democratic leadership
of a country in transition, we must nevertheless demand that all that
can be done about truth and justice *within those limits* be undertaken.
Most emphatically, we must object to democratic leaders who are
disposed to add further, unnecessary limitations to those with which
they already have to live.

Societies faced with a legacy of human rights violations must
strive to fulfill four obligations that the state owes to the victims and

to society. The first of these is an obligation to do justice, that is, to prosecute and punish the perpetrators of abuses when those abuses can be determined to have been criminal in nature. The second obligation is to grant victims the right to know the truth. This implies the ability to investigate any and all aspects of a violation that still remain shrouded in secrecy and to disclose this truth to the victims of injustice, to their relatives, and to society as a whole. The third obligation is to grant reparations to victims in a manner that recognizes their worth and their dignity as human beings. Monetary compensation in appropriate amounts is certainly a part of this duty, but the obligation should also be conceived as including nonmonetary gestures that express recognition of the harm done to them and an apology in the name of society. Finally, states are obliged to see to it that those who have committed the crimes while serving in any capacity in the armed or security forces of the state should not be allowed to continue on the rolls of reconstituted, democratic law-enforcement or security-related bodies.

The realization of these four obligations must be seen as a process, and not simply as a result. More important than the fact that a perpetrator is finally forced to serve time is the way in which his particular criminal liability is determined. The obligations mentioned above must be viewed, in the familiar distinction made in civil law, as "obligations of means" and not of "results." In other words, a government fulfills its obligations by conducting a process, even if in the end, the whole truth cannot be established or the known perpetrators are themselves acquitted. The outcome of either truth-telling or the search for justice cannot be predetermined. To attempt to do so would be to taint the whole process by marking it with a lack of credibility. For the same reason, we must be ready to accept both acquittals and the fact that some crimes will never be completely clarified. Much as it may hurt us to see known criminals go free, it is more important that we uphold fundamental principles of human rights—even in favor of those who once trampled on them—than in meting out well-deserved punishment to possible offenders.[18] The role played by the Hungarian Constitutional Court in rejecting extensions on statutes of limitations (with the exception of crimes against humanity) is a good example of the worth of such a rule.[19] Such a decision does not mean that we are allowing particularly heinous crimes to go unpunished. It merely shows that we emphatically insist there will be no shortcuts to justice.

Naturally, any condition of legitimacy that consists of a scrupulous respect for due process and fair-trial standards poses a very difficult dilemma in those cases in which the state confronting the legacy of abuse must rely upon untrustworthy courts. The courts may be unable to conduct fair trials because of a lack of independence, a long-standing tradition of ineptitude and corruption, or simply because the recent past has left them bereft of the material or human resources to handle momentous trials. This was the case in Haiti immediately after the return to power of Jean-Bertrand Aristide. On the one hand, the international community could not demand immediate prosecution and punishment for the crimes of the Cedras regime unless it was also willing to cooperate in bringing the Haitian courts up to acceptable standards of impartiality, independence, and competence. On the other hand, outside observers are agreed that courts typically affirm their independence and credibility in society—and thereby contribute enormously to the consolidation of democracy and the rule of law—precisely by taking on hard cases and living up to the expectations of fairness that society places on them. In cases like this, where one can appreciate the arguments both for and against transitional justice, it is imperative that we find ways of building up the courts' independence simultaneously with efforts to recover the truth and do justice to the wrongs of the past. It appears in retrospect that with adequate international support, the Haitian Truth Commission could have been designed to give the courts the precious time they needed to rebuild and reach adequate standards of due process, while at the same time assembling all the evidence required for future prosecutions. But unfortunately, the stages of accountability rarely present themselves in such neat compartments. The Truth Commission of Haiti, which finished its work in May 1996, apparently let its historic opportunity pass, providing us with little more information than was available when it began its work about the ills and abuses of the country's past.

A more clear-cut case of illegitimate accountability—and one that is much more distressing as well—has been the attempt at domestic prosecutions in Rwanda following the genocide and the ouster of the regime that brought about the terror in the first place. More than 76,000 persons have been arrested and not a single trial has started; the prisoners are held in the most appalling and life-threatening conditions. Much as we insist that the new Rwandan government has a right and an obligation to punish genocide, we must also condemn the attempt to do so by the means employed so far. Rwanda must build up its court system and then prosecute only under conditions of rigorous due process; even after achieving that objective, the persons held pending trial or after conviction must live in conditions that satisfy the minimum international standards of incarceration. It would also be helpful if Rwanda officially renounced capital punishment for these crimes (even if not obliged to do so by international law). To allow any deviation from norms of fair trial and of humane detention, or to apply the death penalty in any case, would delegitimize the process of accountability in Rwanda. Unfortunately, the international community has contributed to these false steps by not providing adequate support to the International Criminal Tribunal for Rwanda. Although the tribunal was set up by the UN Security Council in 1994, it is only now barely getting off the ground.

At the same time, the fact that accountability is a process and not a result also entails a condition of legitimacy that extends in the opposite direction. Efforts to comply with these obligations must be made in good faith and not as an exercise predestined to failure.[20] Even in less extreme cases, we should be wary of efforts at establishing only a partial truth, prosecuting only some perpetrators, compensating only some of the victims, or dismissing only some criminals from the forces. There can certainly be reasonable and understandable bases for some selectivity, but we must ensure that the process of selection does not result in tokenism or scapegoating.

Tokenism can result from conceiving any of these obligations as a symbolic gesture or a rite of the transition, largely designed to allow politicians to claim that reconciliation has been achieved by decree. Good faith measures to promote accountability are based on an understanding that the facts should speak for themselves and that the process must allow the facts to do just that. No aspect of the recent reality should be suppressed to suit any particular interpretation.

This is not to say that evidence cannot be organized in a way that makes analytical sense; on the contrary, a truth report is all the more meaningful—and effective in promoting social awareness of a recent tragedy—if its narrative approach helps to make sense of the facts, provided that the analysis is soundly based on the evidence. Most important, the victims, their families, and everyone in society with something to say about past events must be given the chance to participate in the reconstruction of this story and in the determination of the policies of redress that are to be adopted. A process of this sort gives meaning to democracy and contributes to the legitimacy and credibility of the new order.

Tokenism can also result from compensation systems that are meager in comparison with the harm done to individuals, even if a justification based on limited resources is offered. Moreover, this obligation has to be regarded truly as "reparation," and not merely as compensation. Of course, reparations may include monetary awards, but also apologies, valued information, and other nonmaterial benefits that, in the aggregate, convey the sense that society recognizes the worth and dignity of the human person behind each victim. Monetary awards that are not conceived in this manner will inevitably be seen as attempts to buy a victim's silence and will rightly be rejected.[21] Tokenism can also happen when a symbolic reshuffling of officers is presented as "the new armed forces," while in fact most abusers of human rights remain in their posts or are routinely promoted.

The most extreme form of tokenism, however, results when a truth commission is proposed as an alternative to criminal prosecutions and not as a step in the direction of accountability.[22] In this case, the preference for truth over justice is misplaced because it equates the pursuit of justice with vindictiveness. Societies that are in a position to provide both truth and justice to the victims of human rights violations should be encouraged to pursue both objectives as much as they can. A truth report that is predicated on the explicit choice not to prosecute even the most egregious abuses will be tainted by that very purpose even before it has begun. Both victims and society as a whole will see it as a disguise for impunity and not as an earnest attempt to disclose what is still mired in denial and secrecy. If nevertheless the truth comes out, this authority will only highlight the injustice of foregoing prosecutions; to avoid this eventuality, the drafters of truth reports may then be tempted to downplay atrocities, to temper them with exculpatory material or contextual background, or simply to soft-pedal their analysis. In all of these cases, the "truth" to result from such a process will be seen as little more than instrumental to a political objective, no matter how lofty the intention. As a consequence, it will fail in its objective of moving society to a higher stage of agreement over a shared history.

The preference for a truth report over trials is also unwarranted for other reasons. In addition to the specific aim of adjudicating criminal acts and imposing sanctions, trials contribute very effectively to society's remembrance of a painful past. If we agree that societies need to confront their past in public, official ways,[23] we must also recognize that trials and the records they create can make a major contribution to that end. To be sure, truth commissions have some definite advantages over trials: they are more free than courts to select the universe of facts to be examined; they can be more friendly to victims because they can treat them as such and not exclusively as witnesses; and they can determine the scope of their inquiries without having to ascertain their relevance to crimes under indictment. But the truth obtained at a criminal trial has its own advantages over a "truth report." Stricter rules governing the admissibility of evidence, the defendant's ability to cross-examine and to offer his own version of the events, and the need to overcome the presumption of innocence, are all factors that convey a special weight and credibility to a verdict obtained at trial. Clearly, there is no infallibility attached to judicial proceedings. But society instinctively attaches a superior quality to the truth found in this process.[24] Naturally, this special credibility depends on whether fair-trial guarantees have been observed, but the same is true for the reports of "truth commissions": they are respected for what they say and for their methodological rigor, not magically because they are the official word. If the proponents of "truth, not trials" were really interested in truth and not in tokenism, they would have to admit that prosecutions have a place in establishing memory against oblivion.

It is far more difficult to imagine a process that punishes the perpetrators of human rights violations without discovering and disclosing the truth, without reparations, and without separation of known perpetrators from police and military forces. Any kind of victors' justice that does away with these other elements would also very likely violate due process. However, to the extent that punishment without truth-telling is at least possible—even if not in violation of due process—this approach to justice should be rejected as a policy option in any case. A conviction obtained in plea-bargaining, for example, could result in hiding the truth. While plea-bargaining should certainly be a feature in any serious process of accountability, it should not be used in a manner that prevents the truth from being known.[25]

When Not to Conduct Criminal Trials

Ordinarily, the universe of criminal offenses and potential defendants will be so large that it is unrealistic to expect that all or even most will be prosecuted. At times, this inevitable selectivity has been singled out as a reason to abandon prosecution altogether.[26] But selectivity by itself does not render the process unfair, unless of course the basis for the selection is deliberately discriminatory, unbalanced, vindictive, or unreasonable. To the contrary, a process of selection based on reasonable and fair criteria is eminently legitimate. To sustain the legitimacy and credibility of the enterprise, however, the choice of cases must be not only fair, but also readily understandable by the public.

The first self-selecting factor will always be the availability of evidence. The public will understand decisions not to prosecute if these choices are clearly explained and if a good faith effort to search for evidence has been made. It is also reasonable to attempt to complete the process in a relatively short time, as long as deadlines are not arbitrary and do not impose impossible constraints on victims, witnesses, and prosecutors. There is a legitimate interest in conducting proceedings within a reasonable time frame, so that their end can be anticipated and the healing of the wounds can begin. In most cases, there are also good reasons to focus the judiciary's limited resources on the most important cases, while declining to prosecute others. The factors that determine the importance of a case can vary widely, but in principle, the decision to concentrate on the most culpable is a valid criterion. The planners, the intellectual authors of terror, and those who effectively had control over state operations constitute a priority under all circumstances. As demonstrated by the two international tribunals created by the United Nations for the former Yugoslavia and Rwanda, it is important to concentrate efforts—as long as the evidence merits it—on those who had command responsibility. These individuals had the power to turn off the killing machine.

In making these selections, however, it is important not to set a regressive precedent by allowing everyone else involved down the chain of command to escape prosecution on the grounds of having followed orders. At least for offenses that qualify as crimes against humanity, it would be a tremendous step backward to allow obedience to be used as a valid defense, especially when we are dealing with orders that exhibited a manifest illegality or when there was a reasonable chance of disobeying these orders without risking life or limb. With these exceptions, the duty of obedience owed by the defendant should be weighed with the rest of the evidence or, at least, in mitigation of liability. In complex operations, it should be legitimate and even necessary to distinguish between knowing and willing participants and those who contributed their presence, and perhaps their firing power, without knowledge of the overall illegality of their actions and without the ability to determine the outcome. The further we go down the chain of command, the more important it becomes to offer leniency in exchange for cooperation, even if this also results in limiting the number of those prosecuted or punished. In the final analysis, if only the leaders are prosecuted, there will always be protests that more needed to be done. But if the opposite is true, that is, if the leaders are allowed to go free while lowly executors are scapegoated, the public will be outraged at the unfairness of the process.[27]

In the end, the legitimacy of all limitations on transitional trials will depend on the transparency of the process by which they are adopted as much as by their reasonableness and accessibility to the general public. For this reason, it is also important to insist that once the general limits in scope have been announced, the process must be conducted in strict adherence to the rules that have been agreed upon. It does great damage to a legal system's credibility if one tinkers with the rules at different times, adapting them to changing circumstances or backtracking from earlier, more ambitious goals as soon as difficulties appear on the horizon.[28]

It is painfully clear that many injustices can be committed in the name of accountability. For example, in some cases, such as the attempts to use Rwanda's domestic jurisdiction to punish the crime of genocide, it is evident that the effort is bound to lead to a miscarriage of justice, and international public opinion must therefore condemn it. The object should not be to discourage a state like Rwanda from prosecuting genocide altogether, but rather to encourage the new government to live up to its double obligation: to punish the genocide and to do so within the bounds of due process of law. In other cases, the line that has been crossed into unacceptable violations of due process is less clear. After long delays, Ethiopia is finally trying forty-six leaders of the Derg regime for many atrocious crimes.[29] Generally, defendants have a right to a speedy trial, but there is no clear time limitation required by international law, and to some extent this obligation is relative to the circumstances involved, such as the complexity of the facts and availability of resources. In 1996, the Ethiopian trial had only just begun and it is thus too early to tell if the process will be fair in the end. In the meantime, the effort to hold the Derg's leaders accountable for their actions should receive qualified but firm support. Under any circumstance, the international community should oppose the application of the death penalty to those convicted.

Other injustices can be committed under the guise of accountability, even if the process of holding people accountable is not designed to apply to the criminal justice system. For example, "lustration" laws have become a controversial feature of many attempts in Eastern Europe to reckon with the legacy of human rights abuse by the old communist regimes. To the extent that these laws are narrowly drawn to administer the secret files of these states' extensive domestic intelligence services, they can serve a useful purpose in a democracy. The public is entitled to make informed decisions about elections and public policy alternatives, and to do this, it must exercise its right to know the content of these files. At the same time, individuals who are wrongly mentioned in the files are equally entitled to a right to privacy, which should allow them to expunge or to correct any mistakes. Unfortunately, many of the lustration laws have gone far beyond these valid purposes and have ended up banning persons named in secret police lists from a variety of positions in public life, from elected office, and from such professions as university teaching and journalism. This type of disqualification is tantamount to a penal sanction, even if it implies a lesser severity than a prison term. Such a penalty should not be applied under any circumstance without due process of law and a fair trial.

As suggested in some of the cases mentioned above, it is clear that the authority of courts can be easily abused to serve the interests of thinly disguised power plays. Thus, it is important that we cast a critical eye over every effort to engage in "exemplary justice," for this approach comes dangerously close to a recipe for scapegoating.[30] Likewise, it is important to resist all attempts to use the courts to realize the misguided demand for immediate justice in the tribunal of public opinion, just as it is wrong to draw a curtain over efforts to do justice only because the majority does not seem interested in it. Still, even if one is properly attentive to these problems and the initial impulse is absolutely valid, efforts can be misguided. For example, trials may well serve the useful purpose of preserving collective memory. But it would be a serious mistake to expect that they should also "settle" a profound social or political conflict in a country's history or contribute to resolving its interpretation. By definition, historic conflicts cannot be "settled" in the sense that debate about them comes to an end. History is and should always be rewritten. Naturally, courts can help advance a more enlightened debate about a historic conflict if they limit their task to deciding the veracity of facts that constitute crimes and individual responsibility for criminal conduct. One debatable aspect of a historic conflict is thus elevated to the rank of indisputable fact, and courts are better equipped than any other institution to contribute to this task. The debate over the interpretation of facts can then proceed on the basis of shared evidence.[31] If, on the other hand, a trial is seen as an opportunity to validate one interpretation of events over another, this is asking the criminal justice system to do something that it is not particularly well equipped to do. Such a charge could result in discrediting the judicial enterprise itself, at precisely the time when such institutions need to be strengthened.

In this regard, ten years later, the historic trial of the junta members in Argentina continues to have a profound effect on that nation's conscience. The reason is not that the proceedings settled conflicting interpretations of the significance of the bloody confrontation that engulfed the country between 1968 and 1979. Rather, the trial appropriately highlighted the illegality and immorality of the methods that were used in Argentina's "dirty war" and then moved the debate onto a higher plane. There is now a more profound discussion about the motives and justifications of each side, but at the same time, each side's respective supporters have had to reckon with society's underlying disapproval of the methods that they chose.[32] In his trial in Germany, the last leader of the East German Socialist Unity Party, Egon Krenz, tried to argue that criminal trials could not be used to settle the historic conflict between capitalism and socialism that initially prompted him to act in the manner for which he faced prosecution.[33] The point that Krenz missed, however, is that no amount of historical significance can ever allow an official to violate the fundamental laws of his country and of humanity. Strangely enough, Krenz's argument seems to rely on the existence of a "superior law" reminiscent of ancient natural law theories. But in fact, his trial had no such grandiose aspirations. Its success lay in persuading Germans of the need to judge the East-West conflict by making clear distinctions between what was legally and morally wrong and what could be defended as the honest pursuit of a political or ideological objective.

The fact that even the best intentions can fail is an argument for being rigorous about what accountability processes can and cannot do. For example, we need to be attentive to the fact that governments may initiate truth-telling experiments because they realize that collective memory is power. If they succeed in implanting their version of events in the public mind, they can expect to govern for a long time. Such a perverse use of accountability should not be underestimated. Postmodernist thought has provided useful insights into the motives behind every political action, and prompts us to exercise a healthy distrust of measures that are justified in high moral tones. But this approach can also make us cynical about quite worthwhile efforts to restore truth and justice. Worse still, it could cause us to lose confidence in the ability of democratic forces to shape events to good effect, even if they cannot always control them. Indeed, even if an accountability process is launched with mean-spirited intentions and motivated by the desire to subordinate others, it can still be made to achieve an important objective in consolidating democracy and promoting social solidarity. In the end, a good faith effort at investigating and disclosing events still mired in secrecy can never be perfectly governed. Yet if the organizations of civil society actively participate in the process (even while holding reservations about some aspects of the undertaking), they can and often do alter the course of events and manage to transcend the initial boundaries of their government's intentions. The circumstances in which these processes unfold will never fully live up to our ideals of what they should be. But as long as the possibility remains open that they might advance the twin causes of truth and justice, they deserve our support and our critical but enthusiastic participation.

NOTES

1. Cynthia Brown and Robert K. Goldman, *Challenging Impunity: The "Ley de Caducidad" and the Referendum Campaign in Uruguay* (New York: Americas Watch, 1989); Lawrence Weschler, *A Miracle, A Universe* (New York: Pantheon, 1990); Joan Dassin, ed., *Brasil Nunca Mais* (New York: Vintage Books, 1986); Servicio Paz y Justicia Uruguay, *Uruguay Nunca Mas: Human Rights Violations, 1972–1985* (Philadelphia: Temple University Press, 1992). The latter two publications are the English versions of nongovernmental efforts in Brazil and Uruguay to document the truth about the human rights violations of their respective military dictatorships.

2. This posture led President Jimmy Carter to his ill-advised offer of a blanket amnesty to General Raoul Cedras and his men, as a condition for Haiti's return to constitutional government.

3. José Zalaquett, "Confronting Human Rights Violations Committed by Former Governments: Principles Applicable and Political Constraints," in *State Crimes: Punishment or Pardon* (Queenstown, Md.: Aspen Institute, 1989), pp. 23–65; and later in *Hamline Law Review* 13, no. 3 (1990): 623–660.

4. Of course, the issue of accountability also arises in settings that are not "transitional" in nature: with regard to ongoing violations or to violations committed in the recent past by the same government that is asked to redress them; as conditions in a peace process designed to end a military conflict; and as lingering issues well after a transition to democracy has

ended. Examples of these nontransitional settings are, respectively: the demands for accountability in countries like Peru and Colombia; the debate about truth and justice in the UN-sponsored processes in El Salvador, Guatemala, the former Yugoslavia, and Rwanda; and the revitalized debate about the duty owed to the families of the "disappeared" in Argentina that has taken place in 1995 and 1996. For this reason, it is probably advisable not to think of these issues strictly in terms of transitions to democracy. After all, even a government that reaches power through complete military victory faces constraints in what it can do to punish its old enemies, in the form of international standards of due process and political pressure from the international community. In addition, restricting our view solely to situations of transition has resulted in assuming too much about the political constraints faced by new democratic governments, at times preventing a clear-eyed and realistic assessment of the threats and of the relative power of democratic forces to overcome them. It is preferable, therefore, to focus our attention first on the obligations that states owe to victims of human rights abuse *in all circumstances*, and then to examine each situation for obstacles that are actual and not imagined.

5. Article 4, International Covenant on Civil and Political Rights, UN General Assembly Resolution 2200-A (XXI) of December 16, 1966; entered into force, March 23, 1976. Under this article, nonderogable rights are: the right to life; freedom from torture and cruel, inhuman, or degrading treatment; freedom from slavery and involuntary servitude; freedom from prison for debts; the right to a fair trial; the right to recognition as a person under the law; and freedom of thought, conscience, and religion.

6. Article 146, IV Geneva Convention Relative to the Protection of Civilian Persons in Time of War, August 12, 1949. (The 1949 Geneva Conventions amend and re-codify previously existing instruments of the body of law generally known as "international humanitarian law.") Although grave breaches once applied only to international conflicts, the obligation to punish and universal jurisdiction over them have been extended to similar acts when committed in conflicts not of an international character. See the Security Council resolution creating the International Criminal Tribunal for Rwanda, Resolution no. 955, November 8, 1995; the International Criminal Tribunal for the Former Yugoslavia, *The Prosecutor v. Dusko Tadic a.k.a. "Dule,"* Case No. IT-94-1-AR72, Decision on the Defense Motion of Interlocutory Appeal on Jurisdiction, The Hague, October 2, 1995; and Theodore Meron, "International Criminalization of Internal Atrocities," *American Journal of International Law* 89, no. 3 (July 1995): 554–577.

7. Diane Orentlicher, "Settling Accounts: The Duty to Prosecute Human Rights Violations of a Prior Regime," *Yale Law Journal* 100, no. 8 (June 1991): 2537; Diane Orentlicher, "Addressing Gross Human Rights Abuses: Punishment and Victim Compensation," in *Human Rights: An Agenda for the Next Century*, ed. Louis Henkin and John L. Hargrove (Washington, D.C.: 1994). See also American Society of International Law, Naomi Roht-Arriaza, ed., *Impunity and Human Rights in International Law and Practice* (New York:

Oxford, 1995). Two Special Rapporteurs appointed by the United Nations have had occasion to explore this obligation in depth: Theo Van Boven, Special Rapporteur on Restitution, Compensation, and Reparations for Gross and Consistent Violations of Human Rights (whose final report on the subject was published by the UN Commission on Human Rights, 45th Session, Provisional Agenda Item 4, UN Doc. E/CN.4/Sub.2); and Louis Joinet, Special Rapporteur on Impunity, whose final report is forthcoming.

8. The most articulate proponents of these two positions are José Zalaquett and Aryeh Neier, respectively. See one manifestation of their long-standing debate about this topic in Alex Boraine, Janet Levy, and Ronel Scheffer, eds., *Dealing with the Past: Truth and Reconciliation in South Africa* (Cape Town, South Africa: IDASA, 1994).

9. Marcelo Sancinetti, *Los derechos humanos en la Argentina post-dictatorial* (Buenos Aires: Lerner Editores Asociados, 1988).

10. Germán J. Bidart Campos, "La víctima del delito y el proceso penal," in *El Derecho*, Buenos Aires, no. 8834, September 14, 1995, p. 7.

11. Adam Michnik, in *Dealing with the Past*, p. 16.

12. The phrase is attributed to Tadeusz Mazowiecki, Poland's first prime minister after the fall of communism. Later, as Special Rapporteur for the UN on the Former Yugoslavia, Mazowiecki contributed strongly to the international community's decision to prosecute perpetrators of genocide. See Timothy Garton Ash, "Central Europe: The Present Past" (review of Tina Rosenberg's *The Haunted Land: Facing Europe's Ghosts after Communism*), in *The New York Review of Books*, July 13, 1995, pp. 21–23.

13. See Michnik, in *Dealing with the Past*, p. 16. This was also the subject of an oral intervention by the author at the Conference on Truth and Reconciliation for South Africa, Cape Town, February 1994.

14. Mark J. Osiel, "Ever Again: Legal Remembrance of Administrative Massacre," *University of Pennsylvania Law Review* 144, no. 2 (December 1995): 463–704.

15. Richard Goldstone, the South African judge and first Prosecutor General for the International Criminal Tribunals for the Former Yugoslavia and Rwanda, recently made this point, in Lawrence Weschler, "Inventing Peace," *The New Yorker*, November 20, 1995, pp. 56–64. A similar point has been made by Kenneth Roth in the introductory essay to Human Rights Watch, *World Report 1996*, New York, December 1995, p. xv. This argument is made specifically with regard to egregious crimes committed in the context of ethnic conflict; I believe it applies, however, *mutatis mutandi*, to other situations in which impunity can cast a shadow over all members of a political, law enforcement, or military elite.

16. Article 19, International Covenant on Civil and Political Rights.

17. In the early days of Chile's new democracy, General Augusto Pinochet laid down this threat in its most blunt form when he declared that democracy was all well and good but that "if a single one of my men is touched [by attempts at accountability], I will put an end to the rule of law."

18. José Zalaquett calls this principle a "condition of legitimacy" of any policy of accountability; see "Confronting Human Rights Violations."

19. See chapter 6 on Hungary in this volume, "Living Well is the Best Revenge," by Gábor Halmai and Kim Lane Scheppele.

20. Inter-American Court of Human Rights, *Velásquez Rodríguez Case*, Judgment of July 29, 1988.

21. See Van Boven's final report, note 7 above.

22. Charles Krauthammer, "Truth, Not Trials," *The Washington Post*, September 9, 1994; Robert Pastor, of the Carter Center, cited in Neil A. Lewis, "Nuremberg Isn't Repeating Itself," *The New York Times*, November 19, 1995; David Forsyth, "The UN and Human Rights at Fifty: An Incremental but Incomplete Revolution," *Global Governance* 1 (1995): 297–318.

23. This is the kind of public ritual that transforms knowledge into "acknowledgement," in the words of Prof. Thomas Nagel, as quoted by Lawrence Weschler in the prologue to *State Crimes*.

24. Carlos S. Nino, *Radical Evil on Trial* (New Haven: Yale University Press, 1996), as quoted by Mark J. Osiel, "Ever Again," p. 472 n. 30.

25. Plea-bargaining can be useful even within a policy of limited clemency, as long as the purpose is accountability and not impunity. An example of this is the process under way in South Africa, by which a Truth and Reconciliation Commission, chaired by Archbishop Desmond Tutu, is charged with presenting a report on the crimes of the apartheid era and with dispensing conditional amnesty ("indemnity") to perpetrators willing to make full confessions. Indemnity will be granted only for the offenses to which they admit and on condition of their truthfulness. A subcommittee on amnesty, entrusted to three separately appointed judges, can deny the benefit if, in the panel's judgment, the crimes were committed with particular malice or for personal gain so that indemnity from prosecution is deemed unwarranted. Although at this writing the work of the Truth and Reconciliation Commission has just begun, it is expected that this conditional amnesty will greatly enhance the ability of the commission to obtain the truth.

26. Forsyth, "The UN and Human Rights at Fifty."

27. See the contrasting decisions by German judges Seidel and Tepperwein, as cited by A. James McAdams in chapter 8 of this volume.

28. For example, several abrupt changes of course by the Alfonsín administration were what tarnished the otherwise historic significance of Argentina's attempt to reckon with the violations of the "dirty war." In this evaluation, I disagree with José Zalaquett, who thinks the problem was that Alfonsín attempted much more than the objective situation allowed (in *Dealing with the Past*, p. 40) and with Aryeh Neier, who thinks that in retrospect it would have been better to prosecute only the leaders of repression under the junta (Aryeh Neier, "What Should be Done about the Guilty?" *The New York Review of Books*, February 1, 1990, pp. 32–35.

29. James C. McKinley, Jr., "Ethiopia Tries Former Rulers in 70s Deaths," *The New York Times*, April 23, 1996, p. A-1. In an unfortunate interpretation of the customary-law rule barring extradition for "political

offenses," Zimbabwe has refused to extradite the dictator Mengistu Haile Mariam, who is being tried in absentia.

30. In the UN-sponsored peace talks on El Salvador, the FMLN representatives insisted on breaking the cycle of impunity by means of "exemplary trials." Though the process did produce an important Truth Commission report, the final outcome was an amnesty law that prevented any of the thousands of crimes of the twelve-year war from ever being examined.

31. Osiel, "Ever Again."

32. Luis Moreno Ocampo, *Cuando el poder perdió el juicio* (Buenos Aires: Planeta, 1996). As striking examples of this enlightened debate, one could cite the many public demonstrations on and around March 26, 1996 in numerous Argentine cities, commemorating the twentieth anniversary of the coup d'état of 1976. With respect to reevaluations of the experience with revolutionary armed struggle, see the documentary "Cazadores de Utopias" by David Blaustein (1996).

33. Stephen Kinzer, "We Weren't Following Orders, But the Currents of the Cold War," *The New York Times*, March 24, 1996, p. E-7.

2

Politics and the Judiciary in the Greek Transition to Democracy

Nicos C. Alivizatos and P. Nikiforos Diamandouros

THE COLLAPSE OF THE Greek authoritarian regime on July 23, 1974 opened the way for the establishment of the most genuinely democratic government in modern Greek history. The circumstances surrounding the installation of this regime and the conditions facilitating the consolidation of democracy in Greece have received limited, though growing, attention from scholars, particularly from political scientists.[1] But the focus of these studies has mainly been on the role of political elites, political institutions, and political forces more generally in making this latest attempt at democratization a success. With only one partial exception, remarkably few efforts have been made to concentrate specifically on the manner in which the new democracy sought to cope with the legacy of its authoritarian predecessor, the subject of nearly complete condemnation and rejection by the majority of the Greek population.[2] Nor have there been many attempts to assess the impact of these policies on the initial stabilization of the government, its eventual consolidation, and the quality of the democracy resulting from the collapse of the "colonels' rule" that had defined Greek politics since the military coup of April 1967.

A distinctive, if not unique, characteristic of the Greek democratization process after 1974 was the central role that the judicial system was called to play in dealing with the country's authoritarian past. Greece stands virtually alone among third-wave democracies in having effectively, and without adverse consequences for its new democratic government, imposed heavy sanctions on a significant number of individuals,[3] including military personnel, found guilty of crimes associated with the preceding nondemocratic regime. In this specific sense, and despite substantive differences, the successful judicial prosecution and subsequent long-term incarceration of these individuals has led some observers to liken the Greek case to that of the Nuremberg trials, which resulted in the long-term imprisonment of the principal figures behind the Nazi dictatorship in Germany.[4]

This chapter constitutes a first attempt to explore systematically the role of justice in the twin processes of democratic transition and consolidation in Greece. In particular, we seek to explain why Greece succeeded in a crucial policy area in which many other states have failed: they either tried to take action but were forced to retreat in the face of determined opposition; or, for whatever reason (e.g., formal pacts or unofficial but binding understandings between the outgoing regime and the incoming democratic leadership), they deliberately elected to shy away from taking action that might risk a severe backlash, endangering newly acquired freedoms and raising the specter of authoritarian involution.

The period of our analysis extends from the end of the colonels' authoritarian regime on July 23, 1974, to December 1975, the point at which the last of the major, so-called "junta trials" took place. These trials dealt with the main individuals implicated in illegal acts under the authoritarian regime. As such, this period straddles the Greek transition and consolidation processes and should be regarded as an integral part of both. The transition to democracy is conventionally understood to extend from July 24, 1974, when the new civilian government under Constantine Karamanlis assumed power, to November 17, 1974, when the first postauthoritarian elections endowed the new regime with democratic legitimacy. The consolidation period had its roots in this transition and was completed sometime between 1977, when the country's newest political party, the Panhellenic Socialist Movement (PASOK), abandoned its semiloyal stance vis-à-vis the democratic government, and 1981, when the same party, having fully accepted the basic rules of the democratic game, triumphantly came to power. It brought with it an end to the almost forty-year-long domination of political life by the Greek Right.[5]

The discrete period that concerns us here spans the m
and precarious moments of the broader processes just de
salient features, which profoundly influenced the partic
tory that the new government traveled on its way to con:
were threefold. The first feature was the threat of war wi... ɪurkey
over the Cyprus crisis, which acted as a powerful demobilization
mechanism for strategically located elites and resulted in the com-
mensurate containment of mass actors. As such, it also imparted a
fragile but critical stability to the Greek transition. The second was
the gradual neutralization of the Greek armed forces as an autonomous political force, due to its patent failure to serve as a credible guardian of national security and to effectively confront the
external military threat in the Cyprus crisis. This process of neutralization was completed in February 1975, when the discovery of a military conspiracy against the new democratic regime enabled the
civilian government to engage in a fairly far-reaching purge, ending
the political autonomy of the armed forces and, for the first time in
almost three decades, ensuring civilian control over the military. The
third feature was the major freedom of movement which was paradoxically provided by these circumstances, both to the new civilian
leadership and, above all, to its leader Karamanlis, who emerged as
the dominant political figure of the transition period and as the ar-
chitect of Greek democratization.

With the benefit of hindsight, we can now see the chief characteristics of Karamanlis's transition and consolidation strategies, which
made his leadership so distinctive. On the one hand, he fought to
promote rapid movement towards early elections to invest the new
regime, its institutions, and his rule with democratic legitimacy.
Through a fair referendum, he also sought to resolve the thorny and
controversial question of the nature of the head of state (monarchy
versus republic), which had repeatedly served as a source of profound division in Greek political life during the twentieth century.
Finally, he pushed for the adoption of a new constitution better
suited to Greece's new political realities. By contrast, the other side of
Karamanlis's transition and consolidation strategy reflected a strong
preference for a gradualist approach to politics. Karamanlis sought
to carefully balance change and innovation with continuity and

tradition in the implementation of policies that he hoped would generate legitimacy for the new regime and ensure its consolidation. As we shall see, this strategy was especially noticeable in those initiatives that were designed to deal with problems surrounding Greece's authoritarian past.[6]

The Judicial Context

The involvement of the judiciary in the new regime's handling of the legacy of its authoritarian predecessor has to be understood within the general political context that we have described above. But in addition, it is also important to take into account the history of the Greek judiciary's relationship with the legislative and executive branches of government.

The Greek judicial tradition is firmly situated within the civil law tradition dominant in Continental, as opposed to Anglo-Saxon, societies. This fact has profound implications for the role, place, social status, and education accorded judges. In sharp contrast to judicial officials in common law countries, who are consciously and deliberately assigned the politically influential role of developing and even creating legal rules, the judge in civil law countries, including Greece, is supposed to act as a mere "operator of a machine designed by scientists and built by legislators." His or her main function is to enforce the law, without openly seeking to acquire real political influence.[7]

A direct by-product of the deep commitment to the civil law tradition in Greece is the powerful and broader legacy of legal positivism that the country inherited primarily from the wholesale introduction of German and French law during the initial period of state-building under the Bavarian monarchy of King Otho I (1832–1862). The most salient characteristic of legal positivism is its propensity to assign a predominant role to the state in its relations with society and to consider the state as the sole source of law as well as rights.

In the Greek case, the prevalence of civil law and legal positivism has effectively translated into a judicial tradition that has been remarkably quiescent vis-à-vis both the legislative and the executive branches. Thus, with rare exceptions, judges have been singularly unwilling to contest the will of the other two branches of govern-

ment, as crystallized in specific acts. Prior to the judiciary's involvement in the trials of individuals prominently associated with the
colonels' regime—which, as we shall see, resulted in both the sentencing and the long-term incarceration of those found guilty—Greek
judges had only rarely found themselves playing such a role in earlier periods of their country's modern history.[8]

The same pattern of quiescence and accommodation was observable during the quarter century following the end of the Greek civil
war (1946–1949). In the parliamentary phase of the post-civil-war
state (1949–1967), a period marked by the ideological ascendancy of
profoundly anticommunist political forces and by systematic state
discrimination against the left and, more generally, against the vanquished side in that war, the courts consistently supported the positions of the right-wing governments of the time. They presented
narrow and formalistic readings of the bill of rights and a broad interpretation of the rules governing the powers of the executive.

This pattern persisted with remarkable consistency during the
authoritarian regime of 1967–1974 and was reinforced and legiti-
mated by legislation dating from the civil war period, which had
been applied by the courts virtually throughout the intervening
years and which greatly restricted civil liberties (e.g., through de-
portations and loyalty controls). This continuity was marked by two
twists. First, in addition to the accommodation typical of the vast
majority in the judicial corps, a small number of prominent judges
actively supported the regime. In the original cabinet appointed by
the colonels on April 22, 1967, a day after their seizure of power, at
least five senior judges occupied prominent positions. These included the premiership itself, held by the incumbent public prosecutor at the Greek Court of Cassation (Areios Pagos), and the
ministries of Justice, Education, Public Works, and Social Welfare
and Health.[9] Second, in a striking and rare break with continuity, the
country's highest administrative court, the Council of State, openly
clashed with the regime in June 1969 over the dismissal, a year earlier, of thirty magistrates considered politically undesirable by the
regime, including the president of the Court of Cassation. The dismissals were effected through a highly controversial procedure involving the suspension, by means of a constitutional act lasting

three days, of the constitutionally guaranteed tenure of judicial magistrates. The Council's 1969 decision to invalidate both the 1968 dismissals and the regime's subsequent denial of the thirty dismissed
judges' right to practice law led to the forced resignation (none was
formally submitted) of the president of the Council of State and the
removal of one of its vice presidents and eight of its members.[10]

Despite the political attention that it inevitably received, the military regime's purge of the judiciary occasioned by this confrontation
with the Council of State was an isolated event that did nothing to reverse either the established tradition of judicial accommodation or
the inclination to heed the political will of successive regimes,
whether parliamentary or authoritarian. As a result, the major problems confronting the judiciary at the time of the 1974 transition to
democracy stemmed from its experience under authoritarianism. On
the one hand, the bulk of its membership was compromised through
its acquiescence to or accommodation with the colonels' regime. On
the other hand, as the 1969 confrontation involving the Council of
State showed, the authoritarian experience had a divisive impact on
the judiciary as a whole.[11]

The Trials and the Prosecutions

Given this political and judicial background, the central dilemma facing the new regime in 1974 was whether or not to make use of the
courts in its attempt to deal with crimes committed by and under its
military predecessor. Karamanlis opted, albeit with some delay, for
using the courts. However, this decision reflected less a newfound
spirit of judicial activism in support of democratic norms than the
presence of a strong political will shared by the overwhelming majority of Greeks, both elites and masses, to end all further experiments with authoritarianism and *democraduras* and to install a
durable and fully democratic regime. Karamanlis's democratization
strategy gave elegant, but also poignant, expression to this pervasive
political will, which will serve as the backdrop to our analysis for the
remainder of this chapter.

The decision concerning the potential use of the courts as an instrument in the Greek democratization process required answers to

three separate questions: (a) whether the government should pursue criminal prosecutions of those responsible for the military regime; (b) what the actual scope of these prosecutions should be, in the event such a course of action was taken; and (c) what the depth of purging in the armed forces should be, as well as in critical sectors of the state mechanism, such as the police, the civil service, the universities, and the judiciary.

To Prosecute or Not to Prosecute?

A major complicating factor affecting the decision whether or not to prosecute those responsible for the seizure of power on April 21, 1967 and for the subsequent establishment of the authoritarian regime stemmed from the phrasing of Presidential Decree 519, which was issued on July 26, 1974, just two days after the assumption of power by the civilian government. Included in this government were prominent conservative and centrist representatives of the preauthoritarian period and of the resistance to the colonels. However, figures from the left were completely excluded. Decree 519 was specifically designed to provide an amnesty to all jailed opponents of the authoritarian regime, but it did not explicitly specify whether it also covered acts undertaken by the protagonists and secondary figures of that regime. Although the point was little noticed at the time, it subsequently acquired major political and legal significance and became the center of fierce debate concerning the new regime's right to prosecute those who had been associated with the worst excesses of its predecessor.[12]

Politically, the issue was repeatedly raised by the radical opposition to the democratic governments of 1974–1975. This challenge was best exemplified by the new political formation of PASOK and above all by its fiery and charismatic leader, Andreas Papandreou, who systematically referred to the vague phrasing of Decree 519 in order to support his argument that the change in regime was nothing more than a change of guard in a NATO-sponsored political arrangement. Legally, the same issue was invoked by the defense (the colonels and their accomplices) during the period of the trials as an argument designed to deny the validity of the prosecutions against the principals of the military regime, on the grounds that they had, in fact, been included in the amnesty provided by decree 519.

The first suit against the leaders of the 1967 coup was not initiated until September 9, 1974. Prior to this date, the issue of prosecution had barely been raised by either the political parties or the mass media. On the very few occasions when it was raised, the calls for action were carefully phrased and did not go beyond measured appeals for "fair trials" or statements concerning the need for "justice to decide." In large part, this caution was mainly due to continuing uncertainty stemming from the threat of a military confrontation with Turkey, which until mid-August 1974 hung heavily over the Greek political scene. In terms of domestic politics, this uncertainty translated into lingering concerns over the military's readiness to acquiesce to punitive action against some of its members and, conversely, the capacity of the new civilian leadership to exercise enough control over events and over the actions of specific individuals to ensure an uneventful unfolding of the transition process.[13]

To give but two illustrations of these circumstances, the strongman of the final, hard-line phase of the Greek dictatorship (November 1973–July 1974), Brigadier General Dimitrios Ioannides, continued to make public appearances as late as the end of September 1974, and he remained free until January 14, 1975. Similarly, George Papadopoulos, the leader of the 1967 coup, also moved around freely until September 25, 1974, when he was initially placed under house detention. He was not arrested until October 23, when, along with four other principals of the fallen regime (S. Pattakos, M. Roufogales, I. Ladas, and N. Makarezos), he was deported to the Aegean island of Kea. And it was not until January 20, 1975 that he was placed under preventive detention and actually jailed. Finally, indicative of the climate of uncertainty and tenuousness which reigned during the initial postauthoritarian period was a statement made by the Minister of Public Order, Solon Ghikas, on September 30, 1974, to the effect that thirty-three specified protagonists of the previous regime were free to travel abroad if they so wished.[14]

In light of the above, it is important to note that the first legal action brought against fifteen principal figures of the 1967 coup was not even initiated by a state agency. Rather, it was undertaken by a private citizen, Alexandros Lykourezos. Although subsequently well known and highly controversial, Lykourezos was at the time a relatively obscure Athens attorney. His action was important in at least four major ways. First, it was timely, in the sense that occurred at precisely the moment when the first calls for movement on this sensitive topic were being aired but before they had acquired the kind of momentum that would make it difficult to contain them or channel them in a direction conducive to the success of the overall democratization process. Second, it allowed the government to "have its cake and eat it too." On the one hand, it forced the state's hand, in the sense that it rendered continuing inaction on this issue more difficult and politically costly. On the other hand, it relieved the government of the burden of having to initiate the proceedings itself and thus lowered the political cost it might have incurred vis-à-vis recalcitrant sectors of the military establishment. In this respect, Lykourezos's action, whether intentionally (on this, there is yet no evidence) or accidentally, carefully balanced the rising expectations for action against concerns about military reaction, and fit neatly within the logic of Karamanlis's gradualist democratization strategy. Third, it opened the way for other private citizens to file additional lawsuits concerning crimes committed by the regime, and thus it affected the scope of prosecution commensurately. Finally, the Lykourezos initiative was important in another way, whose long-term implications were difficult to assess at the time. In allowing for the criminal prosecution of individuals associated with the imposition of military rule in Greece, it forced actors from both elite and mass sectors into a course whose logic and dynamic would later make extrication very difficult and costly. In so doing, it affected the character of the country's democratization process in a significant manner.[15]

The specific accusation leveled against Papadopoulos, Pattakos, Makarezos, Ioannides, and their closest collaborators was high treason, a charge carrying a maximum penalty of life imprisonment. A military judge with the rank of general, E. Plevrakes, was placed in charge of the judicial inquiry concerning this matter. The question that arose immediately (and that was indicative of the complexities implicit in the choice to involve the courts in the democratization process) was how the newly appointed chief of the armed forces,

General Dimitrios Arbouzes, who was by law the competent authority to initiate criminal proceedings against individuals accused of
crimes in their military capacity, would act. Would he choose to go
forward with the action or, conversely, opt to close the file on the
case? At this point, the government stepped in.[16]

On October 3, 1974, the Karamanlis government issued a new
constitutional act, its sixth since assuming power. It explicitly excluded the "protagonists" ("those primarily responsible," or *pro-
taitioi*) of the military regime from the July 1974 amnesty decree and
charged the Athens Court of Appeals with the responsibility for investigating, prosecuting, and adjudicating the case. On November 1,
1974, the court's more than one hundred members decided in ple-
nary session to prosecute the case and assigned responsibility for the
investigation to Judge Georghios Voltes, a moderate conservative.[17]
The investigation phase was completed in spring 1975. On July 28,
1975, a full year after the collapse of Greece's authoritarian regime
and almost ten months after the initial filings of the pertinent suit, the
trial began before the five-member Athens Court of Appeals.

The Scope of Prosecution

The scope of prosecution was an even more delicate issue. Although
the number of those investigated for potential complicity in the
April 21, 1967 seizure of power reached approximately one hundred, only twenty-four of these were eventually charged. Charges
against the rest were dropped on grounds of insufficient evidence.
To a large extent, the court's decision to confine prosecution to such
a small number was due to the narrow wording used in the constitutional act of October 3, 1974. But it also reflected Karamanlis's
own position on the matter.[18]

Private citizens were the moving force as well in the initiation of
two major prosecutions dealing with the bloody suppression of the
student uprising at the National Technical University of Greece
(commonly known as Athens Polytechnic) on November 17, 1973,
and the torturing of political prisoners. Thirty-two individuals
were finally charged with complicity in the first case. They included

G. Papadopoulos, the regime's top man until the student uprising, and Ioannides, the hard-liner who toppled Papadopoulos and put an end to the tightly controlled civilianization of the regime which the latter had set in motion after his election to the position of head of state in an uncontested referendum held in July 1973. The case concerning the events at the Polytechnic held great symbolic significance, both because the uprising was by far the most serious collective act of resistance against the regime and because of the large, though indeterminate, number of persons who were killed in the course of the suppression, most of whom were young. This case was also heard before the five-member Athens Court of Appeals, beginning on October 16, 1975.

The most striking fact about the so-called torture trials was their initially large number. More than one thousand individuals were charged by victims or alleged victims. Of these, however, only a small number were actually tried before competent courts. A series of factors combined to bring about this outcome. By far the most important of these was the gradual emergence of a political will at the governmental level to limit the scope of trials involving alleged torturers, even if this meant that large numbers of malefactors would go unpunished.

In great part, this unstated policy reflected a particular refinement of Karamanlis's strategy for a balanced and gradualist approach to the overall democratization process. The new regime was deeply concerned about the potentially disruptive, derailing, and politically costly impact of developments or events that might get "out of control," and it was driven by an intense determination to contain them. More than any other proceedings against officials of the authoritarian regime, the torture trials held a distinct potential for proliferation— hence, the decision to restrict them. In line with this logic, the government placed, by law, a time limit on the filing of private lawsuits against alleged torturers, allowing six months for high regime officials and three for others. It is worth noting that, according to Amnesty International, which closely monitored the torturers' trials, this time limitation resulted in the eventual dismissal of two-thirds of the privately initiated cases on the technical grounds that the plaintiffs missed the deadline for filing complaints by one day.[19] Nonetheless, the two trials of torturers in the military police (ESA) still received the greatest public attention. A total of fifty-five active and retired officers, petty officers, and conscripts were eventually brought before the military court of Athens in August and October 1975.

The government's preference for gradualism and containment in dealing with offenses associated with the past regime was especially observable in the case of the calls for purging the broader state mechanism of holdovers from the old regime. The first changes in the leadership of the military were restricted to the army alone, and even then did not take place until almost a month after the collapse of the junta. At that time, August 19, 1974, one four-star, five three-star, and four two-star generals, all in the army, were retired. Deeper purges, as well as the handling of individuals potentially dangerous to the nascent democratic regime, took much longer to effect. Again, the pertinent decisions were notable for their caution. For every step the government took, its actions were accompanied by carefully phrased rationales designed to minimize, if not to eliminate at the formal level, the punitive impact of the action taken. Thus, the decision to retire Ioannides was taken on August 24 on the notable grounds that it was necessary in order to promote younger brigadier generals without violating seniority. Another month passed before the hard core of Ioannides' collaborators were placed on temporary suspension; in fact, their final dismissal did not occur until the discovery of a conspiracy against the new democratic regime in February 1975. This event gave the government the golden opportunity it needed to bring about the retirement of a broad range of individuals associated with the fallen authoritarian regime.[20]

Things moved faster in the case of the police. By August 1, E. Mallios and P. Babales, two of the most prominent members of the security branch of the Athens police, who had distinguished themselves in pursuing opponents of the regime, were reassigned to insignificant posts carrying menial responsibilities. At the same time, the chief of the notorious Special Investigating Section of the Military Police (EAT-ESA), Major A. Spanos, was transferred to a unit at the Greek-Bulgarian border. On September 11, 1974, seventeen of the more prominent officers in the security branch of the Athens police were relieved of their duties for periods ranging from four to twelve months. The fate of lower-ranking policemen implicated in the persecution of opponents of the regime remains unclear. It would nevertheless appear that very few, if any, among them faced any consequences for their activities.[21]

The Depth of Prosecution

The scope of purges in the judiciary, the civil service, and the wider public sector conforms to the general pattern we have already described. Trials were limited to the upper echelons of all three bodies and did not touch the bulk of their personnel, despite evidence to support the fact that during the period of authoritarian rule, many had not strictly confined themselves to the execution of their duties. In the case of the judiciary, those dismissed by the military regime were reinstated to the positions they would have attained had they not been dismissed or reached the mandatory retirement age. In addition, the leaders of all three high courts (the Court of Cassation, the Council of State, and the Cour des Comptes) were replaced by new appointees of the civilian government. In the case of the Council of State, which in 1969 had become embroiled in a celebrated confrontation with the military regime, the new leadership was drawn from among those who had been dismissed and subsequently reinstated. In the case of the Court of Cassation and of the Cour des Comptes, the new leadership was selected from the ranks of those serving at the time.[22]

On the other hand, and in line with the policy of contained retribution, the decision to accept appointment as a prosecutor in the authoritarian regime's military courts was not regarded by the democratic civilian leadership as an act constituting a disciplinary infraction. All in all, only twenty-three justices sitting in the country's three highest courts were summoned before the standing judicial council responsible for disciplinary offenses. Significantly, charges brought against these individuals, in accord with express provisions of the constitutional act of September 5, 1974, were confined to those promoted to

higher ranks by the military regime or those who accepted a ministerial appointment under the colonels. This was despite the fact that the
same act armed the Minister of Justice with discretionary power to en-
large the scope of disciplinary action to be taken against those found
guilty of having engaged in "disrespectable acts or behavior within or
outside their duties, in a manner offending the status, or prestige of
the judicial branch of government."[23]

In the banking sector, as well as in the wider public sector, which
consisted primarily of the public utilities, the purges assumed the
form of the dismissal of the top leadership without compensation.
This occurred in early August 1974. Prefects and mayors were replaced in September. In the civil service itself, the major issue of contention was more the reinstatement of those dismissed by the
authoritarian regime than the dismissal of those accused of complicity in pro-regime activities.[24]

Interestingly, the only sector in which purges reached below the
top layer was that of the universities. The constitutional act of September 3, 1974 provided for disciplinary action not only against those
members of the academic staff who had accepted ministerial and/or
other senior political appointments (e.g., bank governors or advisors
to ministers) but also against those of whom "well-grounded indications" of political collaboration with the regime could be adduced.
This greater depth in the purges in the case of the universities can be
attributed in part to the creation of student committees of "dejuntification," which were tolerated, if not instigated, by the new civilian
leadership in the Ministry of Education.[25]

It is also worth noting in this context that the universities and the
judiciary were the only two areas in which the prosecution of those
implicated for collaboration with the authoritarian regime was assigned to individuals who had been its victims. In the case of the judiciary, prosecutorial responsibility was assigned to disciplinary
councils that included judges who had once been dismissed by the
colonels. In the case of the universities, the responsibility for prosecution was entrusted to an ad hoc disciplinary council. Both bodies
were presided over by Justice G. Marangopoulos, the first postauthoritarian president of the Council of State, who had been one of
the judges dismissed by the colonels in 1968.

Trials and Selective Punishment

Of the many trials involving individuals implicated in activities favoring the authoritarian regime, by far the most important was the one dealing with the principal figures in the April 21, 1967 seizure of power. Charges were initially leveled against twenty-four former officers, whom the Athens Court of Appeals labeled as the "protagonists" of the 1967 coup. The indictment brought against them was high treason (in accordance with Article 134 of the criminal code of 1950) and sedition (as defined in Article 63 of the military code of 1941). Twenty of the twenty-four were actually tried. Three of the remaining four had gone into hiding, thus escaping arrest, and one (Th. Theofylogiannakos) was, at virtually the same time, tried on allegations of torture. In addition to Papadopoulos, Pattakos, and Makarezos, who formed the dominant troika of the regime prior to the internal coup carried out by the hard-liner Ioannides in November 1973, the most prominent members in this group were Ioannides himself; G. Spandidakes, a senior general, who at the time of the coup held the crucial position of chief of the army and whose decision to join the insurgents as the putsch was unfolding greatly aided their cause; G. Zoitakes, another general and, in 1967, head of the powerful Third Army Corps, who was appointed regent following the failed royal countercoup of December 13, 1967 against the colonels and King Constantine's departure from Greece; and O. Angheles, the third of only four generals to have sided with the colonels, who served as the regime's chief of the armed forces and, after July 1973, as deputy head of state.[26]

The court of appeals consisted of five judges and two alternates. It was presided over by Ioannes Degiannes, a respected senior judge, who had a liberal-centrist reputation and whose career had not been adversely affected by the authoritarian regime. The remaining justices were also known for their professional integrity and for their moderate political views. The public prosecutor was C. Stamates, also a career judge, who simultaneously held a tenured position in the law faculty of the University of Athens. The judges, as well as the public prosecutor, were selected from among their peers sitting in the Athens Court of Appeals. To date, there is no evidence suggesting any direct attempt by the government to influence the selection procedure by which the court was composed. Long-standing regulations concerning this appointment procedure, however, assign to the president of the Court of Cassation responsibility for selecting, from its own membership, the head of the court of appeals, who in turn selects the particular panel to adjudicate a case. Thus, to the extent that a new leadership of the Court of Cassation had been recently appointed by the civilian government, the possibility that an indirect influence was exercised on the selection of the panel which presided over the trial of the authoritarian regime's protagonists cannot be excluded.[27]

The trial lasted from July 28 to August 23, 1975, and was held in specially arranged quarters in the women's section of the Korydallos penitentiary in Athens. Security considerations dictated the choice of location. While allowing access to journalists, such a location and the amount of security checks that it necessitated made it easier to discourage attendance by the wider public. The trial was covered by closed-circuit television, which was available to the Greek and foreign press corps, but not to the Greek public.

Of the nineteen court sessions that were devoted to the trial, eleven were spent on the examination of the sixty-five witnesses for the prosecution, who mainly consisted of the civilian and military leadership that either held office or occupied prominent political positions on the early morning of April 21, 1967. The civilian group, which covered the entire spectrum of political parties legally operating at the time of the coup, included P. Kanellopoulos, the incumbent prime minister on April 20, 1967; P. Papalegouras and G. Ralles, senior ministers of the last preauthoritarian government; G. Mavros, a senior member of the Center Union party that had won the last preauthoritarian elections by a landslide, and leader of its post-authoritarian incarnation; A. Papandreou, chairman of PASOK and son of the Center Union's preauthoritarian leader; and Elias Eliou, head of the lone legal party of the left (United Democratic Left or EDA) in the preauthoritarian period.

The court narrowly interpreted the provisions of the constitutional act of October 3, 1974 and of Parliamentary Resolution D of January 15, 1975, which confined prosecution to only the "protagonists" of the 1967 coup. It focused its attention exclusively on two items: first, the preparation of the conspiracy leading to the coup, and second, the events of the night of the coup. These events were the arrest of the prime minister as well as the members of both the government and the opposition; "impeding the head of state in the exercise of his legal duties" and securing his reluctant acquiescence to the coup; and the arrest and subsequent detention of more than 6,500 civilians.[28]

The majority of the accused accepted responsibility for their acts in bringing about what they called the Revolution of April 21, but they also followed Papadopoulos's formulation in declaring that they "did not intend to take part in the proceedings." Most refused to appoint defense attorneys, thereby forcing the court to do so on its own initiative in the case of sixteen out of twenty defendants. Finally, the majority of the accused declined to take the stand in their own defense. This behavior contrasted sharply with the defense strategy pursued by the accused during the pretrial period, when many of the same individuals had disputed the legality of both the warrants leading to their arrest and of the indictment itself. In response to the court's charges, they claimed that (a) the prosecution was illegal, since their acts in April 1967 were covered by the amnesty decree issued by the civilian government immediately following its assumption of power in July 1974; (b) they were being prosecuted on the basis of retroactive, and hence unconstitutional, rules, and they were being judged by a court which lacked jurisdiction to hear their case; and (c) their seizure of power had not been a coup but a successful revolution, which created its own legal, and hence legitimate, order.

These arguments were heard before the start of the trials (in spring 1975) by both the Athens Court of Appeals and subsequently by the Court of Cassation. Both bodies rejected them. On the issue of the amnesty, the two courts accepted that the wording of Presidential Decree 519 of July 1975 had been "imprecise" and could, therefore, legitimately be interpreted as extending to the perpetrators of the coup as well. However, they went on to argue that both the national unity government headed by Karamanlis and the parliament issuing from the first postauthoritarian elections of November 17, 1974 legally held constituent powers. As a result, they were free to interpret, even retroactively through a constitutional act and a parliamentary resolution, the imprecise clauses of the amnesty decree in a manner that rendered possible the exclusion of those deemed as coup "protagonists" from the scope of the amnesty.[29]

Concerning the retroactive character of both the constitutional act of October 3, 1974 and Parliamentary Resolution D of January 15, 1975, both courts held that these acts did not set up new crimes but merely provided for the enforcement of legislation in place at the time of the coup. Instead of changing substantive rules, the two acts introduced new procedural rules concerning the court that could have jurisdiction to prosecute and try the cases. More specifically, to the extent that the constitution did not prohibit retroactive changes in court jurisdiction and procedural rules—as opposed to substantive rules—both the prosecution and the trying of the protagonists' case by the Athens Court of Appeal were declared to be legal.[30]

The legal nature of the seizure of power by the colonels was by far the thorniest of the problems facing both courts and brought forth slightly different, although ultimately converging, interpretations. In rendering their respective opinions, the two courts based their reasoning on the widely quoted language contained in the preamble as well as in Article 1 of Resolution D adopted by the first postauthoritarian parliament on January 15, 1975. The pertinent phrase in the preamble proclaimed that the Greek people had "remained steadfastly devoted to democratic principles, not for a moment giving in to tyranny." As a result, the preamble stated, "democracy had never been abolished *de jure*." On the other hand, Article 1 of Resolution D specifically labeled the seizure of power in 1967 a coup d'état "which aimed at the usurpation of the power and of the sovereign rights of the people. The resulting governments were based on violence [and not on law]."[31]

The two courts traveled different legal routes on their way to similar conclusions about this matter. The Athens Court of Appeals did not confine itself to labeling the seizure of power a "coup d'état." In fact, it went on to construct a rather flattering image of popular resistance to the regime and used that construction as the basis for its finding that, since the Greek people had never "adhered" to the regime, its seizure of power could not be considered a revolution; and as a result, it did not possess the legitimacy to rule. By contrast, the Court of Cassation adopted a more realistic position. It stuck to the wording of Resolution D and determined that, since the colonels' advent to power was the result of a coup, the regime issuing from it could therefore not have created its own legal order. On the basis of these converging interpretations, both courts rejected the defendants' claims.[32]

In the actual trial, the Court of Appeals based its verdict on these same arguments. Having established, after lengthy deliberations, each defendant's involvement in the perpetration of the coup, the court sentenced Papadopoulos, Pattakos, and Makarezos to death on grounds of sedition and to life imprisonment for high treason. Eight additional defendants received life sentences, while seven were condemned to prison terms ranging from five to twenty years. Two were acquitted.[33]

One of the most salient features of the trial was that it served finally to clarify the scope of the term "protagonist." Of the ninety-six individuals, mostly former military officers, originally named in the private suits that launched the proceedings, only twenty-four were eventually indicted and eighteen found guilty. Charges against the remaining seventy-two were dropped because the available evidence concerning their complicity in the preparation and execution of the coup was not sufficient to qualify them as protagonists in the sense adopted by the court. On this issue, the Court of Cassation defined protagonists, in the sense of Article 1 of the constitutional act of October 3, 1974, as "those who conceived of the idea of the coup, who drew up the relevant action plan, and proceeded with its execution on April 21, 1967, either on their own or through third parties directed by them, as well as those who adhered to the action plan after it had been drawn up, and those who played a decisive role in its successful execution."[34]

Flowing naturally out of this narrow approach was the court's decision on the same date to drop charges against 107 other individuals who had served as ministers in successive governments of the authoritarian regime but who had not been involved in the planning or execution of the coup. The court's reasoning was that high treason constitutes a "momentary" rather than a "continuing" crime, which legally comes to an end with the execution or attempted execution of specific acts, whereas a posteriori support for the regime does not constitute complicity in an act of high treason. As a result, it concluded that no indictment could be brought against these individuals, despite their deep involvement in the regime during the seven years of its duration.[35]

As we have already indicated, the remaining trials that attracted the greatest attention were the ones dealing with the suppression of the students at the Athens Polytechnic and with the torturers in the military police (ESA). The implication of senior figures in the regime in the first of these trials, and of known and widely detested torturers in the second, accounts for the symbolic significance of the proceedings as well as for the wide publicity they received. The Athens Polytechnic case was heard before the Athens Court of Appeals, though with a different composition than in the protagonists' trial. Among the thirty-two defendants were G. Papadopoulos, Ioannides, and Colonel N. Dertiles, the commander of the forces that stormed the grounds of the Polytechnic. The indictment mentioned the names of twenty-four civilians killed during the suppression of the uprising and its aftermath. The charges against most of those indicted were homicide in the first degree, attempted homicide, moral responsibility for the above, and other common crimes falling under the provisions of the criminal code. Half of the accused were former military officers, four were civilians, and the rest policemen. This trial lasted the longest, for the court heard testimony from 237 witnesses for the prosecution and forty-nine witnesses for the defense. It sat for sixty-one sessions, beginning on October 16 and ending on December 31, 1975, the date on which it delivered its verdict. In rendering its decision, the court made use of the legal arguments formulated in the protagonists' trial and handed down sentences based on the facts of each case. Twenty individuals were found guilty and twelve were acquitted. In the former group, three, the most prominent being Ioannides, received life sentences; while four, among them Papadopoulos, were sentenced to twenty years imprisonment. The remaining thirteen were given sentences ranging from two years to five months.[36]

The prosecution of the torturers in the military police involved two separate trials. Both were heard before the five-member Athens

Permanent Court Martial, the majority of whose members, including their presidents, were career military judges. Both trials were initiated as a result of legal action taken by victims. In the absence of legislation specifically identifying torture as a special crime, the prosecution in these trials was based on the criminal code provisions concerning the abuse of power and bodily damages, whether light or heavy.[37]

The first trial centered upon acts of violence which occurred between February 1972 and August 1973 in the Athens premises of the special investigative section of the military police, located near the United States Embassy. Thirty-one persons faced charges: fourteen were commissioned and noncommissioned officers; the remaining were conscripts assigned to the military police during their regular military service. There were 123 witnesses for the prosecution and sixteen for the defense. The court met in twenty-two sessions from August 7 to September 12, 1975. Fourteen of the defendants were eventually found guilty. The three most notorious among them, Colonel Th. Theofylogiannakos and Majors N. Hadjizissis and A. Spanos, received prison sentences amounting to 23, 22, and 17 years respectively. The sentences for the rest extended to a few months in prison and in some cases were suspended.[38]

The second trial covered the period from May 1973 to the fall of the regime in July 1974 and concerned acts of torture, which had taken place not only in Athens but also in quarters of the military police found in three locations outside Athens, Bogiati and Dionysos very near the capital and Tripoli in southern Greece. In this case, there were thirty-seven defendants, of whom thirteen had already faced charges for various acts in the first trial. There were 115 witnesses for the prosecution and twenty for the defense. The court held forty-three sessions, which lasted from October 13 to December 6, 1975. Twenty-three individuals were found guilty and received sentences ranging from seven years to three-and-a-half months in prison. The sentences of nine persons were suspended.[39]

A host of other trials dealt mainly with members of the urban police and of the gendarmerie. These were held before ordinary criminal courts and were distinguished by three major characteristics. the highly circumscribed number of individuals finally indicted; the small number of those found guilty; and the fact that most sentences were either suspended or converted to monetary fines. A good example of the pattern perceptible in these trials is the case that dealt with the Athens security police torturers, including such notorious police officers as C. Karapanagiotes, P. Babales, and E. Mallios. The fact that the trial was held in November 1975 in Chalkida, a provincial town situated at a distance of approximately a hundred kilometers north of Athens, effectively inhibited large numbers from attending. The harshest verdict handed down by the court was the ten-month sentence, convertible into a fine, received by Mallios.[40]

The Aftermath

On August 23, 1975, just a few hours after the sentencing of the chief figures in the coup had been made public, Prime Minister Constantine Karamanlis issued an official announcement. Among other things, he stated that "in the fair state, the work of justice is completed by the final procedure . . . which permits the reduction of sentences. In this final phase, a high sense of political responsibility must prevail." He went on to signal the government's decision to recommend to the president of the republic that the death sentences against G. Papadopoulos, Pattakos, and Makarezos be commuted to life imprisonment.[41]

    This announcement provoked a sharp reaction from the opposition parties in parliament and from the opposition press. Andreas Papandreou saw in the commuting of the sentences the "completion" of the amnesty scenario inaugurated a year earlier with the issuance of the July 26, 1974 amnesty decree. Furthermore, he unhesitatingly assigned political responsibility for this step to Karamanlis himself, called for immediate elections, and added that "with this last act, the government [had] finalized its mockery of the people and of justice and [had] become historically identified with the junta from which the Prime Minister received the baton of power." A few days later, addressing a military officers' audience, Karamanlis made a statement, which has since become famous, concerning the protagonists' conviction, specifying that "when we speak of a life sentence, we mean a life sentence."[42]

More than two decades have now elapsed since the summer of 1975, and four key figures in the 1967 coup remain in prison, G. Papadopoulos, his brother Constantine, Dertiles, and Ioannides. One of the original protagonists was freed after having requested and received a pardon. The rest were released on various dates, having either invoked the threat of "irreparable damage to their health" as a result of continuing confinement or having served the legal minimum of their sentences. Table 1, (pp. 50–51) based on official data provided by the Greek Ministry of Justice, shows the fate, as of July 1996, of the most important of the former military officers convicted in the various trials discussed in this chapter.

Conclusion

Based on the preceding analysis, there are three distinguishing characteristics of the Greek democratic regime's handling of its authoritarian predecessors: the severe sentences that were handed down against senior figures of the authoritarian regime; the long-term incarceration of these persons; and finally, the acquiescence of the Greek military *as an institution* to the court's verdicts and the absence of any overt challenge of these decisions on its part.

The role of the judiciary in these events, and in the Greek transition and democratization processes more generally, was undoubtedly central and even constructive. Certainly, from one perspective, there can be little doubt about the enormous symbolic as well as political significance of the courts' decisions for the new democracy or about their profoundly legitimating impact. The judiciary's positive involvement in dealing with the authoritarian past made it possible for the new regime to claim "justice" as one of its allies and to be perceived as just by a Greek people who were eager to exorcise the memories of a detested regime. In addition, this perception had a benign impact upon the judiciary itself, allowing it to invoke its positive contribution to democratization as evidence of its substantive dissociation from the old order and even as proof of its democratic credentials.

These observations notwithstanding, a careful and nuanced reading of the situation suggests a more complex and, in many respects,

Table 1
Principal Military Officers Convicted in Greek Trials
Name, Charge, Sentences*, Status (R=released), Date of Release

1. **Angheles, Odysseas M.**
   High treason, sedition
   20 yrs
   Suicide while incarcerated
   March 22, 1987

2. **Balopoulos, Michail N.**
   High treason, sedition
   Life
   Died
   March 3, 1978

3. **Dertiles, Nikolaos V.**
   Sedition, high treason, willful
       homicide
   Life
   Continued incarceration

4. **Gandonas, Nikolaos K.**
   High treason, sedition
   15 yrs
   R-Good conduct
   March 27, 1986

5. **Hadjizissis, Nikolaos D.**
   Abuse of power, torture
   22 yrs
   R-Good conduct
   July 11, 1994

6. **Ioannides, Dimitrios A.**
   High treason, sedition,
       homicides, attempted
       homicides
   Life
   Continued incarceration

7. **Karaberes, Stephanos E.**
   Sedition, high treason
   20 yrs
   R-Good conduct
   January 12, 1990

8. **Konstandopoulos, Georgios K.**
   High treason, sedition
   12 yrs
   R-Sentence ended
   May 23, 1987

9. **Ladas, Ioannes E.**
   Sedition, high treason
   Life
   R-Irreparable health damage
   May 23, 1988

10. **Lekkas, Andonios D.**
    High treason, sedition
    Life
    R-Irreparable health damage
    October 14, 1980

11. **Lyberes, Ioannes M.**
    Willful homicides (2), attempted
        homicide
    25 yrs
    R-Good conduct
    August 6, 1993

12. **Makarezos, Nikolaos I.**
    Sedition, high treason
    Death, life, dishonorable
        discharge
    R-Irreparable health damage
    June 22, 1990

13. **Papadopoulos, Constantine C.**
    Sedition, high treason
    Life
    Continued incarceration

* With the exception of G. Papadopoulos, S. Pattakos, and N. Makarezos, only the most important sentence is cited for each individual. All sentences, other than death, refer to imprisonment.

14. **Papadopoulos, Georgios C.**
    Sedition, high treason,
       complicity in willful
       homicides (7), attempted
       homicides (38)
    Death, life, dishonorable
       discharge
    Continued incarceration

15. **Pattakos, Stylianos G.**
    Sedition, high treason
    Death, life, dishonorable
       discharge
    R-Irreparable health damage
    August 13, 1990

16. **Roufogales, Michail S.**
    Moral responsibility for death
       through torture, sedition,
       high treason
    Life
    R-Irreparable health damage
    March 11, 1988

17. **Spandidakes, Gregorios E.**
    Sedition, high treason
    Life
    R-Irreparable health damage
    August 5, 1990

18. **Spanos, Anastasios G.**
    Abuse of power (1972–74),
       torture (1973–74)
    17 yrs
    R-Good conduct
    April 27, 1989

19. **Stamatelopoulos, Demetrios S.**
    High treason, sedition
    5 yrs
    R-Pardoned
    April 20, 1977

20. **Theofylogiannakos,
    Theodoros D.**
    Abuse of power, torture, moral
       responsibility for torture
    23 yrs
    R-Irreparable health damage
    January 14, 1992

21. **Tsakas, Evangelos D.**
    High treason
    8 yrs
    R-reason unknown
    Unknown

22. **Tsallas, Georgios A.**
    Torture, abuse of power, direct
       complicity in abuse of power
    16 yrs
    R-Good conduct
    May 9, 1991

23. **Zoitakes, Georgios K.**
    Sedition, high treason
    Life
    R-Irreparable health damage
    March 24, 1988

Source: Ministry of Justice. Official communication to the authors, May 22, 1996.

different explanatory framework concerning the role of justice in the Greek democratic transition. We believe that the judiciary's role becomes more intelligible if it is placed in the context of a broader process of rupture with the past.

Shorn to its essentials, this process involved nothing short of a structural transformation in Greek politics beginning in 1974. In concrete terms, this process was the product of six closely intertwined developments. First of all, the anticommunist strategy that had been the dominant political paradigm in Greece since the end of the country's civil war in 1949 and that had reached its apogee during the authoritarian rule of the colonels' regime had proved its complete political exhaustion and moral bankruptcy. Second, the monarchy, once a controversial and politically-divisive institution, had been eliminated as a powerful actor in Greek politics. Third, the military had withdrawn from political activity as well. Fourth, the duration of its rule had been short. For most of Greece's adult population, this effectively translated into strong historical memories of the predecessor parliamentary regime of 1950–1967 and reinforced the determination of elites and mass actors alike to search for a democratic alternative to the pathologies and impasses of the recent past. Fifth, there was a universal clamoring for a genuinely democratic regime that would at long last bring Greece into line with the political and constitutional realities prevailing in Western Europe after World War II and that would ensure the rule of law. (Dissenters, namely those who voted in the November 1974 elections for the single party still linked to the authoritarian past, barely exceeded 1 percent of the electorate.) And sixth, the strong normative and political preference for democracy already dominant within the regional European context, but also discernible at an international level, was greatly enhanced by the demise of Western Europe's only two remaining authoritarian regimes, in Spain and Portugal, and the advent of democracy in these countries.

Taken in combination, these factors served as powerful facilitating conditions that invested Greece's new civilian governments after 1974 with the requisite sense of legitimacy and helped generate a strong political will to pursue democratization strategies. Within this overarching political and historical context, therefore, the role of the

courts in the Greek transition should be read more in terms of continuity than of rupture. In fact, this continuity was firmly inscribed in
the logic of legal positivism which prompted the Greek judiciary to
follow the preferences and political will of the country's leadership
rather than to take the initiative in matters that concerned it. Put
somewhat differently, the use of the courts to facilitate the Greek
transition should be regarded as the deliberate outcome of a political
decision to enforce the rule of law in Greece and to underscore a perceived collective commitment, expressed by the new governments of
the time, to move decisively away from the authoritarian practices of
the past and to adhere to the rules of a democratic order.

Seen in this light, the specificity of the Greek transition, as far as
the country's judicial system is concerned, lies not so much in the
involvement of the courts per se in the democratization process.
Greece's tradition of legal positivism always made this a distinct
probability. Rather, the emergence, firm establishment, and continuing persistence of a novel and potent political climate in support of
the rule of law and of democracy best explains the courts' involvement in this process. This fact was borne out by their subsequent role
in ensuring the long-term imprisonment of the principal figures in
the colonels' regime.[43]

The impact of the persisting tradition of legal positivism on the
quality of Greek democracy is beyond the scope of this chapter. Nevertheless, it is worth noting that in the last decade or so, certain quarters of the judiciary have exhibited a tendency, unprecedented in
Greek history, towards greater emancipation from the tradition of acquiescence to the state. This has been especially true of the Council of
State, a body heavily influenced by French traditions of legal positivism favoring the state's role as the guarantor, and not merely the
source, of rights. In the absence of further evidence, it is too early to
gauge the long-term significance, if any, of these developments. Nevertheless, it would appear that the roots of activism in the judiciary
can, however tentatively, be traced to the growing recognition by
politicians and public alike that the application of the rule of law in
ever-widening areas of Greek life is a necessary concomitant to the
deepening of democracy. To the extent that this is so, this change,
which profoundly affects the role of the judiciary in the Greek politi-

cal system, should be welcomed as one of the most important by-products of the Greek democratization process, which was inaugurated in the *annus mirabilis* of 1974.

NOTES

We would like to thank Arghyris A. Fatouros for his critical reading of an earlier version of this chapter and for his very valuable comments and suggestions.

1. For works dealing with the transition to, and consolidation of, democracy in Greece in the 1970s, see Nicos C. Alivizatos, "The Difficulties of `Rationalization' in a Polarized Political System: The Greek Chamber of Deputies," in *Parliament and Democratic Consolidation in Southern Europe*, ed. Ulrike Liebert and Maurizio Cotta (London: Pinter, 1990), pp. 131–153; Constantine Arvanitopoulos, "The Political Economy of Regime Transition: The Case of Greece" (Ph.D. diss., The American University, 1989); P. Nikiforos Diamandouros, "Regime Change and the Prospects for Democracy in Greece: 1974–1983," in *Transitions from Authoritarian Rule. Prospects for Democracy*, ed. Philippe C. Schmitter, Guillermo O'Donnell, and Laurence Whitehead (Baltimore: The Johns Hopkins University Press, 1986), pp. 138–164; Georges Kaminis, *La transition constitutionelle en Grèce et en Espagne* (Paris: Librairie Générale de Droit et de Jurisprudence, 1993); Spyros Makres, "Oi diadikasies syngroteses tou metapoliteftikou politikou systematos. 24/7/74–19/6/75" [The Construction Processes of the Postauthoritarian Political System: July 24, 1974–June 19, 1975] (Doctoral diss., University of Athens, 1996); and Harry J. Psomiades, "Greece: From the Colonels' Rule to Democracy," in *From Dictatorship to Democracy. Coping with the Legacies of Authoritarianism and Totalitarianism*, ed. John H. Herz (Westport, Conn.: Greenwood Press, 1982), pp. 250–273. For a recent comparative study of democratic consolidation which includes Greece, see *The Politics of Democratic Consolidation: Southern Europe in Comparative Perspective*, ed. Richard Gunther, P. Nikiforos Diamandouros, and Hans-Jürgen Puhle (Baltimore: The Johns Hopkins University Press, 1995).

2. For the one work specifically dealing with the handling of the authoritarian past in Greece, see Psomiades, "Greece." The lack of support for the legacy of the authoritarian regime can be gauged by the fact that in the first democratic elections of November 17, 1974, barely over 1 percent of the electorate voted for the single party still linked to the authoritarian past.

3. Actually, the number of individuals punished was small relative to the total of those implicated, but it was still significant.

4. Undoubtedly, a major difference between the Greek and the Nuremberg trials is that the former were confined to the national level, while the latter were handled by an international court, which based its rulings on international law and was convened as a result of an international agreement. In this sense, a closer resemblance with the Nuremberg trials is

to be found in the tribunals currently investigating events in Bosnia and Rwanda.

5. Authoritative accounts of PASOK's evolution as a party include Michalis Spourdalakis, *The Rise of the Greek Socialist Party* (London: Routledge, 1988), and Christos Lyrintzis, "Between Socialism and Populism: The Rise of the Panhellenic Socialist Movement" (Ph.D. diss., London School of Economics and Political Science, 1983). See also Gunther, Diamandouros, and Puhle, *The Politics of Democratic Consolidation*, pp. 30–31, 113–114, 390.

6. Legally speaking, the two acts which launched the transition to democracy in Greece were the constitutional act of August 1, 1974, published in the *Ephemeris tes Kyverneseos* [Government Gazette] A213, which reestablished the validity of the 1952 constitution, except for the provisions concerning the head of state; and the constitutional act of August 5, 1974, published in [Government Gazette] A217. Both acts empowered the executive to exercise almost unlimited constituent and legislative powers via constitutional acts and legislative decrees respectively. (All future references to the official journal of the Greek government will be cited as [Government Gazette]). Please note that all citations of dates refer to the date an official act was either issued or, in the case of parliament, voted upon. For a discussion of Karamanlis's consolidation strategy, see P. Nikiforos Diamandouros, "Transition to, and Consolidation of, Democratic Politics in Greece," in *The New Mediterranean Democracies: Regime Transition in Spain, Greece and Portugal*, ed. Geoffrey Pridham (London: Frank Cass, 1984), pp. 59–65.

7. For the quotation, see John Henry Merryman, *The Civil Law Tradition*, 2d ed. (Stanford: Stanford University Press, 1985), p. 81.

8. For good discussions of the civil law and legal positivism traditions in Greece, see Nicos C. Alivizatos, "The Presidency, Parliament and the Courts in the 1980s," in *Greece, 1981–89: The Populist Decade*, ed. Richard Clogg (New York: St. Martin's Press, 1994), pp. 70–72, and Adamantia Pollis, "The State, the Law, and Human Rights in Modern Greece," *Human Rights Quarterly* 9 (1987): 587–614. The one and probably lone exception to the judiciary's lack of prior involvement in trials of individuals associated with a nondemocratic regime concerns General Theodore Pangalos, a military officer of liberal political persuasions, who briefly assumed dictatorial powers in Greece in 1925–26 and who was subsequently sentenced to two years imprisonment, significantly enough on grounds other than the abolition of the parliamentary regime of the time. Let us also briefly note, in this context, that the courts' involvement in the sentencing of collaborators with the Axis occupying powers after the Second World War was qualitatively different from the case discussed here, in the sense that those found guilty, though sentenced and incarcerated, were amnestied, pardoned, or simply set free for political reasons after the start of the civil war in 1946. Finally, the scope of these trials was more narrow than the ones dealing with the colonels' regime.

9. The members of the judiciary who served in the first government of the Greek authoritarian regime were C. Kollias, Prime Minister;

L. Rozakes, Minister of Justice; K. Kalabokias, Minister of Education and Religious Affairs; L. Tsarouches, Minister of Public Works; and E. Poulantzas,
Minister of Social Welfare and Health. The first was the public prosecutor at
the Court of Cassation. All the rest were justices of that same body.

10. For the dismissal of the thirty justices by the military regime and
the 1969 confrontation with the Council of State, see Nicos C. Alivizatos, *Les
institutions politiques de la Grèce à travers les crises, 1922–1974* (Paris: Librairie
Générale de Droit et de Jurisprudence, 1979), pp. 497–501; and Michalis N.
Pikramenos, "He krise tes dikastikes anexartesias sten Hellada. He dokima-
sia tes periodou 1967–1974" [The Crisis of Judicial Independence in Greece:
The Trying Period of 1967–1974] (Doctoral diss., University of Athens, 1990),
pp. 135 ff.

11. A narrowly focused, but nevertheless politically sensitive, issue bequeathed by the authoritarian regime to its democratic successor concerned
the fate of the thirty judges dismissed in 1968 and of the councillors of state
forced to resign in 1969. All were rehabilitated.

12. For decree 519 of July 26, 1974, see [Government Gazette] A211.

13. The first calls for prosecuting those responsible for, or associated
with, the authoritarian regime were issued by the resistance organization,
Democratic Defense, and cited in the Athens daily, *To Vima* [The Tribune], on
September 3, 1974. On September 4, the same newspaper cited Andreas
Papandreou's carefully worded call for justice. A few days earlier, on Au-
gust 28, 1974, it had also published his appeal for a "fair trial," citing the
Washington Post as its source.

14. On Ioannides' continued freedom of movement until late September, see *To Vima*, September 27, 1974; on the deportation of G. Papadopoulos
and his close collaborators to the island of Kea, see *To Vima*, October 24, 1974;
and on Ghikas's statement concerning those free to travel, see *To Vima*, October 1, 1974.

15. For Lykourezos's suit against the protagonists of the regime, see *To
Vima*, September 10, 1974. Additional suits by private citizens were filed on
October 9 and 11. The former brought charges against thirty-five individuals
and the latter against fifty-five. Finally, additional suits were brought by private citizens against torturers and persons implicated in the suppression of
the student uprising at the Athens Polytechnic.

16. On General Arbouzes and the more general question of prosecution, see *To Vima*, September 28, 1974.

17. For the constitutional act of October 3, 1974, see [Government
Gazette] A277. Judge Voltes' appointment was made by the Plenum of the
Athens Court of Appeals in its decision no. 12, dated November 1, 1974 and
based on Article 29 of the criminal procedure code.

18. On Karamanlis's statement concerning the narrowing of prosecutions to the protagonists of the coup, made at the officers' club in the north-
ern Greek city of Thessaloniki, see *To Vima*, October 27, 1974.

19. The technicality that caused such a large number of individuals to
miss the deadline for filing by a day stemmed from the fact that when apply-

ing the pertinent phrasing of the law establishing time limitations for private suits, the courts determined that each month had thirty days, thus ignoring the fact that two of the actual calendar months involved in these cases had thirty-one days each. On this point, see *Torture in Greece: The First Torturers' Trial 1975* (n.p.: Amnesty International, 1977), p. 68, and Psomiades, "Greece," p. 273 n. 32.

20. On the retirement of the various high ranking generals, see *To Vima*, August 20, 1974; on that of Ioannides, see *To Vima*, August 25, 1974; and of his close collaborators, thirty-six *in toto*, who were placed on temporary suspension "for reasons relating to the interests of the service," see *To Vima*, September 22, 1974. Finally, on the February 1975 conspiracy, see Psomiades, "Greece," p. 263; *To Vima*, February 26, 1975; and the same newspaper's report of February 28, 1975 quoting the French journalist, Marc Marceau, as saying in a dispatch to *Le Monde* that the goal of the conspirators was to negotiate a general amnesty.

21. On Mallios and Babales, see *To Vima*, August 2 and 3, 1974; on Spanos, see *To Vima*, August 2, 1974; on the seventeen security officers relieved of their duties, see *To Vima*, September 12, 1974. Concerning the lack of clear information relating to the fate of policemen in lower ranks, see Psomiades, "Greece," p. 263.

22. For the rehabilitation of those justices dismissed by the authoritarian regime, see the constitutional act of September 5, 1974, in [Government Gazette] A238.

23. For the twenty-three justices summoned before the standing judicial council, see Pikramenos, [The Crisis of Judicial Independence], p. 225. For the quotation from Article 10 of the constitutional act of September 5, 1974, see [Government Gazette] A238.

24. For the dismissal of the top leadership in the banking sector, see *To Vima*, August 10, 1974; for the same in the case of prefects and mayors, see *To Vima*, September 13 and 17, 1974.

25. Approximately thirty of roughly three hundred senior academic members from the two top ranks in the universities' academic hierarchy were either dismissed (about twenty) or temporarily suspended (about ten). For the text of the constitutional act of September 3, 1974, see [Government Gazette] A237. Article 10 of the same act specifically provides for disciplinary action in the case of "well-grounded" indications of collaboration with the regime. Finally, for the student committees on "dejuntification," see Pikramenos, [The Crisis of Judicial Independence], p. 467, and *To Vima*, September 18 and 21, 1974.

26. Extensive accounts of the protagonists' trials, though not strictly speaking minutes, can be found in P. Rodakes, ed., *Hoi dikes tes hountas. He dike ton protaition* [The Trials of the Junta: The Trial of the Protagonists], 4 vols. (Athens: Demokratikoi Kairoi, 1975). See 1:10 of this work for a discussion concerning those who had gone into hiding.

27. The other voting members of the court of appeals were P. Logothetes, P. Constandinopoulos, I. Grivas, and G. Plagiannakos. E. Giannopou-

los and D. Tsouras were the alternates. Stamates' alternate as public prosecutor was Sp. Kaninias.

28. For the text of Parliamentary Resolution D of January 15, 1975, see [Government Gazette] A6. According to Greek constitutional practice, only constituent or revisionary assemblies can issue such resolutions, which have constitutional force.

29. For the rejection by the Athens Court of Appeals of the defense appeals against the warrants of arrest and the indictments concerning the protagonists, see, respectively, the court's decisions 118/75 and 414/75 in *To Syntagma* [The Constitution] 1 (1975): 326 ff and 483 ff. For decision 683/75 of the Court of Cassation, see ibid., pp. 896 ff.

30. Ibid, pp. 896 ff.

31. For the quotations from the text of Resolution D, see [Government Gazette] A6.

32. For the arguments of the Athens Court of Appeals, see the court's decisions 118/75 and 414/75, cited in note 29 above. For those of the Court of Cassation, see decision 683/75 in the same note.

33. See the lengthy verdict of the actual trial in Rodakes, [The Trial of the Protagonists], 3: 1123 ff.

34. On the dropping of charges against seventy-two of the accused, on grounds of insufficient evidence to qualify them as protagonists, see decision 414/75 of the Athens Court of Appeals, *To Syntagma* 1 (1975): 483 ff. For the opinion of the Court of Cassation on this issue, see the court's decision 683/75 in ibid., pp. 896 ff.

35. For the text of decision 684/75 of the Court of Cassation, concerning the "momentary" nature of high treason, see *To Syntagma* 1 (1975): 686 ff.

36. For the trial concerning the suppression of the uprising at the Athens Polytechnic, see P. Rodakes, ed., *Hoi dikes tes hountas. He dike tou Polytechneiou* [The Trials of the Junta: The Polytechnic Trial], 5 vols. (Athens: n.d.). On the court's decision in this trial, see 5: 2009 ff.

37. For a lengthy account of the torturers' trials, see P. Rodakes, ed., *Hoi dikes tes hountas. Hoi dikes ton vassaniston* [The Trials of the Junta: The Torturers' Trials], 3 vols. (Athens: Demokratikoi Kairoi, 1976). For the first trial, see also the Amnesty International report cited in note 19 above.

38. On the sentences handed down in this case, see Rodakes, [The Torturers' Trials], 2: 770 ff.

39. On the second trial of the torturers, see ibid., 3: 1180 ff.

40. The one exception to the pattern observable in these other trials was that which dealt with six commissioned and noncommissioned naval officers accused of having engaged in torture aboard the cruiser *Elli* in 1968. These individuals were tried between December 8 and 12, 1975, before the Piraeus Permanent Naval Court and received sentences ranging from eight years to six months. See Rodakes, [The Torturers' Trials], 3: 1187 ff. On the trial of the torturers in the Athens security police, see ibid. 3: 1249 ff and 3: 1553 ff for an account of the reactions voiced by the student organizations close to the opposition concerning the court's verdicts declaring a number of

defendants innocent of the charges leveled against them. Both Mallios and Babales were assassinated by terrorist organizations, the former in December 1976, the latter in January 1979.

41. For Karamanlis's statement concerning the conversion of death sentences to life imprisonment, see *Facts on File*, August 30, 1975, p. 637. This statement aptly captures the astute logic of Karamanlis's search for policies expressing decisiveness and effectiveness while avoiding punitiveness or excess that might provoke those affected by them to react in ways capable of adversely affecting the course of democratization. Though addressing a different topic, Takis S. Pappas provides insightful comments concerning Karamanlis's policies during this period in his "The Making of Party Democracy in Greece" (Ph.D. diss., Yale University, 1995).

42. For Papandreou's statement, see Rodakes, [The Trial of the Protagonists], 3:1367. For that of Karamanlis, see 3:1375. Papandreou's utterances notwithstanding, there is no evidence to date of a covert pact between Karamanlis and the military in charge of the authoritarian regime. However, as long as access to pertinent archives, such as Karamanlis's own, remains restricted or impossible, a number of turning points in the democratization process will continue to beg for clarification. One of these is whether or not the controversial ambiguity in the wording of the amnesty decree of July 26, 1974 was an oversight linked to the pressures of circumstances. Karamanlis has vehemently denied the existence of any understanding involving the outgoing regime and there is no reason to doubt him. The fact remains, however, that, to the extent that the phrasing of the amnesty decree appeared to include principals of the authoritarian regime and thus provided them with an additional incentive to remain quiescent, it afforded the incoming civilian leadership precious breathing space during which to proceed with the implementation of its democratization strategy.

A second event of major significance that remains unexplored is the February 1975 conspiracy against the government, whose uncovering provided the latter with the opportunity to deal decisively with many of its remaining opponents. To date, we lack sufficient details concerning the conspiracy's depth and scope to evaluate its significance. Politically, it constituted a high point in Karamanlis's strategy for eliminating potential threats to the new democratic order and a complete reversal of the precarious situation that prevailed during the initial months following his arrival in Greece, during the summer of 1974, when he was forced to spend his nights on naval ships off the coast of Athens. Clarification on these points, when and if it comes, will help us better to understand the specificities of the Greek transition to democracy and to assess Karamanlis's critical role in this process.

43. The continuing adherence of the courts to a narrow and formalistic perception of their role during the period that concerns us here, and their inclination to exercise self-restraint and to operate within the general terrain defined by the political elites, is clearly borne out by their failure to act in a more emancipated fashion in areas where that was quite possible. Examples of such areas include the possibility of enlarging the scope of the trials and

the handing down of harsher sentences in the torturers' trials. The fact that they did not reflects the absence of a will for such action at the level of the political elites.

The long-term (and in four cases, continuing) imprisonment of the authoritarian regime's protagonists raises the sensitive issue of pardons, which by law fall exclusively within the jurisdiction of the executive. With one exception, that of D. Stamatelopoulos, in which a pardon was asked for and was granted, the remainder of those convicted have steadfastly refused to apply for pardons on the grounds that this would be tantamount to an admission of guilt, which they have always denied. The position of the civilian governments, on the other hand, would appear to be that the granting of a pardon without a prior request from its potential beneficiaries implies acceptance on the part of the democratic regime of the convicted former officers' refusal to accept the legitimacy of the trials and of the verdicts these produced. Conversely, the democratic governments have readily agreed to granting release, upon request, on grounds of "irreparable damage" to one's health. In practical terms, this has resulted in the continuing incarceration of the four protagonists who have refused to ask for a pardon and the release of most others on real or ostensible medical grounds.

3
Democracy Dignified and an End to Impunity:
Bolivia's Military Dictatorship on Trial

René Antonio Mayorga

THE USE OF THE JUDICIAL PROCESS against the Bolivian military dictator, García Meza, was a momentous event, both in the country's democratic history and in Latin America. For the first time, Bolivia's political and legal institutions showed themselves equal to the task of conducting an "accountability trial" against the principal agents and collaborators of a de facto military government that ruled the country from July 1980 to August 1981.[1] Within Bolivia, the event was accurately labeled "the Trial of the Century" for bringing before the bench and convicting those who had violated the Constitution and basic human rights by violently overthrowing a democratic regime. It was also the first time that the democratic system, restored in October 1982, was able to utilize its legal system fully to confront a dictatorial past. In doing so, it established an important legal and political precedent contributing to the consolidation of Bolivia's democratic institutions. All of this made the trial a watershed in the political and democratic history of the country.

As we shall see later in this essay, this attempt to pursue transitional justice, that is, to use Bolivia's constitution and its legal codes to prosecute the individuals responsible for a destructive political act— a military coup—and for their part in flagrant human rights abuses was unique in Latin America. When Bolivian democracy was restored, following a complex and circuitous transition process that lasted five years, the country's leaders confronted a number of troubling questions. Given Bolivia's long history of political instability and de facto government, should they ignore the criminal nature of the García Meza dictatorship, or should they instead confront the endemic problems of human rights violations and the usurpation of democracy? Should they merely attempt to forget the crimes of the past and grant an amnesty to all those responsible, or should they instead seek to establish a political and legal precedent by prosecuting a military regime that had blatantly violated the Constitution? The political significance of the trial that ensued rests precisely in the manner in which the Bolivian parliament resolved this dilemma, by deciding to move against the dictatorship. Reasoning that the consolidation and stability of the democratic system would depend to a large extent on their success in pursuing justice, they chose to use the tools of the judicial system and to send an unmistakable message in defense of democratic institutions.[2]

The objective of this essay is to analyze the legal and political significance of the judicial proceedings against the García Meza dictatorship, highlighting in particular the restoration of democratic values in Bolivia. First, we shall examine the indisputable political logic behind the trial, which was emphasized in the formal congressional indictment that led to the proceedings: to strengthen democratic institutions by means of a judicial process capable of revealing the concealed aims and the antidemocratic and criminal methods of the dictatorship. Second, we shall demonstrate that this decision to take action against an arbitrary and capricious dictatorship created a precedent that was not only political and judicial but ethical as well. In this way, the essay seeks to illustrate the extent to which the logic of politics was intertwined with the judicial logic inherent in Bolivia's legal order. In these cases, politics was subordinated to the law.

The third goal of this essay is to address the political and institutional significance of the García Meza trial along two dimensions: both as an extraordinary historical, political, judicial, and ethical precedent for strengthening democratic institutions, and as a substantial reinforcement of the constitutionally-mandated subordination of the armed forces to civilian power. Without a doubt, if there existed any unfinished business in the consolidation of Bolivian democracy, it was the need to subordinate the military to civilian control.[3] A fourth objective of this essay will be to examine the two sides to the Supreme Court's role in the process, whose actions spurred changes in the distribution of state power but also revealed continuing deficiencies in the Bolivian judicial system. Finally, this essay touches upon the singularities of the Bolivian record in pursuing retrospective justice in comparison with the experiences of other Latin American countries, particularly Argentina.

The García Meza Dictatorship:
The Violation of the Constitution and of Basic Human Rights

The long wave of military dictatorships that swept Latin America beginning in the 1960s took the form in Bolivia of eighteen years of military rule (1964–1982), the most extensive period of military government in the country's agitated, twentieth-century history. Nearly as difficult as the dictatorial era was Bolivia's troubled transition process, which was shaken by a rapid succession of four military coups between July 1978 and July 1980. Of these, only one of the coups (that of General Padilla against General Pereda in September 1978) included among its objectives the restoration of conditions propitious for redemocratization.[4] But of all the coups, that of General García Meza in July, 1981 stands out as the most bloodthirsty and cruel in Bolivia's history. The coup fractured the transition process, first by overthrowing the provisional constitutional government of Lydia Gueiler and then by abolishing the June 1981 elections, which in turn prevented the change of government scheduled for August of that year. Then, it unleashed an unprecedented reign of terror and corruption.

The García Meza dictatorship was not just another attack against the democratization process. It was also the culmination of a process of sustained decomposition in the armed forces in which a kleptocratic gang with ties to drug-trafficking had come to dominate those officers, the so-called "institutionalists," who still defended the constitutional regime and advocated the military's definitive return to the barracks. The group led by García Meza represented the most conservative and reactionary sector of the military and opposed the country's democratization. Its paramount interest was in keeping the armed forces in power in order to utilize the resources of the state apparatus for personal benefit. This interest coincided with the apprehension and distrust felt by other antidemocratic sectors, both in private enterprise and in those political parties that feared that the democratic process would strengthen leftist and syndicalist tendencies in Bolivia. Because of the indisputable influence of these latter tendencies in the Unidad Democrática y Popular (UDP) populist front, which won the 1980 general elections by a relative majority, the conservatives rejected democratization as a threat to the armed forces and to the continuation of private property.[5]

In fact, the strength of the UDP and the resurgence of the labor union movement (a significant actor in Bolivia since the 1952 revolution) contradicted the military strategy laid out in the last years of the Banzer dictatorship (1971–1978). This strategy, which sought to "liberalize" existing power arrangements while maintaining the armed forces as the nucleus of power and private enterprise as the key social and economic actor, fell apart during the transition process, accounting to some extent for the vicious circle of repeated openings and closings experienced by the Bolivian political system between January, 1978 and October, 1982. This instability, in turn, dramatically aggravated the country's economic crisis, heightening political tensions.[6] It was during this destructive period that the armed forces split into contending factions, some demanding the military's return to its proper constitutional role, and other, reactionary factions refusing to abandon the privileges of arbitrary power. The catastrophic culmination of the confrontation between these military factions, which intensified along with the democratic forces' struggle to maintain the constitutional order, was the García Meza dictatorship. Through the use of insubordination, pressure, and even mutiny against the executive power, and the deliberate violation of the rules governing military promotions, García Meza forced through his appointment as commander-in-chief. He then placed his allies in strategic positions of command and deployed paramilitary groups in a criminal wave of terrorism against union organizers, political leaders, and journalists, thus creating the conditions for a coup d'état.

Among military authoritarian regimes, the García Meza dictatorship clearly stands out for its criminal and terrorist nature and its direct links with the Argentine military dictatorship of General Viola. This was not just another coup. It was the product of a premeditated plan against the democratic process supported by Argentine military officers and executed by paramilitary groups, assisted even by Italian fascists and by the notorious head of the Gestapo in Lyons during World War II.[7] The overthrow of Lydia Gueiler's constitutional government brought with it the total suppression of the Constitution. Parliament was shut down, judicial magistrates dismissed, political parties and union organizations banned, and a wave of terror unleashed in which dozens of political leaders, union leaders, and common citizens were killed.[8]

García Meza's coup was unofficially supported by members of some of Bolivia's most important political parties (Acción Democrática Nacionalista [ADN], and the Movimiento Nacionalista Revolucionario [MNR]), and by certain sectors of the entrepreneurial and middle classes. In this sense, the coup was no different from the majority of military coups, in which close civil-military collaboration has been the norm. But in three other respects, the coup stands out. First, it installed a dictatorship with direct links to the illegal drug trade, transforming the state apparatus into a support network for drug-trafficking and the illicit acquisition of wealth. The García Meza dictatorship was, in fact, the first Bolivian government openly associated with the drug-trafficking mafia.[9] Second, as already noted, the preparation of the coup and its success were closely linked to the enormous amount of logistic and political support that it received from the Argentine military dictatorship. Finally, this was the first time in Bolivia's history that the actions of coup leaders were actually determined by a strategy of state terrorism. Under García Meza, constitutional guarantees evaporated, the country was literally converted into a "military zone," and the population was subjected to a state of generalized fear and intimidation through the indiscriminate action of irregular armed groups.[10]

Like other Latin American dictatorships, however, the García Meza dictatorship was inspired by the ominous "national security ideology," taking the principle of "security" to such unprecedented extremes that political action was defined as the physical destruction of the "enemy." The dictatorship labeled political and union leaders committed to democracy and all other opponents of the regime "extremists" and "subversive delinquents."[11] In appealing to this ideology, it used the well-known justifications for legitimizing military intervention, arguing that the coup was necessary to overcome the political chaos and social turmoil into which the country had fallen due to ultra-leftist subversion and international extremism, a situation which threatened the existence of the armed forces and of the nation. The dictatorship attributed the supposed demise of the democratic process to such imaginary defects as "partisanship," "foreign intervention," and electoral fraud. From this "diagnosis," it concluded that its duty was to banish anarchy and impose order by overcoming the defects of "formal democratism." The crude alternative it imposed was described as the construction of an "unprecedented and authentic democracy" serving as the foundation of a "national reconstruction" government based on "consensus."[12]

The cynical use of this ideological mantle to conceal the profound inversion of moral and democratic principles represented by the military's intervention was one thing. The true nature of the dictatorship was something else—a military gang that terrorized the country in order to enrich itself through drug-trafficking and pillage. Just as Bolivia had never before experienced such a dramatic assault on human rights, neither had it seen such systematic corruption and plundering of the state economy as that undertaken by the army in its assault on the public patrimony. As a result, the regime's human rights record was a cause for profound dismay. It included the destruction of media headquarters and labor union offices, the suppression of union and political activities, a general prohibition of the rights to free speech and association, as well as numerous arbitrary detentions, torture, and disappearances.

Given this background, it is not surprising that the García Meza dictatorship discredited the armed forces and eroded their legitimacy. Having failed to garner solid institutional backing, the dictatorship not only provoked the institutionalists in the military, who would finally overthrow García Meza in August 1981. It also precipitated its complete rejection by society. Throughout the dictatorship, the country's leading social and political organizations engaged in continuous and extensive mobilization demanding a return to democratization. Indeed, it was this mass mobilization, coinciding with the growing political and moral exhaustion of the armed forces, that determined the principal character of the final phase of democratization, that of a "transition through rupture." As a result, the military lost all possibility of negotiating its withdrawal from power and of maintaining an influential position in the democratic system.[13] Instead, parliament honored the June 1980 presidential election results and named Hernán Siles Zuazo, head of the center-left UDP alliance, President of the Republic in October, 1982. Ironically, it was precisely the ascent of this alliance that the García Meza coup had tried to prevent.

The Accountability Trial of the García Meza Dictatorship and Its Collaborators

From the first, the political conditions for a trial of the García Meza dictatorship were favorable because the Bolivian military had been weakened, due to the type of transition that occurred in October 1982. Only with this type of transition, a transition through rupture, or total collapse (as occurred in both Argentina and Bolivia), has it historically been possible to open the space necessary to bring military dictators to justice. In cases of negotiated transition, by contrast, in which the military has retained fundamental positions of power (as in Chile, Brazil, and Uruguay), the tendency has been to apply amnesties and other practices that impede prosecution. Furthermore, due to the long duration of the Bolivian trial, as well as the institutional changes that coincided with it, the trial itself did not serve to force the democratic regime to compromise with the military, as was the case in Argentina. Instead, it ratified and strengthened a process of military subordination already underway.[14]

Given the notorious and illegal nature of the crimes committed by the dictatorship, society's demands for justice rapidly made themselves felt once Bolivian democracy was restored. The violations of the Constitution and of basic human rights had been so flagrant that there was a widely perceived and deeply felt need to submit those responsible for such crimes and abuses to the judicial process. The feeling was also widespread that this course of action represented less of a risk to the stability of the democratic regime than the prospect of continued impunity. There was little risk of provoking a destabilizing military reaction, since the armed forces had totally lost control of the political process and were divided and weak. In addition, Bolivia's international context had changed fundamentally. Thus, those who advocated punishment rather than reconciliation (the latter arguing that a still fragile democracy needed military backing) constituted a very powerful current.[15]

The initiative to undertake an accountability trial came from two left-wing political parties, the Movement of the Revolutionary Left (MIR) and the Socialist Party (PS), each of which had been harshly persecuted during the dictatorship and endured the assassination of key leaders. Supported by compelling evidence, these parties presented a formal indictment against García Meza and his principal collaborators to the House of Deputies at two of its sessions, on February 13 and February 16, 1984. In taking this action, they also had the support of numerous civil organizations, including the Permanent Organization for Human Rights (APDH), the Association of Relatives of the Disappeared (ASOFAM), and the Bolivian Workers' Central. All of these groups later came together to form an unofficial mobilizing body, known as the Comité Impulsor (Driving Committee), which campaigned to promote their views and publicize the trial.

From this point, the proceedings next passed to the Constitution and Justice Commission of the House of Deputies, which issued an initial Writ of Instruction on March 1, 1984. Despite Article 2 of the 1944 accountability law, which requires a response within fifteen days, this commission then took more than two years to release its opinions and conclusion, a delay due in large part to a grave political crisis that afflicted the government of the UDP, of which the MIR was a part. However, on February 25, 1986, the Congress finally decided (after several postponements due to the lack of a quorum) to submit a formal indictment against García Meza and fifty-five of his collaborators to the Supreme Court. In this way, they were fully in accord with the procedures established by the Constitution. These procedures delegated to Congress the right to indict former presidents and ministers of state for crimes committed in the exercise of their duties (Article 68, paragraph 12). They also stipulated that the Supreme Court could only render a verdict in an accountability case after a formal indictment had been decreed by Congress (Article 127, paragraph 6).

The congressional resolution presented to the Supreme Court in February 1986 accused the dictatorship of eight types of crimes. The principal indictment was against the former president Luis García Meza, his Minister of the Interior, Luis Arce Gómez, and the other ministers of the first cabinet, which charged them with crimes against the Constitution, including sedition, armed uprising, usurping the rights of the people, organizing paramilitary groups, and defying the Constitution and the legal order. The indictment also accused the ex-dictator and the former Minister of the Interior of assassinating political and labor leaders, of committing genocide in the massacre of a group of eight MIR leaders, and of various crimes against the economy perpetrated in collaboration with other governmental functionaries. Among the latter crimes were the clandestine trafficking in minerals, theft from the General Treasury, and the clandestine sale of semiprecious stones. Yet, the congressional resolution not only named the former dictator and his ministers. The indictment was addressed to a total of 56 persons, who may be divided into three groups based on their role in more than 45 specific crimes: 1) the former president, García Meza, and 18 ministers of state; 2) the former Minister of the Interior, Arce Gómez, and 20 paramilitary operatives; and 3) 13 other functionaries involved in illicit businesses.[16]

It should be noted that the congressional indictment was preceded by widespread social and political debate in which various political and legal arguments were advanced, not all of them in favor of bringing an accountability trial before the Supreme Court. One of the most serious disagreements concerned the juridical nature of the trial that should be pursued. For example, the two human rights groups, the APDH and the ASOFAM, sought to elicit a declaration by the La Paz Superior Court of Justice that would have had García Meza and his accomplices tried not as ex-dignitaries but instead as common delinquents. Their central argument, which was legally sound but politically untenable, was that an accountability trial applied only to legitimate, democratically elected governments and hence not to that of García Meza.[17]

Despite certain political inconsistencies, Congress was able to establish two key points of agreement, one regarding the political and historical need for the trial, and another regarding its juridical nature. The congressional resolution began by setting forth the fundamental principle, both political and ethical, that democratic systems needed to be able to reestablish justice following periods of dictatorship and state terrorism. The resolution also affirmed the idea that a democratic state should be able to defend itself against future attempts to undermine its constitutional foundations. Thus, a failure to prosecute the dictatorship would have posed an irreparable threat to the democratic system.

In addition, the resolution also appealed to a double historical-political and judicial argument that was brought up by the attorneys (the so-called "civil party to the indictment" [*parte civil de la acusación*]) representing the various social organizations who had called for the trial. Their argument was based on two main points. Juridically, they argued that only by applying the legal system (the Constitution, the accountability laws, and the penal code) would it be possible to prove the existence of offenses that were punishable under the law given sufficient evidence of guilt. But politically, they also asserted the ethical and historical importance of using legislation to protect republican institutions against anyone who might endanger the survival and democratic continuity of the state.[18] Establishing justice was seen as equivalent to strengthening a collective moral conscience about the dictatorial past. It would restore historical memory and national dignity by reconstructing the truth about the deeds that had occurred during the dictatorship, and it would generate public confidence in democratic institutions.[19] For both governmental and civic actors, therefore, the use of the judicial process against the dictatorship transcended strictly legal objectives. By taking steps to bring a sinister period in Bolivian history to an end, they hoped to establish legal precedents against any future violation of democratic principles.[20]

The second point of convergence in Congress was in regard to the juridical nature of the trial. After debating the issue, the body decided to prosecute the defendants in an accountability trial, and not for common crimes. Those political parties and civil organizations that supported the congressional decision argued that the crimes of the dictatorship were crimes against the Constitution, committed in order to install a regime of state terrorism. Therefore, they concluded, the trial should be carried out by the Supreme Court in accordance with Article 126, paragraph 6 of the Constitution. Nevertheless, this decision contained serious deficiencies. Bolivia's accountability laws of 1884 and 1944, both of which were called into question from the beginning due to their obsolete character, had been promulgated to demand accountability from democratically elected officials and not from usurpers of power. In addition, these laws were never backed up by specific procedural codes that would facilitate their efficient application. As we shall see, this inconsistency, along with other inadequacies in the law, would have pernicious effects on the judicial process and would lie at the heart of many procedural difficulties encountered along the way.[21]

In the congressional debates leading up to the indictment, it is also important to note that there were important differences in the positions taken by the various actors supporting the trial. There can be no doubt that not everyone shared the same goals or, afterwards, the same degree of commitment to the trial. For example, when the new democratic government was first installed, there was little immediate evidence of the political will necessary to bring the García Meza dictatorship to trial. Faced with fragile democratic institutions and a vexing social and economic crisis, a kind of compromise strategy initially prevailed between politicians and the military. Under this tacit agreement, the dictatorial past would not be condemned, nor would the crimes of the dictatorship be prosecuted, in exchange for which the military agreed to subordinate itself to the democratic order. Nevertheless, thanks to the political initiative of the MIR and PS parties and backed by a broad societal demand for justice, this strategy was reversed and the decision was reached to try the dictatorship at the highest possible level, that of an accountability trial.

It is undeniable that the congressional indictment also reflected the partisan political positions of the dominant political parties. More than a clear legal decision to expedite the punishment of the guilty parties, it represented a controversial political accord between those parties that initiated the indictment and the parties of the governing coalition. MIR, the party that initiated the process, had been a direct victim of the dictatorship and was determined to broach the subject of submitting the García Meza dictatorship to justice. But the ruling political parties in the 1985–1989 period (the MNR and the ADN) succeeded in limiting the scope of the trial based on a political calculus. They would accept the MIR indictment only on the condition that prominent members of the governing parties who had held responsible positions during the dictatorship and who now occupied high political positions in the new government not be included in the trial. Their reasoning was both pragmatic and a matter of survival. The ruling parties did not want their work to be obstructed, nor did they want the legitimacy of their leaders seriously questioned. Nearly all of their leaders had been implicated in past military coups, for example, the former president Victor Paz Estenssoro and the de facto former president Hugo Banzer Suárez. Of all the democratic political parties, only the MIR was free from suspicion and had not been involved in any dictatorial government. Thus, although the governing parties unambiguously accepted the indictment in April 1986, they clearly limited its reach to persons directly responsible for the dictatorship or implicated in overtly criminal acts of violence and killing. An additional consequence of the political accord that underlay the congressional resolution was the exclusion of drug-trafficking charges. This was a serious omission, given that one of the principal crimes of the García Meza government was precisely that it was a "narco-dictatorship," the first Latin American government openly tied to cocaine-trafficking mafias.[22]

The military accepted the proceedings against García Meza only reluctantly, out of weakness. It is obvious that they would have preferred a general amnesty law. On various occasions, they even asserted that the armed forces had nothing to do with the coup.[23] But when a Military Justice Tribunal gathered sufficient evidence on the concealment and illegal sale of the diaries of guerrillas Ché Guevara and Pombo, which had been captured in the 1976 military campaign in Ñancahuazu and were considered "war trophies," the military reacted as though its institutional dignity had been violated. The commander in chief of the armed forces himself sent the case to Congress for processing, and in September 1988 Congress initiated a second accountability trial against García Meza and two others.

The Institutional Context:
Democracy, Human Rights, and the Role of Justice

The judiciary is responsible for two essential functions executed in a democratic system: the administration of justice to protect and guarantee the security of society, and the guardianship of the constitution, as a way of controlling, when necessary, the actions of the executive and legislature and guaranteeing the constitutionality of laws and political decisions. In these respects, the García Meza trial represented an important opportunity for the Bolivian justice system to demonstrate its capacity to fulfill these functions. Yet, despite the chance to redeem its negative image, the trial occurred at an exceptionally difficult juncture in Bolivian history, revealing both the ongoing institutional problems of the judicial branch as well as its conflicts with other state powers.

The congressional proceedings against García Meza highlighted the responsibility and constitutional competencies of the Supreme Court. In accordance with the Constitution, the Court was not only the highest appeals court, it was also the appropriate authority to try accountability cases against state officials. Its decision was final, without appeal. In this sense, the new democratic juncture gave the Supreme Court the opportunity for the first time in history to play an autonomous role in relation to the executive branch, setting the groundwork for a progressive institutionalization of judicial power. In accord with the Constitution, the democratic regime had already begun to appoint both Supreme Court and District Court judges, steps that naturally encouraged a reduction in the judicial branch's traditional dependence on the executive (a trait that had only been exacerbated by García Meza's decapitation of the judiciary). As a result, when the trial opened, only two of the magistrates had been named by the García Meza government; the others had been constitutionally appointed in 1982 when the Siles Zuazo and Paz Estenssoro administrations reconstituted the Court.[24] Furthermore, the decisive phase of the trial took place during the Paz Zamora administration (1989–1993) under a Supreme Court the majority of whose members were not politically associated with the political parties in power.

Nevertheless, despite the fact that the trial against the dictatorship was an enormously important opportunity for the autonomous development of the Supreme Court, it would be wrong to imagine that all of the evils endemic to the Bolivian judicial system had been overcome. The recently restored democracy was in no condition to change or reform the obsolete nature of the nation's laws, codes, and procedures. Moreover, the trial itself served to reveal the antiquated character of the country's legal system as well as to highlight many of its traditional vices.[25] When the proceedings began in 1986, the Bolivian legal system faced numerous problems, including the contradictory, incoherent, and obsolete character of its codes and procedures, making modernization an urgent matter; inadequate legislation in defining the roles of the different actors within the judicial system, for example, the role of the attorney general; restricted access to the administration of justice and to the protection of individual liberties resulting from socioeconomic inequalities, the ethnic and cultural heterogeneity of the country, and the propensity of the entire judicial system to corruption; limited resources for the efficient administration of justice (until 1990 the judicial system received less than 1 percent of the national budget); and, finally, widespread corruption.[26]

The Judicial Process: Characteristics and Procedural Difficulties

The García Meza trial passed through three seemingly interminable stages. The first stage of preparatory hearings required more than two years (April 1986–May 1988). The second, most prolonged stage was the presentation of evidence (July 1989–September 1992), and the third and final stage consisted of summaries and sentencing by the Supreme Court (October 1992–April 1993). At the end of the first year, the civil party to the indictment launched severe criticisms at the state for the extremely slow pace of the proceedings, echoing the frustration felt by many of those most interested in seeing the dictatorship punished. The prosecution pointed to three major problems: the lack of coordination between state powers, especially between the executive and legislative branches; indecisiveness and an absence of political will to grant jurisdictional support to the Supreme Court; and the impotence of the Supreme Court itself due to a lack of special procedures.[27] Nor did the press fail to express its disapproval of the trial's discouragingly slow progress. At the end of the trial's third year, an editorial in an important newspaper complained that there was no will to carry the procedure to its ultimate conclusions and spoke exaggeratedly of the total failure of all those involved—the judges, the lawyers, the government, the legislative branch, and even the prosecutors.[28] Despite these criticisms, however, the Comité Impulsor at least expressed its conviction that the judicial process had become a socially unrescindable and juridically irreversible process.[29] When five years had passed and the Supreme Court was paralyzed by a serious institutional conflict between the executive and judicial branches, Juan del Granado, the principal lawyer representing the civil party to the indictment, used dramatic terms in describing the accountability trial as "delayed, complex, full of obstacles, with indecisive judges, ineffectual prosecutors, and complacent police, [and] taking place in a weakened, indifferent, and almost complicitous democratic institutional context." It was, he added, once again "a faithful reflection of the hundreds and thousands of trials that never resolved anything and that failed to fulfill the litigant's expectations of justice. It is an amplified and condensed portrait of our entire judicial system, a judicial system that contradicts the existence of democracy and is far removed from the needs of the collectivity."[30]

To this climate of suspicion, discouragement, and lack of confidence that were shown by both the civil party to the indictment and public opinion, another worrisome factor was added: a countervailing campaign of threats, intimidation, and violence directed against judges, the attorney general, and the civil party prosecutors by persons allied with García Meza and even by the ex-dictator himself. Lawyers representing the civil party to the indictment were repeatedly threatened with death and, on one occasion in Sucre, García Meza himself threatened Juan del Granado with violence.

Given the historical deficiencies of Bolivia's judicial system and its lack of credibility, it was no surprise that the trial took place in a permanent climate of skepticism directed toward the Supreme Court by the civil party. The civil party and the press spoke frequently, and rightfully so, of the "leaden feet of justice" and of the need for "more social control over the trial" in order to accelerate the process. In fact, however, the adverse political and institutional context of the trial was due not only to the Supreme Court's lack of will or to its incapacity to administer justice, but also to equally serious institutional problems and tensions between parliament and the executive that erupted into a serious institutional crisis and confrontation between November 1989 and May 1990. This crisis, the most serious endured by the democratic process to date, pitted the legislative and executive branches against the judiciary. Using its parliamentary majority, the government even voted to subject eight of the twelve Supreme Court magistrates to an accountability trial of their own, accusing them of evasion.

The cause of this conflict was not the tardiness of the trial, however, but rather a quite unrelated decision by the Supreme Court to declare unconstitutional an increase in taxes for the production of beer that had been included in the government's 1989 budget. It seems that the MIR and ADN coalition government decided to take advantage of this controversial, though juridically sound, decision to bring the Court under its control, intending to rid it of those magistrates who, in the coalition's view, were linked to the principal opposition party, the MNR. The majority of the Supreme Court magistrates had been appointed by the Siles Zuazo and Paz Estenssoro governments, and the ruling parties felt that they did not have the political support they desired in the Court. In itself, this was a positive indication that the institutionalization of the democratic system had already generated an unprecedented separation of powers and that the decisions of the executive could be challenged and revised by the judicial branch. Nonetheless, the institutional conflict paralyzed the Court for eight months, endangering the continuity of the proceedings against the former dictatorship. Eventually, however, the government itself had to dismiss the case against the magistrates for lack of evidence. The civil party held that the "secret motive" behind the congressional action had been to obstruct the Supreme Court so that a sentence against García Meza could be avoided. It also accused the government of deception and of protecting those responsible for the 1980 dictatorship.[31]

During a decisive phase in the trial, therefore, it is not surprising that these conflicts combined to produce a hostile environment replete with mutual attacks and accusations between members of the *Acuerdo Patriótico* government, Supreme Court magistrates, and the prosecution, throwing into doubt the will of the government and of parliament to support the trial. Even the press and the Comité Impulsor had suspicions about the judges and accused them of acting irresponsibly and of accepting bribes to prevent the Supreme Court from passing sentence. Certain Court magistrates were even accused of conniving with the ex-dictator himself, since he had been forced by judicial order to reside in Sucre, the site of the Court. For all of these reasons, the "trial of the century" threatened to become a "century of trial."

As we have pointed out before, the fact that the legal foundations and procedures for conducting a successful accountability trial were inadequate did not make matters any easier. The accountability laws themselves were obsolete and not based on any special procedural code. There were no specific mechanisms designed to direct judicial procedures against former state officials who could only be tried by the Supreme Court. For this reason the Court had no choice but to turn to the penal code as it was applied in ordinary trials in searching for insights into its application in this specialized case. According to Edgar Oblitas, the president of the Court, the "Gordian knot" that provoked such delays in the trial was precisely this need to apply an ordinary judicial process to a special law, equivalent to admitting that no adequate regulation existed.[32] In an open letter released when the trial had already entered into its final stages, the Supreme Court rejected the accusations of inefficiency made by the press and numerous politicians, basing its argument on the obsolescence of the laws and noting that the Congress had never bothered to regulate the procedure. The Court further speculated that Congress had acted with premeditation, knowing that under these conditions the trial would take a long time. The Court accurately pointed out that an accountability trial against fifty-six defendants had never before been initiated in Bolivia.[33] The civil party agreed, emphasizing through its principal lawyer that the delay in the judicial process should be attributed to the procedural shortcomings of Bolivian law.[34]

One of the major drawbacks of relying on the ordinary penal code for direction was that all of the trial's transactions tended to be multiplied by the number of defendants. This helped to make the process interminable. To correct this and other inadequacies, the Supreme Court as well as the civil party and the Comité Impulsor urgently solicited Congress at the beginning of the trial to promulgate a special procedural law to cover accountability trials. However, the Congress failed to take action, and as the trial unfolded the Supreme Court continued to insist that this oversight constituted the parliament's gravest error with regard to the trial. Another congressional error, they regularly pointed out, was to lump together former state dignitaries directly responsible for the dictatorship with lower-ranking officials and, worse yet, with paramilitary forces involved in the repression and crimes committed by the dictatorship. For this reason the president of the Supreme Court appropriately referred to the "authentic Greek gift" that the legislative branch had bequeathed it when it accused fifty-six persons and forced it to superimpose an accountability trial on an ordinary judicial process involving paramilitary agents.

It is not surprising, then, that in these circumstances the judicial process was accompanied by constant debate regarding the appropriateness of the trial, a debate that highlighted the most important judicial errors of the congressional resolution. These were its mistaken application of Article 68, paragraph 12 of the Constitution that states that accountability claims can only be brought against the president, the vice president, state ministers, the heads of diplomatic missions, and the general comptroller; and its failure to consider Article 89, paragraph 3, which prohibits active members of the armed forces from being elected president or vice president, suggesting that those responsible for the military dictatorship could not be considered ex-dignitaries of the state.

Nonetheless, the fact that the marathon trial turned into a true work of Sisyphus for the prosecution and the magistrates of the Supreme Court and also into a seemingly interminable obstacle course does not admit of a simple explanation. The most apparent cause was associated with the cumbersome procedures in the investigatory phase and the delaying tactics that the trial procedures permitted. Yet, while the length of the trial was due in large part to structural deficiencies in the judicial system, the delay must also be

attributed to broader factors, namely, the difficult reinstitutionaliza-
tion of the government and particularly the varying degrees of commitment to democracy held by various political actors.

In the first place, it was never possible to dispel suspicions that
certain magistrates lacked commitment to the process and that they
were applying delaying tactics in order to slow the trial and perhaps
suspend it once and for all. Added to this were the undeniable delaying tactics used by García Meza himself and the other defendants,
which were designed to call into question the democratic and jurisdictional will of Congress and even to deny the competence of the
Supreme Court to try the dictatorship.[35] It is also clear that some of
the obstacles and interruptions of the trial were secretly provoked by
various politicians, military officers, and businessmen who were indebted to García Meza and still occupied influential positions in all
three branches of the democratic government. A reasonable, though
not easily verifiable, hypothesis insistently voiced by the prosecution
referred to the existence of a "protective triangle . . . a triple politico-
economic and military structure" acting at all state levels to protect
García Meza. What is known is that prominent civilian members of
the García Meza government who belonged to the ADN and the
MNR parties were once again in positions of executive and legislative power.[36] It was perhaps for this reason that Congress did not
order the capture of García Meza when the indictment was issued
against him, even though it was required by law to do so. Also, the
police were unable to force him to remain in Sucre during the trial or
to prevent his escape at the end of 1988.[37] Finally, the civil party attributed other judicial delays to the failure of Supreme Court magistrates, some of whom had been named to their posts during the
dictatorship, to demonstrate institutional initiative. In the first year
of the trial, the principal lawyer of the civil party, Juan del Granado,
asserted that the magistrates were not playing an active role and that
they "lacked a deep conviction of the national and patriotic importance of this trial" in which democracy itself stood in the balance.[38]
All of this compounded the grave institutional conflicts that we have
already witnessed between the Supreme Court and the legislative
and executive branches.

Despite these obstacles, however, Bolivia's institutional crisis was

resolved and the trial was able to advance against wind and tide into
the decisive phase of presenting evidence, a phase that lasted more
than two years (July 1989–September 1992). The civil party presented
nearly two thousand pieces of documentary evidence, including all
of the confidential decrees and resolutions issued by the dictatorship
in its destruction of the constitutional order, as well as other evidence
including expert testimony, circumstantial evidence, and confessions
from more than one hundred witnesses for the prosecution. To all of
this must be added the strong interest, commitment, and support
provided by prominent human rights activists and by multilateral
organizations such as the United Nations, the Organization of American States, Amnesty International, and the International Labor Organization, which introduced a truly international dimension to the
proceedings and contributed numerous supporting documents analyzing and denouncing the García Meza dictatorship.[39]

Summations and Sentencing by the Supreme Court

In the decisive final phase of judicial summations, the principal foundation for the Court's verdict rested on the evidence and arguments
provided by the prosecution. In contrast, the summation of the attorney general, as the chief prosecutor representing state and society,
did not add anything that would have enhanced the case against
García Meza and the other defendants. Instead, he pointlessly repeated that the Supreme Court should resolve the jurisdictional
questions concerning the appropriateness of an ordinary trial versus
an accountability trial, insisting that it clarify the criteria for undertaking an ordinary trial that might treat García Meza and his collaborators as common criminals without the right to special treatment. In
his conclusion, the attorney general stated that the evidence contributed by his office and by the civil party to the indictment had
demonstrated that García Meza, his ministers, and the low-ranking
functionaries had committed the crimes of which they were accused,
though, curiously, he did not at any point expound upon the evidence provided by the civil party.

Because of the juridical nature and political context of the trial, the
summation provided by the civil party to the indictment constituted

the most complete, convincing, and forceful testimony ever provided in a Bolivian accountability trial. This was a significant historical and juridical document not only because it reconstructed the most salient aspects of the dictatorship but also because it used solid judicial argumentation to analyze the evidence on which the legal criteria for imposing sanctions against the dictatorship were established. The civil party used the Constitution and the penal code as its fundamental reference points rather than the accountability laws of 1884 and 1944, an understandable decision given that the latter were inadequate to sufficiently specify the dictatorship's crimes. Article 17 of the 1884 law had defined in very general terms the reasons for which state officials could be held accountable, but unlike the Bolivian penal code, it did not identify specifically punishable offenses. The civil party's argumentation, therefore, was based largely on various articles of the penal code as well as on Articles 2 and 4 of the Constitution; these latter articles were concerned with the division of power among the three branches of government and the sovereignty of the people as exercised through their representatives, as well as the crime of sedition committed by any armed force that usurps the sovereignty of the people. Among the penal code's provisions, the most relevant for specifying and sanctioning the most significant crimes were the following: Articles 121 (the crime of sedition), 124 (the usurpation of the rights of the people), 146 (the use of undue influence), 153 (illegal and unconstitutional decrees), 150 (conduct incompatible with the exercise of public office), 221 (contracts harmful to the State), 252 and 132 (the crimes of assassination and felonious association), 292 (deprivation of liberty), and 296 (crimes against freedom of the press). The crime of genocide, which is not specified in the penal code, was considered and sanctioned on the basis of the November 27, 1968 United Nations Covenant that considers genocide to be an imprescriptible crime against humanity.[40]

Ultimately, the legal and political argumentation that the Supreme Court used to justify its verdict was not essentially different from that expressed in the civil party's summation, and it called for the imposition of corresponding punishments for the offenses committed by those responsible for the military dictatorship. But in addition, the Court also emphasized the goals of the 1884 and 1944 accountability laws whose point, according to the magistrates, had been to prevent powerholders from committing criminal acts of corruption with impunity.[41] Based on this interpretation, and using standards that were upheld by the civil party, the Court elaborated four central criteria to support its verdict:

1. the political and historical need to bring the accountability trial to a successful conclusion as a vital procedure for strengthening the democratic institutional system;

2. the need to impose sanctions for crimes committed against the Constitution and human rights, and to show respect for international treaties to which Bolivia was a signatory (including the United Nations' October 1983 Convention on the Non-Applicability of Statutory Limitations to War Crimes and of Crimes against Humanity, and the 1993 Economic and Social Council Resolution on the protection of liberty, security, and the recognition of the juridical personality of human rights);

3. application of the principle of shared responsibility, rejecting as inadmissible the excuse that García Meza's collaborators were "following orders"; and finally,

4. the importance of the judicial process and the condemnation of those responsible for crimes committed by the dictatorship, based upon the distinction between individual responsibility and the institutional responsibility of the armed forces.[42]

After more than seven years of judicial proceedings, the Supreme Court's historic sentence was read on April 21, 1993, which the government declared a "Day of National Dignity." The Court sentenced the former dictator, García Meza, and his principal collaborator, Arce Gómez, to thirty years in prison without parole, the most severe punishment permitted by the Constitution, for the crimes of sedition, armed uprising, genocide, anti-constitutional decrees, and economic damages against the State.[43] Of the ministers in García Meza's first cabinet, the former Minister of Peasant Affairs and the former Minister of Planning were each sentenced to six years imprisonment. Waldo Bernal, a member of the first junta and former Chief of the Air Force, was sentenced to five years for contracts damaging to the state and for decrees contrary to the laws and the Constitution. Finally, the remaining ministers were given prison sentences of two years. Eleven para-military agents implicated in both the assassination of labor and political leaders and in the genocide of MIR leaders were sentenced to between twenty and thirty years in prison without parole.[44]

Concluding Reflections

Several important conclusions can be extracted from the experiences accumulated during Bolivia's legal confrontation with the García Meza dictatorship. Despite ongoing debate regarding the validity of the accountability procedures, it is clear that the trial was unprecedented in its importance. It was the first successful attempt in Latin America by a democratic system to "settle accounts" with a legacy of military dictatorship, of which García Meza was only the most recent and most negative example. From this point of view, it was a notable example of the way democratic institutions may be used to establish a definitive break with a history replete with military assaults on government and the abuse of the state apparatus for personal and arbitrary ends. Today, Bolivia is no longer in the same position as it was before this verdict was delivered, for it is now probable anyone responsible for a future coup d'état against the democratic order will have to account for his actions before the halls of justice. In this way, the judgment against García Meza may prove to be an essential guarantor of the rule of law, helping to preserve the dignity of Bolivian citizens and prevent the return of future dictatorships.[45]

Although the trial was undertaken with many different intentions and even against the will of some political leaders, it corresponded to an unquestionable demand for justice by Bolivian society. Its significance lay in confronting years of arbitrariness and political chaos with the rule of law, creating a precedent that was not only juridical and political in nature but also ethical. The political logic of the trial was intermeshed with its judicial logic, since the legal order itself was used to defend Bolivia's democratic institutions. Importantly, the political logic of defending democratic institutions was articulated by appealing to a judicial logic that was based on the laws in effect at the moment the democratic process was interrupted and not on any ex post facto or retroactive legislation. Despite various inconsistencies in the congressional resolution that initiated this process, the choice of an accountability trial can therefore be seen as a justifiable "middle way" of pursuing backward-looking justice. In the final reckoning, the trial resulted in a sentence that may help to prevent future abuses of power.

In at least two respects, the García Meza trial may also have contributed to the strengthening of Bolivian democracy. On the one hand, it affirmed the constitutional role of the Supreme Court in fulfilling its fundamental purpose of promoting the rule of law. As we have seen, the Court was able to live up to its mandate by carrying the accountability trial to its final phase of sentencing. In so doing, the trial's outcome may also have helped to overcome a prevailing sense of skepticism in Bolivia, demonstrating that the judiciary could in fact play an impartial and autonomous role even in the face of opposition from the executive branch. To this extent, the trial was a crucial step in the Court's efforts to repair the atrophied reputation of the judicial branch.

Nevertheless, and despite the Court's best intentions, the trial also revealed unacceptable defects in the Bolivian legal and justice system.[46] As long as these defects persist, it is clear that the Bolivian judiciary will be unable in any complete sense to fulfill the role demanded of it in an institutionalized democracy—the impartial and efficient administration of justice which guarantees respect for basic human rights and for the Constitution.

On the other hand, the use of the courts to try the former dictatorship was still a very important step in the process of subordinating the Bolivian armed forces to the democratic order. As we have seen, the reestablishment of democracy took place in a context in which the military was extremely weak and discredited. This "transition through rupture" was a key factor favoring the progressive subordination of the military to the constitutional order. The military did not even attempt to secure itself against future judicial action by dictating amnesty laws or laws of "national pacification," as was done by the Argentine, Uruguayan, and Chilean militaries. Even so, the Supreme Court's verdict against the García Meza dictatorship represented a decisive push in this process of subordination. Through it, the military as an institution was forced to recognize the high cost of dictatorship, and in response, high-ranking military officers reaffirmed their obedience to civilian power and their loyalty to democracy.[47] Subsequently, the armed forces publicly recognized the constitutionality and legality of the sentence against García Meza and, implicitly, the antidemocratic and criminal nature of the dictatorship. Thus, the accountability trial was important not only for its part in reinforcing the constitutional role of the military but also for distinguishing between the crimes of the García Meza dictatorship and the armed forces as an institution.[48]

No less important is the fact that the trial also prompted a process of political and moral recovery for Bolivian society as a whole, and particularly for members of a political class that had grown accustomed to conducting its business under the protective arm of the military and that was itself seriously compromised by the coups d'état that had taken place in Bolivia between 1964 and 1980. Despite the decision not to prosecute many of the civilian participants in the dictatorship and the mild penalties given to many of García Meza's ministers, the trial's historical contribution was in drawing a clear dividing line between the present and a bitter dictatorial past for which civilians as well as military personnel were responsible. In this sense, the political and ethical value of its verdict lay in its implicit warning against any future attempts by members of Bolivia's political class to arrive at power through illicit means.

Admittedly, given the trial's limitations, this lesson was not as forceful as it might have been. From some critics' perspective, the highest authority and his principal collaborators were not punished strongly enough for their offenses; additionally, the sentences of the former cabinet members were commuted almost immediately after the verdict;[49] and, above all, party militants who had cooperated with the dictatorship were also exempted from the trial (an indefensible decision, given the role that civilians have played in past coups and the fact that they continue to engage in politics with impunity). Moreover, another limitation of the trial was its failure to prosecute the dictatorship for the crime of drug-trafficking even though, as the first narco-dictatorship in Latin America, it inflicted serious moral and political damage on the state and society.

Still, we can appreciate the significance of the Bolivian case by placing it within its Latin American context. In so doing, we cannot avoid an obligatory reference to the Argentine experience. In contrast to Chile, where the legal system operative under the Pinochet dictatorship is still in force and where it took years for the regime to permit judicial proceedings against any of the country's former oppressors (but not against Pinochet and other military members of the dictatorship), and to Uruguay, where an amnesty law was ultimately declared, Bolivia and Argentina are the only two Latin American countries that have tried military officers in connection with egregious human rights violations. In both countries, the political context, "transition through rupture," and strong demands for justice by civil society organizations made it possible to bring the dictators to trial. Nonetheless, the resulting trials also represented two very different judicial processes utilizing their own procedures and producing distinctive results. Bolivia's trial was an "accountability trial," initiated by congressional resolution and carried out by the Supreme Court. In contrast, the Argentine trial was a summary trial initiated by the executive branch and prosecuted by the Federal Court of Buenos Aires against the top commanders of the dictatorship that ruled the country from 1976 to 1979. While it utilized ordinary legal procedures, this trial only came about after a confrontation between the government, which initially gave the military the opportunity to judge itself using military tribunals, and various human rights organizations and judges.

In Bolivia, two of the principal leaders of the dictatorship were sentenced to imprisonment without parole, as were several ministerial collaborators and other agents of state repression. Neither amnesty laws nor laws of due obedience were enacted, and it is thus unthinkable that such laws could be legally enacted now. For these reasons, Bolivia remains the only country in Latin America where a former dictator and his collaborators are currently imprisoned for their crimes. This represents a notable contrast with Argentina, where a similar trial was limited by "full stop" and "due obedience" laws passed during the Alfonsín government. All five of the military junta members who were convicted were subsequently pardoned through a de facto amnesty declared by the Menem government.[50]

For all its faults and limitations, therefore, the judicial process against García Meza was without a doubt a historical landmark in the Latin American context. Bolivian democracy demonstrated its ability to meet a difficult legal, political, and ethical challenge by responding to the demand for justice voiced by individuals and social institutions seeking to restore basic dignity to the men and women victimized by the dictatorship. Not only did the Supreme Court rescue these individuals from dishonor and oblivion in handing down its decision, but it also provided an invaluable service to both the construction of democracy and the rule of law in Bolivia.

Translated by Carol Stuart

NOTES

1. Throughout Bolivia's history, there had been twenty-five previous attempts to conduct accountability trials, most of them against the republic's presidents. Yet of these, only one (against former Minister of Agriculture Jorge Mercado in 1944) resulted in a verdict, serving as a precedent of minor importance.

2. Juan del Granado, a key prosecuting attorney in the trial, described the connection in the following terms: "The reestablishment of peace, democracy, and peaceful coexistence among Bolivians . . . will only be possible based on justice" (Informe Especial, *Los Tiempos*, Cochabamba, September 20, 1991). He also noted that "Dictatorial impunity strips the democratic system of credibility, reduces its potential, and severely distorts justice" ("Impunidad del ex-dictador . . . violenta principios democráticos y derechos humanos," *Ultima Hora*, La Paz, December 16, 1990).

3. On this theme, see Raúl Barrios Morón and René Antonio Mayorga, *La cuestión militar en cuestión: Democracia y Fuerzas Armadas* (La Paz: CEBEM, 1994).

4. For more information on this stage, see James Dunkerley, *Rebellion in the Veins: Political Struggle in Bolivia 1952–1982* (London: Verso, 1984); René Antonio Mayorga, *De la anomia política al orden democrático? Democracia, estado y movimiento sindical en Bolivia* (La Paz: CEBEM, 1991); and James Malloy and Eduardo Gamarra, *Revolution and Reaction: Bolivia 1964–1985* (New Brunswick: Transaction Books, 1988).

5. See René Antonio Mayorga, "Democracy and Private Business as Key Political Actors in Bolivia," in *Organized Business in Latin America: Response to Changing Times*, ed. Francisco Durand and Eduardo Silva (Boulder, Colo.: Westview Press, forthcoming).

6. Mayorga, *De la anomia política al orden democrático*.

7. The former Chief of the Argentine Army, General Leopoldo

88 BOLIVIA'S DICTATORSHIP ON TRIAL

Galtieri, was directly implicated in planning the coup, and Argentine army officers participated in repression and torture. See *Newsweek* and *New York Times* journalist Martin Edwin Andersen's *Dossier Secreto: Argentina's Desaparecidos and the Myth of the Dirty War* (Boulder, Colo.: Westview Press, 1993); "Gobierno de García Meza 'fabricado en Buenos Aires'," *La Razón*, La Paz, March 4, 1993.

8. The statistics on human rights violations during the thirteen months of the García Meza dictatorship, though only approximate, are sobering: 196 assassinations, 554 wounded, 87 disappearances, 3500 arbitrary detentions, and between 440 and 1500 exiled. See Federico Aguiló, *"Nunca Más" para Bolivia* (Cochabamba: IESE-UMSS, 1993).

9. Various publications have revealed abundant evidence of the financial backing given to the García Meza coup by drug-traffickers. See Andersen, *Dossier Secreto*, especially its chapter on "the cocaine coup" in Bolivia. According to Michael Levine, a former agent of the U.S. Drug Enforcement Agency (DEA), the CIA also supported the coup with the goal of operating the cocaine factory in Huanchaca (the largest such factory in Bolivia, discovered in 1986) and using its profits to fund its secret activities, especially those against Nicaragua. See Michael Levine and Laura Kavanan-Levine, *La guerra falsa: Fraude mortífero de la CIA en la guerra de las drogas* (Cochabamba: CEDIB, 1994), as well as their statements at the "Observatorio geopolítcio de las drogas" colloquium held in Madrid, proceedings published in *Cambio 16*, Madrid, March 1993. See also R. W. Lee, *El laberinto blanco* (Bogotá: Ed. CEREC, 1992); Instituto de Estudios Políticos para America Latina y Africa (IEPALA), *Narcotráfico y política* (Madrid: 1982); and Dunkerley, *Rebellion in the Veins*, pp. 321–325. The North American judicial proceedings against former Minister of the Interior Arce Gómez also revealed far-reaching connections between drug-traffickers and the García Meza government.

10. This is how the situation was described in a dramatic pastoral letter from the Catholic Church, released October 10, 1980, cited in Justicia y Dignidad, *Alegato presentado por la parte civil en juicio de responsabilidades* (Sucre: 1992), 104.10.

11. García Meza declared in a speech that "Bolivia will be the tomb of extremists" and threatened to "make them disappear, because we do not need those people." Almost simultaneously, Arce Gómez announced the promulgation of a new national security law that would apply the death penalty to extremists, adding that "all those who infringe upon this law should walk with their will under their arm" (ibid., pp. 311–312).

12. See "Declaración de participación de las Fuerzas Armadas en el proceso político para la reconstrucción nacional," cited in the verdict of the Supreme Court, in Corte Suprema de Justicia, *El juicio del siglo* (Sucre: Editorial Judicial, 1993), pp. 56–57; Daniel Salamanca, "Del caos a la construcción," in Justicia y Dignidad, *Alegato presentado por la parte civil*, pp. 47, 49–52; Resolutions of the Armed Forces (ibid., pp. 68–72); and *Bolivia: Cronología de una dictadura* (Quito: PADI, 1982), p. 327.

13. Barrios Morón and Mayorga, *La cuestión militar en cuestión*.

14. When the trial began, the military officers linked to the García Meza dictatorship had already been reassigned by the UDP government. They did not maintain positions of power nor were they responsible for guaranteeing the security of the democratic regime. The military high command under García Meza had been demoted, as had thirty officers implicated in drug-trafficking. The high command installed by the UDP government was led by García Meza's adversaries, the institutionalists.

15. On these alternative viewpoints, see Jamal Benomar, "Justice after Transitions," *Journal of Democracy* 4, no. 1 (January 1993): 3–6.

16. "Resolución Congresal," in Corte Suprema de Justicia, *El juicio del siglo*, pp. 27–31.

17. The APDH also pointed out that the congressional resolution violated the penal law and the 1844 and 1944 accountability laws by failing to formally detain the accused ("Juicio de responsibilidades: Informe especial," *Presencia*, La Paz, March 22, 1988).

18. Justicia y Dignidad, *Alegato presentado por la parte civil*, pp. 3–5, 157–158.

19. According to the Bolivian penal code, the goal of criminal punishment is not to rehabilitate but to prevent crimes by dissuading potential violators.

20. In its summation, the civil party stated: "It is precisely now, when the Bolivian judicial system is experiencing one of its worst crises and the population exhibits great skepticism about the application of laws, that reason and motive must be provided to restore faith in democracy's institutions, so that our people regain their self-esteem and turn our country into one populated by sensitive and devoted persons who give and merit respect" (Justicia y Dignidad, *Alegato Presentado por la Parte Civil*, p. 497).

21. The summation points out the enormous difficulties that the decision to hold an accountability trial implied for the administration of justice. The legal system had not foreseen this excessive form of criminal behavior and therefore, "this special kind of criminality, taking the form of permanent and continuous illegal conduct by persons bent upon subverting the constitutional machinery of government, violating the judicial order in its entirety, and using the state apparatus and its governing mechanisms as privileged instruments for the commission of crimes, was not sufficiently developed in [Bolivia's] penal doctrine" (ibid., p. 5).

22. The civil party's final summation emphasized that the Writ of Congressional Proceedings, "though significant, is barely a pallid reflection of the many aspects of social and political life that were assaulted by the de facto government." Many crimes were not taken into account. "The accusation of drug-trafficking was absent even though this detestable, illegal activity formed the backbone of the regime." Nor does it mention the assassinations and massacres in Caracoles and other mining districts or name the most prominent or flagrant authors or co-authors of the crimes (ibid., p. 3).

23. Declarations by the Commander in Chief of the Armed Forces (*Presencia*, La Paz, August 1, 1990).

24. The two magistrates referred to are Edgar Oblitas, president of the Supreme Court during the trial, and Hugo Galindo.

25. After several years of political debate, the reform of the judicial branch has recently begun. It was instigated by the August 1994 Constitutional Reform Act, which called for the creation of a Constitutional Court and a new procedure for naming magistrates, based on the approval of two-thirds of Congress. The latter reform seeks to redress the dominance of political forces and the executive branch in the functioning of government. The reform has proceeded very slowly, however, and it has only been hesitantly applied to codes and procedures.

26. See Eduardo Gamarra, *The System of Justice in Bolivia: An Institutional Analysis* (Miami: Florida International University, 1991); C. Castro Rodríguez, *Historia judicial de Bolivia* (La Paz: Los Amigos del Libro, 1987).

27. Declarations by Juan del Granado in *Los Tiempos*, Cochabamba, December 18, 1988.

28. "Consecuencias del juicio de responsibilidades," *Presencia*, La Paz, January 29, 1989.

29. "Juicio de responsabilidades: Balance de la gestión 1989," *Hoy*, La Paz, December 30, 1989.

30. "Conflicto por Corte Suprema puede favorecer impunidad del ex-dictador," *Los Tiempos*, Cochabamba, April 14, 1991.

31. "Conflicto por Corte Suprema puede favorecer impunidad del ex-dictador," *Ultima Hora*, La Paz, April 14, 1991. No sooner had the trial begun than Freddy Vargas, an MNR Congressman, made an attempt to bring all of the magistrates to trial for prevarication, endangering the continuity of the process. At that time it was said that the "trial of the century" was going to be "a century of trial." In a letter to the president of the House of Deputies, the Supreme Court rejected this effort and affirmed that it was clearly committed to carrying the accountability trial forward, since the future of the polity would depend on its results ("Corte Suprema pide resolución de juicio de responsibilidad," *Presencia*, La Paz, September 24, 1988).

32. Declarations by Edgar Oblitas in *Los Tiempos*, Cochabamba, May 30, 1988 and in *El Mundo*, Santa Cruz, October 4, 1988.

33. Corte Suprema de Justicia, "Una explicación necesaria al pueblo de Bolivia," *Hoy*, La Paz, November 15, 1992.

34. "La verdad amenaza la impavidez del ex-general García Meza," *Los Tiempos*, Cochabamba, February 20, 1988.

35. Justicia y Dignidad, *Alegato presentado por la parte civil*, pp. 6–7.

36. Among the numerous examples that can be cited, the most notorious include the following: Mario Rolón Anaya, an ADN member, the minister of foreign relations under García Meza and ambassador to the OAS during the government of Paz Zamora; Guillermo Fortún, also an ADN member, a key member of the Advisory and Legislative Commission in the government of García Meza and president of the Senate in the Paz Zamora

government; and Fernando Valle, comptroller of the University of La Paz during the dictatorship and minister of defense during the government of Paz Estenssoro.

37. The civil party attacked the Paz Estenssoro government "for not assisting the legal proceedings and for undertaking actions that tended to reinforce impunity such as failing to hand over the reports and confidential documents of the dictatorship as solicited by the Supreme Court, and especially for ignoring the Supreme Court's instructions to arrest García Meza" (Juan del Granado in *Presencia*, La Paz, June 12, 1988).

38. Declarations by Juan del Granado in *Presencia*, La Paz, June 12, 1988.

39. Among the most important of these documents was a report on "The Human Rights Situation in Bolivia" by Héctor Gross Espiell, special envoy of the Inter-American Human Rights Commission to Bolivia, presented to a session of the OAS in March, 1981. This report thoroughly documents the criminal aspects of human rights violations during the dictatorship.

40. Justicia y Dignidad, *Alegato presentado por la parte civil*; Corte Suprema de Justicia, *El juicio del siglo*.

41. Corte Suprema de Justicia, *Sentencia contra Luis García Meza y sus colaboradores* (Press documents, *La Paz*, April 25, 1996), p. 15.

42. Ibid., pp. 3, 7–8.

43. If the Constitution and the penal code would have permitted the accumulation of sentences, they could have been condemned to more than 220 years for the crimes committed. García Meza was sentenced in absentia. Almost a year later, he was captured in Brazil where he was living clandestinely under a false passport. The Brazilian government extradited him to Bolivia in March 1995. Since then, García Meza has been serving his sentence in a maximum security prison. When Arce Gómez was sentenced, he was already in prison in the United States, condemned to thirty years for drug-trafficking after being taken prisoner in Bolivia by DEA agents and transported directly to the United States without extradition. At the time, the Paz Zamora government justified the surrender of Arce Gómez with the deprecating argument that the Bolivian Supreme Court could not be trusted. Although the Court's sentence called for Arce's extradition from the United States, the Bolivian government has not initiated any formal proceedings.

44. The civil party's summation referred to those who had been excluded from the congressional resolution that began the accountability trial. The Court's sentence also made an explicit reference to the need for the attorney general to begin ordinary criminal proceedings against those collaborators for whom there was sufficient evidence of criminal activity but who were not included in the congressional resolution. Nevertheless, for understandable reasons, neither the attorney general nor the civil party has taken any initiative in this direction.

45. The future is essential to the administration of justice. The function of law implies a temporal dimension that has to do with the fact that legal

norms constitute a "framework of generalized symbolic expectations" for society's adaptation to an uncertain future (Niklas Luhmann, *Das Recht der Gesellschaft* (Frankfurt/Main: Suhrkamp Verlag, 1995), pp. 125, 130.

46. It is clear that the successful conclusion of this trial does not imply that the many problems endemic to the judicial system (delays, inequity of verdicts, corruption) have been overcome. Nevertheless, the trial has been a relevant factor in pushing the dominant political parties to begin a modernization program for the judicial branch as an integral part of its Constitutional Reform Act of August 1993. Judicial reform, including the creation of a Constitutional Court, is slowly being implemented, though its results are still uncertain. During the debate on judicial reform, the Supreme Court took very conservative positions including opposition to the creation of a Constitutional Court.

47. During the trial, the Military High Command repeatedly asserted that the armed forces as an institution had nothing to do with the García Meza coup *(Presencia*, La Paz, August 1, 1990). In this way, they rejected every attempt by García Meza to involve the military institution in his dictatorship. Nevertheless, declarations by military personnel acting as witnesses for the prosecution established the individual and institutional participation of the armed forces. After sentencing, several active-duty and retired officers, among them de facto ex-president Banzer, expressed their "pain and concern" over the verdict (*La Razón*, La Paz, May 7, 1993).

48. The armed forces collaborated in this work by asking Congress to initiate a second trial for the theft of the diaries of the guerrillas, Ché Guevara and Pombo. The civil party asserted in its summation that the trial contributed to the reinvigoration of the armed forces as an institution, reasserting its constitutional functions and "the military honor of deserving officers" by establishing the personal responsibility of the accused and transforming those who "acted against military honor" into "the real enemies of the armed institution" (Justicia y Dignidad, *Alegato presentado por la parte civil*, pp. 14–15).

49. The civil party denounced the verdict against the ministers in García Meza's first cabinet, labeling it inadequate. In this writer's opinion, the legal argument they expounded, based on general considerations of penal law and on Article 20 of the penal code, remains irrefutable: "Of those crimes that were tried, and especially of those of the first group, the participation of all those involved in the criminal enterprise was subject to a general plan. . . . [T]his indicates that all those who participated in the uprising and in the unlawful deeds and acts that followed, played a supporting role in the criminal enterprise . . . and the support of each one of them in accordance with the plan was necessary" (ibid., p. 155).

50. See Carlos Acuña and Catalina Smulovitz, "Guarding the Guardians . . ." in this volume (chapter 4), and Andrés Fontana, "La política militar del gobierno constitucional argentino," in *Ensayos sobre la transición democrática en la Argentina*, ed. José Nun and Juan Carlos Portantiero (Buenos Aires: Puntosur, 1987).

4

Guarding the Guardians in Argentina:
Some Lessons about the Risks and Benefits of Empowering the Courts

Carlos H. Acuña and Catalina Smulovitz

IN THE CONTEXT OF Latin American politics, the Argentine democratic transition has been exceptional. The trial and conviction of those individuals most responsible for human rights violations during the years of military dictatorship was a first sign of this singularity. In spite of a political process which, in successive stages, conspired to limit the reach of legal sanctions and finally led to the pardon and freeing from incarceration of the convicted, the impact of these trials on Argentine democracy could not be totally reversed. Once the focus on a "juridical logic"[1] had transformed historical facts into proofs, neither a pardon nor an amnesty could ever return the human rights situation in Argentina to one in which investigation and judgment are of no consequence. The second sign of Argentina's singularity is that it remains the only Latin American case in which the military leadership has publicly recognized the illegitimate character of the repression and systematic human rights violations carried out during the years of dictatorship. Although the admission was late in coming, on April 25, 1995, the Chief of Staff of the Army, Lt. General Martin Balza, publicly recognized that the country's armed forces had engaged in acts of torture and murder during the confrontations of the 1970s. In his apology, he declared: " He who violates the constitution commits a crime. He who imparts immoral orders commits a crime. He who complies with immoral orders commits a crime. He who uses unjust and immoral means to seek a goal that he believes to be just commits a crime."[2] Subsequently, Martin Balza's words had an important domino effect on other prominent social actors, the Navy, the Air Force, and the Catholic Church, which, although with varying degrees of clarity, then issued public statements admitting to their own complicity in carrying out or collaborating with state terrorism during the period.

The object of this chapter is to analyze and explain the dynamics of the political struggle over human rights and civil-military tensions in Argentina, from the military's coup in 1976 until the present. We propose to show not only why the actors did what they did, and how and why their differing actions shaped the country's politics, but also to demonstrate the significance of this process for the successes and shortcomings of Argentina's democratic consolidation. We shall contend, first of all, that the politics of criminal prosecution which characterized the initial stage of the Argentine transition was *not*, as is commonly understood, the simple consequence of the policies of the presidency of Raúl Alfonsín. Rather, it was the result of a number of different strategies implemented by all the intervening actors in the course of moving away from the military dictatorship. Second, we shall argue that the direction followed in this process did not correspond to the ideal choice of any of the actors involved, but was instead marked by a series of unanticipated developments which strengthened the hand of numerous societal forces, including the Argentine judiciary. Third, we maintain that the resolution of this struggle over human rights in Argentina has led *in the long run* to the subordination of the military to constitutional rule. Finally, we contend that in spite of the well-known concessions granted by the governments of both Alfonsín and, later, Carlos Menem, the high costs and high risks suffered by the armed forces as a result of the investigation and judicial conviction for human rights violations are central reasons for the military's present subordination to constitutional power.

To Sanction Past Human Rights Violations or "Turn the Page": The Political Dilemma of Democratic Transitions

In political debates about transitional justice as well as in disputes among academics, the problem of how to treat those responsible for state terrorism and, simultaneously, ensure the transition to democracy and the consolidation of democratic institutions may be seen as a choice between two contradictory strategies. Some suggest that in order to neutralize the opposition of those actors formerly connected to an authoritarian regime, it is necessary to diminish the uncertainty that the democratic *apertura* (opening) implies for them. Therefore, the proponents of this position claim that for the armed forces to be willing to collaborate, or at least not to sabotage the democratic transition, its members must receive benefits which eliminate the uncertainties that the democratic process poses for them. If one's priority is to reduce the risks which threaten the democratic consolidation, a strategy of not bringing the military to judgment for human rights violations, i.e., of "turning the page," appears to be almost a logical conclusion.

We argue, in contrast, that under certain conditions the use of judicial means to address human rights violations is the most appropriate approach for the successful consolidation of a constitutional regime. This position does not arise merely from ethical considerations, nor does it imply a "juridical" understanding of the relations of power. Rather, our position is based on the effects that judicial punishment of state terrorism may have on the political costs and benefits apparent to authoritarian elites.

How are these effects produced? The judicial process is characterized by the application of universal and abstract criteria based on the principle that all citizens are equal before the law. Even though a juridical interpretation of the law admits a range of possible resolutions, the criteria which characterize judicial proceedings limit the space in which actors in conflict may negotiate and exchange political costs and benefits. This does not mean that the effects of these proceedings are neutral, for a law generates differential costs among diverse social groups. Still, laws reorganize the form of conflict resolution, redefining the cost/benefit matrix determining the probability that each of the diverse social groups involved will realize their interests.[3] Even though a law does not have a particular or concrete beneficiary—that is, even though it does not constitute a selective threat—it can establish the magnitude and universality of the costs that will confront those who decide to violate it. In a democratic "game," the actors tied to a former authoritarian regime do not have the certainty that the judicial process will produce selective benefits. However, they can be assured that they will incur costs if they decide to desert such a game. Therefore, if the judicial process can establish that the costs of deserting the new rules of democracy are greater than the costs of acting within it, then the trials of those responsible for past human rights abuses become a mechanism for deterring future authoritarian strategies and, consequently, an important factor in reproducing democratic stability.

In a nutshell, can constitutional rulers punish former human rights violators who are still the armed "guardians" of the country? Or is impunity the price for democratic stability? When do democracies put their stability at greatest risk, when they punish or when they pardon human rights violators? Since Plato's time and the emergence of the polity, the question of how to guard the guardians has been a central question, both for political theorists and for those struggling for political power. In transitions from a repressive authoritarian regime to a democracy, the dilemma about how to place the guardians under democratic rule becomes more acute than ever. On the one hand, there is the question of whether the guardians will accept being punished for the crimes they committed while in government without revolting against the newborn regime. On the other hand, there is the question of how a new democracy can survive if it fails to demonstrate that all citizens are equal before the law. The ethical foundations of democratic rule establish that all criminals should be brought to justice, particularly when they have followed an authoritarian strategy and when their crimes have been massive. Nevertheless, covering up genocide and other atrocities has been a systematic part of many new democracies' efforts to achieve stability in the twentieth century, especially when the old authoritarian rulers have been perceived as fulfilling important functions in the transition to democracy.[4]

For these reasons, it is important to see what recent experiences can teach us about the relationship between the treatment of past human rights violations and its effects upon the legitimacy and stability of emerging democratic regimes. Our analysis begins with the record of state terrorism in Argentina from 1976 to 1983, when democracy reemerged, and with the military government's first attempts to devise a political "exit" that would serve its interests.

The Repressive Methods of State Terrorism in Argentina

The political strategies of the Argentine military leadership evolved in three very different stages during the dictatorship. In the first stage, from 1976 to 1978, the military's main goal was to violently subordinate society to state control. The second stage, running from 1978 to 1982, had as its goal the design and implementation of a series of measures to ensure a future political order in which the military would play a major tutorial role. The third and final stage, from 1982 to 1983, was characterized by the pursuit of minimal goals in the context of the crisis that resulted from the Malvinas (Falklands) fiasco and the retreat of the armed forces from government.

In 1976, when the armed forces seized power in Argentina, their diagnosis was that the Argentine crisis was due not only to the guerrilla threat, to the "lack of control" of trade union activism, and to the Peronist political movement, but also to a semi-closed statist economy that subsidized industry and promoted "politicization" and a highly inefficient, intersectoral transfer of resources. Subsequently, the military's strategies led researchers and analysts to underscore the intertwined nature of the economic and political objectives of the military, at times however, at the cost of losing sight of the specificity that the political process acquired. In this section and in the next, we will underscore the political plans of the armed forces and their consequences.

When the junta seized power, it announced the suspension of all constitutional authority, it modified the rules of political competition and the functions of governmental power, and it established comprehensive regulations for the operation of state institutions. The junta dissolved the Congress and the provincial and municipal legislatures. It gave legislative powers to the presidency, modified the composition of the National Supreme Court and of the higher provincial courts, and declared all judges subject to immediate removal on the decision of the military authorities. Finally, it eliminated the right to freedom of assembly and suspended political parties, outlawed political activity by trade unions, restricted the freedom of the press, and granted military courts the power to issue swift indictments for any cases involving the disruption of public order.

The junta also defined the institutional mechanisms that would govern the decision-making process, to guarantee that political power would be exercised by the military corporation in a shared way.[5] As the highest authority of the state, the junta itself was empowered to establish general government directives and to designate the president, the members of the Supreme Court, and all other government officials. This joint exercise of power implied a division of the state apparatus into various jurisdictions assigned to the three branches of the armed forces: each force was entitled to be in charge of one-third of government positions. The point of these provisions was to avoid intra-military conflicts in presidential succession and the risk of a personalization of power, a feature that had characterized previous Argentine military governments.

Although all these features were important to the character of the Argentine regime, it was the nature and magnitude of illegal repression that set this dictatorship apart from previous ones in Argentina's history. In 1984, the National Commission on the Disappearance of Persons (Comisión Nacional sobre la Desaparición de Personas, or CONADEP) documented the disappearance of 8,960 people, though it made clear that it estimated that the actual number of victims exceeded 9,000 cases. Amnesty International estimated that the number of victims surpassed 15,000 cases, while other human rights organizations have maintained that the number of victims reached as high as 30,000.[6]

When the coup was in the making, the commander in chief of the Army decided, in September 1975, that the coming repression was to be predominantly clandestine. Furthermore, it was to be used not only to neutralize but to physically exterminate all militant opposition, regardless of whether suspected opponents were involved in armed struggle.[7] This decision was reached in order to foreclose the possibility that subsequent civilian governments might later release opponents to the regime who could then return to generate a counteroffensive, as had been the case in the 1973 democratic opening. The clandestine nature of repression had various objectives.

Among these, the government hoped to delay protests and international pressures of the kind that confronted the Chilean dictatorship, to prevent possible checks and controls of military power, and to paralyze popular reactions through terror. But it also entailed some risk. As the military commanders knew—French and American military specialists had so warned them in 1975—the strategy's concealed character meant that some sectors of the Argentine military would probably gain organizational autonomy, and might use their autonomy to obtain personal economic benefits. Given the type and structure of repression, the military foresaw even before the coup occurred that the expected internal consequences of their choices would be corruption and breaches in the chain of command. Yet, despite the fact that their chosen strategy set the structural bases for the erosion of military institutions, they followed the course of action because of the high political benefits and military efficiency it offered in the short term.

At the earliest stage, the sheer magnitude of the repression and the lack of action on the part of political parties, trade unions, the church, and the press left citizens helpless. A few months after the coup, some groups and organizations[8]—most of them born as a consequence of the retreat of other institutions arose to denounce the government's policies. At first, the government was able to neutralize the public visibility of these accusations at the national level. Nevertheless, and particularly in the international arena, it became increasingly more difficult to offset the effectiveness of these charges. Towards the end of 1976, an Amnesty International mission visited the country, and when the Carter administration took office, U.S. military help to Argentina was reduced.

The Military's Political Plans
and Their Impact on the Democratic Opening

The second stage of the Argentine military regime began in 1978, when the junta determined that it had achieved a military victory against all the revolutionary organizations. Between 1978 and 1982, the military rulers concentrated their efforts on designing and then constructing a political order that would allow them to hand over political power to a future civilian government without impairing their tutorial rule over society. In the process of pursuing this strategy, several competing political projects emerged within the military leadership. However, they all had one factor in common—they required full civilian approval of the military's repressive methods and an understanding that "the past" would not be open to scrutiny.

The first attempt to whitewash the government's repressive methods involved an international organization, the Inter-American Commission of Human Rights (Comisión Interamericana de Derechos Humanos, or CIDH). From the government's perspective, and based on the assumption that its close relationship with the presidency of the Organization of American States (OAS) would influence the CIDH, a visit from the commission was to serve as proof that repression was part of a necessary though restricted "war" to defend Argentina, a war which had now come to a close. Nonetheless, these intentions backfired. For not only did the legal members of the commission show significant autonomy vis-à-vis the OAS, but the report that followed their visit to Argentina, first scheduled for December 1978 but finally concluded in September 1979, turned out to be much more critical than the armed forces expected, thus preventing them from achieving closure on the issue. For like reasons, the junta also initiated a so-called "Political Dialogue" in 1979 that was designed to secure the support of the more conservative elements in the Argentine party structure. According to the armed forces, their "victory in war" had granted them the right to claim a major and permanent institutional role in politics. In particular, they envisioned fulfilling a tutorial function in the future democratic regime, in which a congenial political force would guarantee the continuity of their policies and their continued presence in government.[9]

Between 1980 and 1982, the military government confronted increasing political and economic difficulties, which limited its capacity to impose conditions on other political and social actors. When the Nobel Peace Prize was awarded to Adolfo Pérez Esquivel in 1980, the growing demands and activities of the human rights movement in Argentina were given greater national legitimacy, forcing a spectrum of politicians and other influential individuals to make public statements about an issue that many would have preferred to avoid. In 1981, the presidential succession, in which General Viola replaced

General Videla, resulted after a short time in a palace coup, which led in turn to the presidency of General Galtieri. While indicating the incapacity of the armed forces to guard the political stability that they pretended to guarantee, the coup also revealed the depth of intramilitary tensions. Argentina's economic conditions were no better. The size of the country's external debt, the decrease in the investment rate, the recession, growing inflation rates, and the growth of the opposition's capacity to mobilize its forces, were all evidence of a crisis that was going to have significant long-term consequences.

Given this increase in political and social tension, the "solution" the military leadership found to freeze the growing opposition was the invasion of the Malvinas (Falklands) Islands on April 2, 1982. The islands represented a long-standing Argentine claim to sovereignty around which there was a significant societal consensus, both between military and civilian officials and left- and right-wing forces. Military planners initially foresaw a bloodless action that was to include the occupation and immediate evacuation of the islands. This strategy sought to avoid a British reaction, compelling the British to initiate negotiations. As is well known, however, once the military operation began, a succession of events encouraged the junta to persist in a confrontation for which it had elaborated no contingency defensive plans. The British decision to use force to defend the islands ended up in a disastrous Argentine military defeat.

After the military defeat on June 14, 1982, the government's situation changed. It lost authority vis-à-vis society, and intra-military conflicts sharpened. Between June and September 1982, the military pact that had existed among the branches of the armed forces broke down. Such divisions reduced the capacity to negotiate with civilian forces. The military could not agree about what should be discussed and negotiated, with whom, and through what means. Consequently, after the Malvinas war, the military government was compelled to redefine its political goals. It abandoned the strategy oriented toward establishing its own right-wing party, which it had hoped would become the first electoral minority, and attempted instead to negotiate a way out of the crisis with the Peronist and Radical opposition.

In November 1982, the military government presented the

political parties with a list of fifteen issues that they were required "to agree on" in order to "conclude the institutionalization of the country." When it was unable to obtain a consensus on these issues, the government unilaterally imposed the contents of those on which it was unwilling to compromise. In May 1983, the military made two announcements. First, it established its position with respect to human rights violations in the *Documento Final* (Final Document), and second, it decreed in an *Acta Institucional* (Institutional Act) that all military operations undertaken by the armed forces should be considered acts of service and thus were not subject to punishment.[10] Then, two weeks before presidential elections were to be held on October 30, 1983, it sanctioned the *Ley de Pacificación Nacional* (Law of National Pacification, popularly known as Law of Self-Amnesty), granting immunity to suspects of acts of state terrorism and to all members of the armed and police forces for crimes committed in the context of the repressions between May 25, 1973 and June 17, 1982.[11] Finally, in its last days of government, the military passed a decree ordering the destruction of documents referring to military repression.[12] In this fashion, the strategy of retreat implemented by the armed forces confirmed the importance of the human rights question for the military and also made the issue a key part of the agenda of transition.

The acceleration that characterized the post-Malvinas political scene, as well as the military government's manifest decomposition, had a paradoxical consequence. It forced Argentina's political parties "to support the regime they had confronted before, in order to give themselves enough time to prepare their orderly accession to office."[13] Thus, there was no explosion or radicalization of social demands during the process of liberalization. The historically majoritarian working-class-based Peronist party, for example, had been ousted from power by the military in 1976 and, given its popular roots, had also been a main target of state terrorism. Yet its candidate for the presidency, Italo Luder, appeared to take for granted his electoral victory, due to the popular character of his party's supporters and its historical electoral record. Hence, he considered that it was not necessary to make the effort to attract those discontented voters who rallied around the demands of human rights organizations. In his view, it was more convenient to minimize future confrontations with the armed forces.

But in contrast, the middle-class-based Radical Party's candidate, Raúl Alfonsín, chose to place a greater emphasis on the human rights question. This may have been because he had no certainty of electoral victory and thus needed to attract the voters that the Peronist candidate had decided to underestimate. Or perhaps he did not need to ensure *ex ante* a peaceful relationship with the armed forces, since the Radical party, unlike the Peronist party, was not perceived as a threat to the military. Whatever the reasons, Alfonsín's decision to set himself apart from the other presidential candidates paid off. In October 1983, to the surprise of many and with the support not only of the middle classes but also of some of the traditionally Peronist popular voters, he won the presidential elections.

Judicial Autonomy and the Trial
of the Members of the Military Juntas

To meet the demand for justice that had set the tone for its electoral campaign, the Radical government designed a strategy that was designed to hold those members of the armed forces who had committed major violations of human rights responsible for their crimes, while seeking simultaneously to incorporate the armed forces as a whole into the democratic arena. The military was to be allowed to sit in judgment upon itself with the expectation that its "self-purification" (*autodepuración*) would at least allow the Radical government to apply judicial sanctions to some of those responsible for violations of human rights. In the process, the government would be able to fulfill its electoral promises without, however, creating a generalized threat to the armed forces. To ensure this understanding, the government and the military carried out a secret exchange which led to the following agreement: the military would hand in a list of about thirty names of officers they were willing to judge and convict, in return for which the government agreed to the suppression of a campaign that the armed forces perceived to be bent upon their destruction. Another important feature of the exchange was the presidency's determination to pardon those convicted for human rights violations before the end of its first term in office, namely 1989.[14] In these respects, the equilibrium that Alfonsín sought to attain was based upon a limited number of prosecutions that would satisfy his campaign promises, relatively low-cost sentences for those who were convicted (whatever their sentences, the military officials were to remain in jail for no more than six years), and finally, a neutralization of the threat represented to the rest of the armed forces.

However, these negotiations immediately fell short for both parties. For its part, the military provided only nine names, those of the former members of the military juntas that ruled the country since 1976. On the other hand, while the government delivered on its commitment and desire to close the judicial chapter as soon as possible, both its leaders and the military were surprised to find that even in a presidential democracy, the executive faced constraints and checks and balances that were bound to frustrate Alfonsín's hoped-for equilibrium.

Initially, the government's plan included the immediate detention of the former members of the military juntas as well as of some military and police authorities that had become public symbols of human rights abuses, the repeal of the Law of National Pacification (or Law of Self-Amnesty), and the enactment of a new law that was to reduce dramatically the scope of penal liability for human rights abuses and the jurisdiction in which the trials were to be held. Aside from these measures, the government also sponsored the formation of the National Commission on the Disappearance of Persons (CONADEP), whose central purpose was to receive denunciations and proofs of disappearances, send them to the justice system, check on the whereabouts of such persons, and finally, to determine the location of lost children of the disappeared. But the constitution of CONADEP also allowed the government to block the formation of a bicameral investigative commission, which was being sought by most of the human rights organizations. From the government's point of view, such a commission would have granted Congress both a larger say in the formation of a human rights policy and the power to investigate those presumed responsible, thereby endangering its understanding with the armed forces about the limits to be imposed on the trials of former military officers. If indeed these reasons explain why the presidency decided on the formation of CONADEP, it should be emphasized that the effects of the commission's work, in terms of the public dissemination of information about past human rights abuses, were quite different from those the government had foreseen at the time of its creation.

On December 13, 1983, the administration's strategy seemed off to a good start when Congress repealed the Law of Self-Amnesty. However, the government encountered its first problems when it sought to sanction the related Reform of the Military Justice Code (Law 23,049). This law was ultimately passed on February 9, 1984 and conferred upon the Supreme Council of the Armed Forces the initial jurisdiction to prosecute military personnel, something the government had wanted all along. However, the parliamentary opposition managed to include a mechanism within the new law that provided for the mandatory appeal of such cases to federal appeals courts in trials that were unresolved after 180 days. In addition, the opposition forces also devised a legal formula that precluded the indiscriminate use of the concept of "due obedience" in cases of particularly infamous or aberrant crimes (*delitos atroces y aberrantes*). This last modification prevented the government from limiting *ab initio* the scope of the trials. Finally, when it became evident that the Supreme Council of the Armed Forces was not going to carry out the self-purification of the military, the Federal Appeals Court of Buenos Aires took the case of the members of the military juntas into its own hands. Civilian proceedings against the members of the military juntas began on April 22, 1985, and once the witnesses for the prosecution were being heard, the Argentine media were flooded with the horrors of state terrorism.[15] From this moment onward, and for several months to come, a juridical logic achieved primacy over the political logic that had previously governed the debate over Argentina's past.

When the trial was concluded on December 9, 1985, former military president Jorge Rafael Videla and the former commander-in-chief of the Navy, Admiral Emilio Massera, were given life sentences, former president Eduardo Viola was given seventeen years in prison, and the junta members for the Navy and Air Force, Admiral

Lambruschini and Brigadier Agosti, were given eight years, and three years and nine months, respectively.[16] The use of judicial means to obtain these convictions, all of which were openly presented and publicized, gave credibility to the narratives of past abuse and established the witnesses' accounts as beyond suspicion. In this sense, the trial turned into an effective mechanism for passing historical and political judgment on the Argentine dictatorship. Furthermore, and contrary to what was expected by the government, instead of closing the human rights question, the trial ended up reopening the issue. The court recommended that all additional leads and information gathered about officers and NCOs accused of any involvement in human rights violations should subsequently be followed up. Naturally, these developments were a blow to the government's credibility among the military. The Army's Chief of Staff had expected that the few sentences imposed would foreclose any future prosecutions by making the principle of due obedience applicable to all those members of the armed forces and police who had acted under the authority of the juntas.

The Presidency's Attempt to Curtail Judicial Autonomy

When the trial of the juntas' leaders came to a close, in a context characterized by increasing discontent and pressure from the armed forces, the Alfonsín government quickly took measures to restrict the scope of the verdict and ensure the military's acquiescence. Of particular note, both because of the administration's aims and, as would later become apparent, its limited successes, were the following steps: the *Instrucciones a los Fiscales Militares* (Instructions to Military Prosecutors), the *Ley de Punto Final* (Law of Full Stop), and the *Ley de Obediencia Debida* (Law of Due Obedience).

First, in 1986, only a few months after the end of the trial, the Ministry of Defense issued instructions to military prosecutors that were designed to radically reduce the number of prosecutions that took place. Among those to be exempted from accountability under the new guidelines were all those accused of torture, kidnapping, or murder in cases in which they could prove (or the context would lead one to assume) that they had acted according to orders. Nevertheless, this initiative immediately gave rise to a wave of opposition across the political spectrum, among the ranks of the Peronist Party, sectors of the governing Radical Party, human rights organizations, and the Federal Court of the Federal Capital.

In a second such measure, the *Ley de Punto Final*, also promulgated in 1986, the government sought to approach the issue from another angle. Instead of considering whether those who violated human rights were liable for their actions, it established a February 1987 deadline for summoning all presumed violators of human rights. Because January is traditionally a holiday month in Argentina, when most judicial activities are suspended, the government assumed the courts would not be able to find the time needed to investigate the cases. Nevertheless, when the law was approved by a slim parliamentary majority, seven federal courts suspended their January holidays in order to work on the pending cases. As a result, by February 1987, when the law's statute of limitations came into effect, more than three hundred high-ranking officers had been indicted. Thus, even though the president had passed the *Ley de Punto Final*, the practical consequences of the law and an increasingly independent judiciary meant that this second attempt to head off prosecutions was really a failure.

The government's final measure, the *Ley de Obediencia Debida*, was approved shortly after a military uprising of April 1987 (the so-called Easter Rebellion). The uprising was headed by the *carapintadas*, or "painted faces," so named because of the dark camouflage used on their faces, who insisted that even the government's limited involvement in human rights prosecutions was evidence of a shrewd strategy to destroy the armed forces. During the uprising, two major facts came to light. First, the uprising showed the strength of the military's demands and the inability of both civilian authorities and the Army Chief of Staff to impose their command. Second, and in marked contrast to this position, the wide and generalized mobilization of civil society that took place in response to the uprisings showed that there was an equally strong level of societal repudiation for the idea that the military should have an impact upon politics or, worse still, threaten to impose its own government.

When the uprising was finally put down, the president appeared personally to have gained by imposing society's democratic will upon the rebellious. However, shortly after the crisis ended, Alfonsín submitted a proposal to Congress for a due obedience law, which demonstrated that, one way or another, a new exchange was in the works between the presidency and the military. The approved *Ley de Obediencia Debida* established that those individuals who at the time of the events were chief, junior, or non-commissioned officers, soldiers of the armed forces, members of security forces, or police and penitentiary personnel were not punishable for crimes that violated human rights, provided that they had acted within the scope of due obedience to the authorities above them. At first glance, one might have thought the government had finally achieved the objective it had sought since 1983. But Alfonsín's victory came at the wrong time, for the new law's political meaning entailed different costs and benefits than the ones the government had intended to achieve at the outset of the process. For most of the population, the law was clear evidence of the fact that the administration had given up one of the key banners that had allowed it to become the principal guarantor of democracy and of the rule of law in 1983. It also suggested that the president's word was untrustworthy. Moreover, the law's approval left unresolved a continuing dispute with the armed forces—the political vindication of the military repression from 1976 to 1982.

Since the Easter Rebellion of April 1987, a new front of conflict had opened in the relationship between the government and the armed forces, allowing the dispute over human rights to overlap the conflict over what should be done with those who had participated in the military rebellion. The preeminence of this new dispute, which was in reality a struggle over the capacity of the emerging rebel sectors to influence the army's decisions, modified the relative weight of the issues being debated. As a result, the question of how to penalize those responsible for past human rights violations was overshadowed by the more pressing debate over how to reinstall the army's chain of command. Thus, even though the government was committed to finding a way of resolving the human rights issue, neither it nor important sectors of the Army High Command were willing to do anything that might have helped to give the *carapintadas* added credibility within the military.

The future of the armed forces came to a head with the further insurrections of "Monte Caseros" and "Villa Martelli," both in 1988, and a final uprising in December 1990, as a result of the *carapintadas'* refusal to accede to the penalties the military leadership established for them. However, following passage of the law of due obedience, it was revealing that the rebel forces encountered growing difficulty in finding followers for their cause among the officer ranks. With the recurrence of incidents in which the military's chain of command was being broken to advance interests that were no longer perceived as related to the needs of the "whole" armed forces, the sympathy that the *carapintadas* originally enjoyed among the officer corps and NCOs had simply eroded.

Menem: A New President Following an Old Strategy

The handling of past human rights violations and the growing tensions with the military were not the only problems the Alfonsín administration had to face. Argentina's economic challenges proved much more complex than expected, and after the government's third economic plan failed, the Argentine economy actually collapsed in 1989. This crisis forced Alfonsín to turn over the government to Carlos S. Menem, the country's newly elected president, several months ahead of schedule. Notably, the speed and the uncontrolled nature of these events prevented the outgoing president from fulfilling his commitment to pardon those who had been convicted for human rights violations.

The 1989 presidential elections created new expectations among the *carapintadas*. They trusted that an electoral victory of the Peronist candidate would bring about the dismissal of the sanctions imposed by the Army General Staff, as well as a governmental position for their imprisoned leader, Colonel Mohammed Seineldín. On October 8, 1989, Menem, who had been in power since July, announced the first presidential pardon. Among the pardon's 277 beneficiaries were military personnel who had been involved in numerous human rights abuses under the dictatorship, others who had been convicted for their roles in the Malvinas war, others convicted for their participation in the military uprisings during the Radical gov-

ernment, and also civilians previously sentenced for guerrilla activities. Yet notably, the former commanders in chief and former junta
members Videla, Viola, Massera, and Lambruschini were not included in this pardon; neither were Generals Camps, Richieri, and
Suárez Mason, or the former head of the guerrilla organization *Mon-
toneros*, Mario Firmenich, although a future pardon was announced.

What were the consequences of this pardon for the intra-military
conflict? A first reading might lead one to believe the *carapintada*
leaders had obtained the results they were after, that is, the imposition of an amnesty for human rights violations during the dictatorship and the advance of their own political cause within the military.
Nevertheless, some days later, it became evident that the pardon
would not reverse the sentences imposed upon them by the Army
General Staff. Although the pardon allowed them to avoid being convicted by civilian courts, it did not grant the *carapintadas* impunity
within the military. Hence, from this point onward, they could no
longer seek to legitimate their behavior in terms of institutional demands. Furthermore, their growing politicization also led to their increasing isolation among their military comrades.

Due to their disenchantment with Menem, to the fact that some of
their own members were shifting towards greater participation in institutional politics, and to their dwindling military influence and de-
creasing control over active army units, the *carapintadas* made one
last effort to gain control of the Army General Staff. Their final uprising, on December 3, 1990, was the bloodiest and most violent of all.
But this time, the government reacted with a forceful suppression of
the rebels. When the fighting had ended, the *carapintadas* had been
both defeated on the military field and neutralized in the political
arena.

What circumstances had changed to produce such a broad and
clear defeat? In the first place, with the government's pardon and
the imminence of a second one, as well as with the growing politicization of the *carapintada* movement, support for the rebel forces
among army officers could only be sustained on the basis of political
loyalty. But the officers in charge of the army now understood that
the repeated challenges to the chain of command and the fact that
carapintada support came primarily from low-ranking and non-

commissioned officers implied a major risk for the survival of the military as an institution.

A few days after the defeat of the December rebellion, a second presidential pardon was made public. This time, the pardon included the first two military juntas as well as Generals Camps, Suárez Mason, and Richieri, along with the former guerrilla leader, Mario Firmenich, and a few other civilians. What reasons did the presidency have to issue a second pardon in the wake of the December 1990 uprising? The pardon reaffirmed the Menemist strategy of forgiving past crimes while punishing present and future acts of disobedience. At the same time, the administration strengthened the Army General Staff by preventing the *carapintada* minority from once again becoming the spokespersons for the demands of the military corporation as a whole.

Feasibility, Risks, Costs, and Benefits of Sanctioning Human Rights Abuses

What conclusions can be drawn from the Argentine case? Were the trials of those military leaders responsible for the systematic violation of human rights a gesture too ethical for the risky conditions of a democratic transition? Will the armed forces' current subordination change as soon as the victorious military sector recovers from its convulsions and is able to make effective use of its recently regained cohesion?

In the first place, it is important to recognize that the criminal prosecution that took place during the Argentine transition contradicted the strategy set forth by the presidency. This is so because, in the process, the government's two central goals were frustrated, namely, to limit from the outset the number of military to be prosecuted and to allow them to sit in self-judgment. Alfonsín sought to foster an equilibrium that would have allowed him simultaneously to punish some of those responsible for human rights violations while obtaining military obedience to the new democratic order. To this end, and in order to facilitate the goal of a limited judgment and the military's self-purification, he developed a strategy aimed at reducing the space in which Argentina's legislative and judicial powers and the human rights movement could act. Yet through congressional action, the opposition parties and the human rights forces frustrated the president's attempt to limit the scope of the trials. Not only did the presidency fail to achieve the passage of the legal clauses aimed at limiting judicial action, it also encountered the military's resistance to judge itself and cleanse its institutions of those members most clearly identified with past repression.

Therefore, the scope and significance of the trial of the former commanders in chief (including the four military presidents of the dictatorship) in a civilian court was radically different from the proceedings originally foreseen by the government. Not only did the armed forces resist self-purification, but the evidence gathered during the pre-trial investigations resulted in the indictment of hundreds of officers from the three forces. Thus, the trial that was supposed to "close" the chapter on state terrorism by declaring guilty a few of those responsible and clearing the image of the armed forces before public opinion instead "opened" an uncertain new juncture in the Argentine political struggle. At this juncture, not only did new and important actors (e.g., the judges and prosecuting attorneys of several federal courts) assume surprising autonomy in regard to the presidency, but all the contending forces in Argentine society encountered a new structure of options[17] and of costs and benefits,[18] as well as new rules for the resolution of conflicts. These new rules, in turn, redefined the efficiency of the resources upon which each actor could rely.[19]

The presidency's successive attempts at reestablishing its control over the judicial process (i.e., the Instructions to Military Prosecutors, the Law of Full Stop) forced the government to modify the ideological foundations of its policies. If in the first stage, the government appealed to ethical reasons and principles as a way of justifying its strategy, in the second stage, *raison d'état* became its foundation. Its new failure, brought about by the reactions of the political parties (including the incumbent Radical party), of the human rights organizations, and of the judiciary, created conditions for the emergence of the *carapintada* actor and for a series of new "strategic conjunctures" which, as we have seen, finally developed into an intra-military conflict. Thus, Alfonsín's government was never able to achieve an equilibrium between the social demand for justice and the military's wish to vindicate the "dirty war."

The evolution of the Argentine transition also shows that the success of the country's human rights organizations and of the political opposition was only partial; that the judiciary saw its primary goals frustrated when the due obedience law was passed; and that, for their part, the armed forces could not obtain their main goals since they proved unable to prevent either the trials or societal condemnation of their past activities. In contrast, at least at the time of this writing, Menem's government seems to have had a greater degree of success in meeting its goals. Arriving late on the scene, and thus with relatively little political erosion, Menem proposed a tacit deal to the parties involved: he would pardon all those accused and convicted for human rights violations or military uprisings, in exchange for which the military would consent to obey the civilian government. Without Alfonsín's electoral obligations, Menem tried to solve the "military problem" by strengthening the Army General Staff while at the same time negotiating with the *carapintadas*. The success of this strategy was only partial. For example, it did not prevent the rebels from resorting to armed confrontation in December 1990. Yet the government managed to suppress the insurgents by using forces loyal to the Army General Staff, and it was also able to reinstall the chain of command. The harshness of the punishment imposed on the officers that participated in this last uprising set the rules that would define Menem's relationship with the military—all crimes committed in the past would be pardoned, but present or future disobedience is to be punished severely.

The Military's Future as a Political Actor in Argentina

What were the effects of this process upon the Argentine armed forces as a political actor? What now prevents the victorious military sector from using the high degree of cohesion that it has achieved to threaten future democratic governments with traditional military pressures? The present position of the armed forces in Argentina is more than simply a product of contingent factors. On the one hand, the armed forces have been forced to confront one of the worst possible scenarios for any military institution—the trial and conviction of their leaders for responsibility in the repressive acts of a former dictatorship. As we have also seen, the political costs for the army increased as a consequence of the conflict between its General Staff and the *carapintadas*. Even though the General Staff succeeded in gaining the benefit of a presidential pardon and was ultimately victorious in its struggle with the *carapintadas*, it was not able to neutralize the profound shift in its relative position before civil society. Nor has it since been able to eliminate the costs and risks resulting from the politicization of military institutions.

On the other hand, it is now recognized that the juntas that ruled Argentina between 1976 and 1983 led to a significant degree of erosion in the military's public image and political legitimacy. In the first place, the armed forces' systematic violations of basic human rights generated strong resentment among the majority of the population against the military. In this sense, the subsequent trial of the military leadership only accentuated a tendency already in place in Argentine society. In the second place, the deep socioeconomic crisis that resulted from the military's economic policies compounded the resentment and caused important segments of the bourgeoisie that had traditionally constituted the core of political and economic support for military governments to distance themselves from the armed forces. As a result, the military ceased being a predictable institution and became a source of new uncertainty in relation to the interests of capitalists.[20] Another example of the risks that the military's behavior entailed for the bourgeoisie and for traditional international allies, such as the United States, was the ill-fated Malvinas adventure. This defeat also generated two deep intra-military cleavages: the breakdown of the relationships among the different forces, on the one hand, and a horizontal tension between the generals, who had exercised politico-military responsibility, and junior officers and non-commissioned officers who were in charge of operational functions.

The internal confrontation that exploded during Easter Week of 1987 unveiled a new scenario for conflicts within the military. In contrast to the confrontations that had taken place in the past, in which the armed forces were divided along vertical lines, this time the conflict emerged as a struggle of low-ranking officers supported by NCOs against "the generals." If the *carapintadas* were not isolated and defeated, this "class struggle" could only end with the destruction of the institution as such, since a victory by the *carapintadas* would have implied the discharge of most high-ranking personnel, while a victory of "the generals" would have meant the dismissal of lower-ranking officers.

Even though the most serious aspects of these internal tensions were resolved and the *carapintadas* defeated, it is clear that the role played by the armed forces during their control of the Argentine government was responsible for their high degree of social and political isolation and the acute internal crisis that took place between 1987 and 1990. Consequently, those who defeated the *carapintadas* have been left with a clear choice about their options. If their priority is the survival of the military as an institution, the armed forces cannot run the risks involved in political intervention. In this way, as a combined result of the crisis that the armed forces themselves helped to promote, thanks to their role in the dictatorship, and of the political and judicial consequences of the struggle for human rights, the military has lost the incentive to challenge future constitutional governments.

The current situation of the armed forces has also been affected both by a transformation in the international scene and by the fiscal crisis of the Argentine state. For one thing, the end of the cold war has resulted in the disappearance of the communist threat, eroding one of the traditional arguments used to justify preventive military intervention in politics. Additionally, the country's economic integration with Brazil and its frontier agreements with Chile have resulted in the transformation of old hypotheses about the sources of social and political conflict and the conversion of potential enemies into allies or at least commercial partners. Argentina's political and economic realignment with the United States as well has led to the dismantling of important military projects, such as the CONDOR missile and the construction of nuclear devices, the latter as a consequence of the signing of the Tlatelolco Treaty. These factors have promoted both the search for new military duties (such as participation in UN peace missions) and a significant redefinition of the military's role in domestic politics.

The changes in Argentina's national and international context have been reinforced by a series of legal modifications providing for a new political and institutional position for the armed forces. Since 1983, the presidency's formal leadership role as commander in chief has been strengthened through the elimination of some of the prerogatives that historically endowed the military with large shares of power and autonomy. Also, the approval of the *Ley de Defensa* (Law of Defense) in 1988 restricted the duties of the armed forces exclusively to defense measures to ward off external aggression.[21] Finally, the fiscal crisis of the state and economic restructuring have resulted in a significant decrease in the military's participation in economic activities. During Menem's first administration many army quarters have been dismantled, nearly all military enterprises have been privatized, personnel have been substantially reduced, the draft has ended, and military budgets have been cut dramatically. All these events have meant a radical transformation in the power of the armed forces as a political actor.[22]

Justice, the Judiciary, and Democracy in Argentina and Elsewhere

Were the Argentine trials a gesture too "ethical" for the difficult and risky features that characterize a process of democratic transition? Did they undermine the consolidation of the democratic process instead of favoring it? To evaluate the effects of the judicial treatment of human rights violations on the democratic process, it is necessary to consider whether, in spite of the covert amnesty of the due obedience law passed during the Alfonsín government and the presidential pardons of the Menem administration, the existence of legal sanctions in Argentina was sufficiently strong to redefine for the military the costs of deserting the democratic game. We believe that the best way to determine whether a pardon has neutralized the deterrent effects of punishment or weakened a society's confidence in the ethical foundations of its government is to look at the conditions under which it was granted, as well as its political meaning at the time.

If a pardon is perceived as a voluntary governmental act, independent of military pressure, its granting may result in the incorporation into the democratic regime of those sectors, such as the military, that have hitherto felt threatened by the new order. Beyond the ethical and political problems involved in pardoning anyone guilty of human rights violations, we acknowledge the possibility that pardons may serve a useful function at some stage in the transition to democracy. In the first stage, the appeal to judicial means allows for a redefinition of the costs to be incurred in case the military should return to authoritarian practices. But at a later stage, a pardon may neutralize the risks involved in the prolonged political isolation of the armed forces. However, in order for this second effect to take place, it is necessary to judge and punish in the first stage. The integrating effect of a pardon is only possible if there have been judgment and punishment in the first place, for, as Hannah Arendt has pointed out, "men are unable to forgive what they cannot punish."[23] Consequently, and in spite of the concessions granted by the Alfonsín government and the pardon granted by Carlos Menem, one of the central reasons for the long-term subordination of the military to constitutional power in Argentina has been the high risks and costs that the judicial investigation and conviction for human rights violations initially signified for the armed forces.

Finally, what does the Argentine case tell us about the role of the judiciary and its relationship to the dilemmas faced by newly emerged democracies? When democratic politicians face the challenge of having to deal with human rights violators that still legally bear arms, they tend to perceive in the autonomy of the judiciary a source of potential danger. No doubt, courts that serve the law before the political needs of the executive can become sources of tension in processes characterized by unstable equilibria. In this sense, politicians are right to be attentive to the risks entailed by autonomous judiciaries. Yet, while there is nothing wrong with being careful about these risks, the politicians' error is to assume that the problem lies with the judiciary per se when, in fact, the challenge is one of getting used to democracy as a regime of governance and conflict resolution. As Adam Przeworski has pointed out, the stability of rules inherent to the democratic struggle creates uncertainty about outcomes.[24] To prioritize the achievement of any outcome over the stability of these rules and over the freedom of action of the judiciary would be to act against the democratic nature of the regime. Hence, if democracy is a regime where all citizens are equal before the law, as a general rule all those responsible for human rights violations should be taken to trial and punished, and all those democratically committed to the collective welfare of the society should be willing to face the risks entailed by the rule of law. It is difficult to imagine a process of democratic consolidation in which politicians and citizens are not willing to face the risk of an autonomous judiciary. Where does the Argentine process stand in this respect?

Clearly, Argentina has ended up in a middle-of-the-road situation. Without a doubt, the trial, conviction, and seven years imprisonment of former military presidents and commanders in chief constitute an exceptional and key element in the country's process of democratic consolidation. Without an autonomous judiciary willing to defy the political strategies of the presidency, as well as without political parties and human rights organizations willing to face the risk of the rule of law, military subordination to constitutional rule would probably not have come about. But on the other hand, Argentina's presidential pardons have also obstructed the cause of imposing punishment for past abuses. Similarly, the due obedience law constitutes a de facto amnesty that violates the right to justice of the victims and their relatives. In short, the Argentine dilemma is not only about past human rights violations but also about present ones. In a nutshell, the story is not merely about how a democracy deals with the past but about the extent to which it is able to defend and realize the rights of its citizens in the present. The dilemma is about the kind of democracy currently being built.

Up to now, the democratic record in much of the world has been either weak or simply bad when it comes to judging the crimes of the guardians. All too often, political scientists and politicians have argued that in order to guard the guardians, we need to avoid the risks that are associated with judging their crimes. But in spite of the shortcomings we have observed in this essay, exceptions like Argentina should be considered a challenge to false dualisms between political efficiency and ethics. They can be celebrated as a victory by all those committed to the defense of human rights and the deepening of democracy.

NOTES

Research for this chapter was conducted within the framework of the project "Human Rights and the Consolidation of Democracy: The Trial of the Argentine Military," carried out by Centro de Estudios de Estado y Sociedad (CEDES) with the support of the John D. and Catherine T. MacArthur Foundation and the Ford Foundation. Some of the arguments in this essay have been previously developed in "Adjusting the Armed Forces to Democracy: Successes, Failures, and Ambiguities in the Southern Cone," in E. Jelin and E. Herschberg, eds., Constructing Democracy: Human Rights, Citizenship, and Society in Latin America *(Boulder, Colo.: Westview,* 1996).

1. A "juridical logic" can be distinguished from a "political logic," among other reasons, by the way it treats the issue of proof, by the way it reduces the margins of negotiation in its resolutions, and by the way it arrives at sentences and punishes criminal actions according to preestablished rules. In each case, actors must adjust to an environment in which the victims become "witnesses" and the perpetrators become the "accused." In this context, parties with strictly political interests are reduced to the role of "observers" of judges, who are presented as "neutral" because they resolve the confrontation between victims and accused through preestablished rules, based on the preferences of congressional majorities and juridical principles.

2. Martin Balza, on the television show "Tiempo Nuevo," TELEFE, Argentina, April 25, 1995, as translated by the BBC in its summary of World Broadcasts, April 28, 1995.

3. Although the approval of a new rule does not necessarily imply the resolution of a conflict, its enforcement can induce new behavior, insofar as it implies a new manner of organizing that resolution.

4. When we consider just the last five decades of world history, numerous examples come immediately to mind: the Western allies' decision not to punish most of the Nazis responsible for human rights violations during World War II, which was justified by the need to maintain a functioning state bureaucracy in West Germany; the U.S. government's decision not to punish members of the Japanese royal family for their role in the genocide of Chinese civilians, in order to take advantage of the symbolic force of the emperor and his family as a legitimating resource for the new democratic order; and the all-too-common support by Western democracies of authoritarian regimes guilty of systematic human rights violations, in the name of preventing the advance of "anti-western" movements.

5. Andrés Fontana, "Political Decision Making by a Military Corpo-

ration: Argentina 1976–1983" (Ph.D. diss., University of Texas at Austin, 1987).

6. For CONADEP's findings, see *Nunca Más: The Report of the Argentine National Commission on the Disappeared*, with an introduction by Ronald Dworkin (New York: Farrar, Straus, and Giroux, 1986). The commission's original Spanish-language report appeared in 1985. For other findings, also see Amnesty International, *Argentina: The Military Juntas and Human Rights* (London: Amnesty International Publications, 1987), and Organization of Inter-American States, Inter-American Commission on Human Rights, *Report on the Situation of Human Rights in Argentina* (Washington, D.C.: General Secretariat, Organization of American States, 1980).

7. See Ramón Camps, "Apogeo y declinación de la guerrilla en la Argentina," *La Prensa*, January 4, 1981; Emilio Mignone, "Derechos humanos y transición democrática en la sociedad Argentina," paper presented at the Schell Center, Yale University, 1990; Daniel Frontalini and María Cristina Caiati, *El mito de la guerra sucia* (Buenos Aires: CELS, 1984), pp. 32–33; Iain Guest, *Behind the Disappearances: Argentina's Dirty War Against Human Rights and the United Nations* (Philadelphia: University of Pennsylvania Press, 1990), pp. 21–22; and Claudio Uriarte, *Almirante cero: Biografía no autorizada de Emilio Eduardo Massera* (Buenos Aires: Planeta, 1992), p. 97.

8. Among the human rights organizations, one should mention: Madres de Plaza de Mayo, Familiares de Detenidos y Desaparecidos por Razones Políticas, Abuelas de Plaza de Mayo, Servicio de Paz y Justicia, Movimiento Ecuménico de Derechos Humanos, Asamblea Permanente por los Derechos Humanos, Centro de Estudios Legales y Sociales, Liga Argentina por los Derechos del Hombre.

9. The congenial political force was supposed to come to power through electoral means by aggregating into one national political party the disparate conservative votes and by dividing both Peronism and Radicalism. For a detailed account of this strategy, see Carlos H. Acuña, "El diálogo del gobierno," *Revista del Centro de Investigación y Acción Social* (August–September 1980), pp. 295–296; and Inés González Bombal, "El diálogo político: La transición que no fue," *Documento CEDES*, Buenos Aires, 1991.

10. See Americas Watch, *Truth and Partial Justice in Argentina: An Update* (New York: Human Rights Watch, 1991), p. 10.

11. See *La Nación*, September 24, 1983.

12. Between 1976 and 1983, the military government sanctioned more than twenty secret laws and at least two secret decrees, of which at least some must have related to its strategy of repression. On this, see Maria Laura San Martino de Dromi, *Historia política Argentina: 1955–1988* (Buenos Aires: Astrea, 1988), especially pp. 208–224. Later, the trial proceedings against the juntas demonstrated the existence of lists and other documents certifying the existence of disappeared persons and the institutional responsibility of members of the armed forces. See Sergio Ciancaglini and Martin Granovsky, *Nada más que la verdad: El juicio a las juntas* (Buenos Aires: Planeta, 1995).

13. Inés González, "1983: El entusiasmo democrático," Buenos Aires, CEDES, mimeo, 1992.

14. A former Chief of Staff during the Alfonsín administration, General Ríos Ereñú, stated in an interview, "President Alfonsín had promised that before leaving office those that had been condemned would be pardoned. . . . This means that I, the Chief of Staff, knew that the maximum that they would have to endure was six years. That during those six years, if things worked out fine, only the military Junta and some Commanders of Army Corps would be sanctioned and that the majority would have no problems" (Deborah Norden, "Between Coups and Consolidation: Military Rebellion in Post-Authoritarian Argentina" [Ph.D. diss., University of California, Berkeley, 1992], p. 256). Joaquín Morales Solá confirms this version when he states that "Ríos Ereñú became enthusiastic with a promise made to him by Borrás [Minister of Defense at the time]. The Minister assured him that the President would decide an amnesty before the conclusion of his government and meanwhile only the military juntas and a small group of commanders . . . would be judged" (Morales Solá, *Asalto a la ilusión* [Buenos Aires: Planeta, 1990], p. 148, our translation).

15. The impact on public opinion was such that the government, in an attempt to reduce it, ordered that all television newscasts were to show the images but not the audio of the trial, something that was possible because at the time the major networks were state owned. It was assumed that the "cold" description by anchorpersons of what was being revealed in the trial would create less anger than the narration by the victims themselves.

16. The members of the junta that governed the country between 1979 and 1982 were acquitted because the court considered the evidence against them insufficient and inconclusive.

17. Consider, for example, the military as an actor. Whereas in the first stage, its options were to pressure the executive or the legislative branch in order to influence the course of events, in the second, once the trials had been initiated, influencing these powers would not have yielded benefits. The military, therefore, had to choose between accepting or resisting the order to appear before a civil tribunal.

18. For example, the costs of options such as the decision to resist a subpoena were very different from the costs of options in the first stage of the process.

19. It is obvious that even if the judges showed themselves more or less susceptible to pressures by various actors, resources such as the mobilization capacity of the military, congressional and presidential lobbying-power, as well as a senate majority, tend to lose weight or influence over the decisions of a court. The latter functions through evidence, the testimony of witnesses and the accused, the actions of the prosecution and the defense, and resolutions according to preestablished rules in a forum in which all those collective actors with interests in conflict behave as mere observers.

20. Carlos H. Acuña, "Politics and Economics in the Argentina of the

Nineties (Or, why the future is no longer what it used to be)," in W. Smith, C. Acuña, and E. Gamarra, eds., *Democracy, Markets, and Structural Reforms in Latin America: Argentina, Bolivia, Brazil, Chile, and Mexico* (New Brunswick, N.J.: Transaction, 1994), pp. 56–68.

21. It should be noted that although the law explicitly prohibits the participation of the armed forces in internal intelligence and security, after a guerrilla attack on military installations in 1988 the Alfonsín government passed various decrees authorizing the armed forces to lend logistical support to the security forces.

22. For a comparative analysis of the evolution and significance of the military industry and resources, see Carlos H. Acuña and William C. Smith, "The Politics of Military Economics in the Southern Cone: Comparative Perspectives on Arms Production in Argentina, Brazil and Chile," *Political Power and Social Theory* 9 (1995): 121–157. The data in this article allow one to infer that while the average military expenditure as a percentage of GDP in the democratic period previous to the military regime was 1.3 (1973–1976), during the military regime it increased to 2.8 (1976–1983), during the Alfonsín administration it was reduced to 1.1 (1983–1989), and during Menem's first government it fell to approximately 0.9 (1989–1995). These percentages do not include the cost of military pensions, which represent around a third of total military expenditures in Argentina.

23. Hannah Arendt, *The Human Condition* (Chicago: University of Chicago Press, 1958), cited in Lawrence Weschler, *A Miracle, A Universe* (New York: Pantheon, 1990), p. 243. Arendt refers to crimes that are so terrible that there is no possible punishment to match the harm done (as in the case of genocide). We thank Charles Kenney of the University of Notre Dame for reminding us of the importance of the difference between the lack of capacity or power to punish a crime, and the impossibility of punishment due to the horrendous and overwhelming nature of a crime.

24. Adam Przeworski, *Democracy and the Market: Political and Economic Reforms in Eastern Europe and Latin America* (Cambridge: Cambridge University Press, 1991), especially chapter 1.

5

"No Victorious Army Has Ever Been Prosecuted . . .":

The Unsettled Story of Transitional Justice in Chile

Jorge Correa Sutil
in collaboration with Francisco Jiménez

THIS CHAPTER seeks to flesh out the role played by the Chilean court system in the protection of human rights during both the military dictatorship of General Augusto Pinochet (1973–1989) and the first years of democracy under Presidents Patricio Aylwin and Eduardo Frei (1989–1995). As I shall contend, the behavior of the courts throughout this period is a major issue in understanding the transition to democracy in Chile. From a very early stage in the military regime, the courts were asked by human rights groups, sponsored by church organizations, both to prevent and to punish human rights abuses that were occurring under the dictatorship. For more than a decade, their response to this challenge varied from a complete refusal to accept this task to a stage of timid protection and limited investigation during the final years of the dictatorship. Later on, as Chile's transition to democracy began, the behavior of the courts was often erratic, ambiguous, and in some ways contradictory. As a result, many of those most responsible for the crimes of the military regime were never punished.

Yet, as I shall argue in this chapter, we cannot simply blame the courts for this failure to prosecute past human rights violations. Even today, the most prominent political actors in Chile and, in many ways, Chilean society as a whole remain undecided about whether to punish past abuses and, if so, how best to accomplish this task. This hesitation has been greatly due to a continuing concern among many

Chileans that any solution that is found to the human rights issue will, in turn, obstruct other political and economic objectives the country is striving to achieve. As a consequence, more than twenty years after the most serious offenses were committed under military rule, Chileans have still not found a neat balance between morality and prudence, and there is still considerable ambiguity regarding the extent to which judicial means can and should be used to redress past wrongs.

In this essay, I propose to show how the Chilean approach to transitional justice has been shaped by the country's peculiar process of democratic consolidation. Unlike many new democracies, in which a former dictatorship has fallen as a result of military defeat or political collapse, the Chilean military was not defeated on the battlefield but at the ballot box. Thus, in assessing the courts' efforts to reckon with the human rights violations of the Pinochet era, I shall endeavor to place their activities within this broader context. In particular, I will treat their behavior as an interactive process with Chile's primarily political actors. In this process, as we shall see, although both sides have frequently been undecided and unclear as to how they should deal with the past, there has been progress in determining the truth about most grave human rights violations. However, only in a handful of cases has it been possible to bring the guilty to trial, and discovery of the whereabouts of those still missing seems more unlikely every day.

This essay is divided into three broad parts. The first describes the role of the courts during the years of dictatorship. The second, which includes several sections, seeks to describe and analyze the activities of the courts and other actors during the first five years of the process of consolidating Chilean democracy. The third, an epilogue, highlights some more general conclusions about the role of the courts in providing justice in Chile.

Justice under the Dictatorship.

On September 11, 1973, in the midst of an economic, social, and political crisis, a *junta militar*, led by the commander in chief of the Chilean army, Augusto Pinochet, overthrew President Salvador Allende's elected government. It soon became clear that the new military regime intended to reorganize the Chilean political system completely and to change the social and economic order fundamentally. To this end, the junta reversed the tendency toward a socialist order in Chile that had begun with a powerful welfare state in 1920 and led to the election of a government with strong Marxist influences in 1970. An open market economy was instituted, and the ideas of intellectuals and politicians, such as Friedrich von Hayek, Milton Friedman, Michael Novak, and Margaret Thatcher, were frequently mentioned as sources of inspiration for Chilean public policies. The new model established deep roots and, with minor changes, it prevailed even after the armed forces left power.

Politically, the military regime was somewhat less successful, although by no means a failure. All along, the junta's political objectives were less clear than its socioeconomic goals. The military frequently oscillated between the attempt to establish a permanent authoritarian regime of a fascist character, on the one hand, and the countervailing desire to pursue a more classic conception of democracy, on the other, with just enough restrictions and safeguards to ensure that the new socioeconomic order would not be challenged. But in October 1988, a surprising event occurred: the armed forces were voted out of office in a popular referendum.

This referendum had been conceived in the provisions of a new constitution that the junta approved and ratified in a plebiscite in 1980—a plebiscite conducted on an exceptional basis during a time of no constitutional guarantees and incomplete electoral rules. By virtue of the constitution's approval, Pinochet was able to continue in his position as president of Chile for eight more years, from 1981 until 1989. Had all gone according to plan, it was anticipated that at the end of this period, another plebiscite would simply rubber-stamp the junta's choice and allow Pinochet to rule the country for eight additional years. Yet unexpectedly, the option to reject the candidate emerged victorious, and Pinochet was defeated. As specified by the constitution, presidential elections were then held in 1990. These led to the defeat of the right-wing candidate, Hernán Büchi, Pinochet's former secretary of the treasury, and Aylwin's election as president of Chile.

From the beginning, Chile's new democratic government was

confronted with the question of how to deal with the massive human rights violations that the military regime had committed for nearly seventeen years. Under Pinochet's rule, for the first time in Chilean history, political differences had been resolved through a systematic policy involving police brutality, censorship, exile, torture, disappearances, and executions. According to official figures, a total of 2,095 individuals lost their lives during this period, and there were 1,102 additional disappearances.[1] Notably, many of these violations were taken to the courts, primarily through writs of habeas corpus and later through requests for criminal punishment as well. However, although Pinochet did not overtly challenge the judiciary's constitutionally protected status, the courts did very little during these years to aid the cause of human rights protection, to punish those responsible for abuses, or even to take steps to prevent violations from recurring in the future.

The Supreme Court chose not to review decisions of the wartime military courts, and until well into the 1980s, Chilean appellate courts invariably rejected writs of habeas corpus that were presented on behalf of political detainees. Despite clear rules to the contrary, the courts also tended to act on these habeas corpus writs only after months had gone by. Even in cases when judges inquired about the fate of detainees, they generally honored explanations given by political authorities as the truth without further investigation. There were no orders to bring those arrested into the courts; and for a long time, judges neglected even to visit detention sites. After the military's fall from power, Chile's National Commission on Truth and Reconciliation came to an unequivocal conclusion about this record of failure:

> Had the Courts respected the constitutional requirement of acting immediately, or had they complied with the legal requirement to issue a decision within twenty-four hours, or exercised the legal power which is the essence of that appeal, namely to physically examine the person detained . . . or finally had they fulfilled the requirement of the ruling that they make a decision before the evil of unjust imprisonment is allowed to take major proportions, many instances of death, disappearance and torture would have been prevented. . . .[2]

Not only did the courts fail to live up to these obligations, the result of their inaction was that many of the worst violators of human rights during the dictatorship were never brought to justice. Although a number of investigations were opened, only a handful of persons were ever actually indicted, and as we shall see, no one was penalized until the mid-1990s.

Among the many reasons for this broad failure of the Chilean court system, one should emphasize the application of the amnesty law of 1978. This sweeping decree was enacted by the military junta on April 18, 1978 and published on April 19, 1978. With few exceptions, it covered all crimes against persons committed in the period between September 11, 1973 and March 10, 1978, including murder, injury, and kidnapping.[3] Although the decree made no distinctions about the individuals it was meant to protect, it was widely criticized as a self-amnesty law, since Chile's left-wing parties had not used violence as a means of resistance during the period in question. At the same time, this was precisely the period when state officials were implicated in the greatest number of human rights crimes.

Another reason for the courts' failure to take a stand on human rights violations was the fact that the junta also approved several statutes that reserved to military courts the exclusive right to investigate cases when the suspect was a soldier. Moreover, judges frequently lacked the assistance of the Chilean police to carry out serious investigations. This was a particularly notable handicap, for in the Chilean judicial system, the judge himself plays the role of both investigator and prosecutor and is therefore dependent upon adequate police support. Yet even if one takes all these factors into account, a final reason for the courts' inability to prosecute human rights violations resided with the judicial institutions themselves, and the unwillingness on the part of both Supreme Court judges and lower court judges to shoulder their lawful responsibilities.[4]

In spite of the legal authorities' weak responses, however, Chilean human rights groups continued to present cases to the courts throughout the dictatorship, both as writs of habeas corpus and as criminal actions. These initiatives were part of a concerted strategy by activists and victims to document instances of abuse, to force the authorities to recognize arrests, and to use all means, whether effective or not, to advance the cause of human rights. Of particular note in these campaigns was the role played by the church-based human rights organization, Vicaría de la Solidaridad, whose fact-finding activities would later prove to be a crucial source for the National Commission on Truth and Reconciliation.[5]

In some exceptional instances, such as the "Lonquén" case, the strategy paid off. In September 1978, the Catholic Church was informed of the existence of human remains in two abandoned lime furnaces in Lonquén, a rural village about fifty kilometers from Santiago. Bodies were found that had been buried in lime to hasten the deterioration of the bones. Once this information was confirmed, the Church formally presented the case to the courts. The shock generated by Lonquén caused the Supreme Court to appoint an appellate court judge, Adolfo Bañados, to take charge of the investigation. After several months of work, Bañados determined that members of a police department had in fact been involved in the illegal detention and killing of fourteen people, though he was not able to identify the names of the perpetrators. He then sent the case to a military court. At the time, August 1979, this judicial decision alone was a notable step forward in the protection of human rights.

From 1984 and 1985 on, minority votes were cast in several appellate courts in favor of accepting writs of habeas corpus. A group of judges took up the investigations of another grave site and initiated procedures to clarify the identity of the "missing" persons whom they had discovered. As one might have expected, none of these cases ever led to an indictment against the perpetrators of the crimes. Pursuant to Chilean law, the judges were obliged to turn the cases over to military courts as soon as it was clear that military personnel were involved. In such a forum, all further investigations would have ceased. Even though this new judicial attitude of the mid-1980s did not lead to charges or convictions, it did bring about some improvement in both the prevention and investigation of human rights abuses.[6] In one case, an appellate court judge went as far as to bring charges against several high-ranking officials, including a former commander in chief of the Air Force, though the decision was later reversed by the Supreme Court.

From 1980 onward, important changes in Chilean politics and society had slowly left their mark on the judiciary. Although the reasons behind the shift in judicial attitude have not been investigated in depth, the most important appears to have been the enjoyment of more freedom in the country once the period of high political repression against the opposition had come to an end. At this point, civilians were beginning to play a more important role in government, and those who had fought for an open market and a liberalized economy were trying hard to bring about some liberalization in the political arena. Within the government, there were continuing tensions between the more authoritarian forces, known as the *duros*, and their opponents who favored more liberalization, the *blandos*. This second group scored an important victory with the approval of the new constitution in 1980. Their aim was to "institutionalize" the regime in order to guarantee the survival of the socioeconomic order after the end of military government and to ensure that it would no longer be dependent upon repression.

A series of external pressures on the government in the early- and mid-1980s provided judges with reasons for involving themselves in the issue of human rights protection. These were the economic crisis of 1982; the *Protestas*, or public protests, against the military regime that began in 1983; and the signing of the *Acuerdo Nacional* (National Agreement) in late summer 1985. The economic crisis of 1982 brought about a period of high unemployment in Chile, the bankruptcy of many companies, and a state of general unrest. According to official figures, annual unemployment reached a high of 30 percent, not counting underemployment. In turn, this situation generated the first of the so-called *Protestas* in 1983. These popular demonstrations initially consisted of people hitting cooking pots in their homes or making other noises for an hour as a way of giving voice to their dissatisfaction. But once the first wave of protests had passed, these demonstrations became increasingly violent. People threw stones at the police, burned tires in the streets, and gave vent to their anger in other ways. The government's response to these manifestations of public discontent was equally violent. At times, during public curfews, unknown individuals driving cars without license plates would fire into shantytowns, causing numerous deaths and injuries. In the city of Santiago, at one notable point, Pinochet sent twenty thousand troops with painted faces and camouflage uniforms into the streets.

The *Protestas* did not fully come to an end until the fall of the dictatorship, and the government showed that it was determined to continue responding to violence with equal levels of repression. However, by the mid-1980s there were significant pressures on the military regime to make room for greater freedom of speech and autonomous political activity. One such impetus was provided by the signing of the *Acuerdo Nacional* in August 1985. In this initiative, the Catholic Church sought to bring together diverse opposition parties, trade unions, and even some of Pinochet's supporters to call for greater respect for human rights and a peaceful return to democracy.

As in the Lonquén case, small strides were made in the investigation of unresolved human rights cases. In one investigation, which involved the murder of three members of the Communist Party in 1985 and came to be known as "Degollados," the judge's decision failed to bring charges against distinct offenders. However, the evidence so clearly pointed to police involvement in the crime that César Mendoza Durán, the director of the police and a member of the ruling junta, was actually forced to resign under political pressure, and a full branch of the police was dissolved.[7] The investigation of this case was reactivated in a civilian court in 1989 and, as we shall see later in this essay, finally led to criminal convictions in 1994, marking an even more important advance in the quality of Chile's transition to democratic rule.

Lonquén and Degollados remained the exceptions to the rule. A majority of other cases that were brought forward during the dictatorship languished in the courts with little or no investigation. In general, there was little justice for the victims of political crimes; seldom was anybody punished. In those few instances when judges did muster the courage to investigate complaints, they invariably found that the police refused serious cooperation. In the even rarer instances when the courts brought charges against individuals, civilian judges declared themselves incompetent to render judgment immediately after the indictment was issued, and the cases ended up in military courts, with the predictable lack of results.

Nevertheless, in spite of the lack of concrete judicial action during the 1980s, it would be a mistake to think that efforts to pursue justice had no impact on the political atmosphere in Chile. The flow of information generated by these cases influenced the mood of a society that was slowly awakening from the bonds of dictatorship. Magazines routinely covered the most prominent cases, and books about their outcomes (or the lack thereof) turned into best-sellers.[8] Gradually, attention to these issues generated subtle pressures on the government, compelling the country's leaders to move slowly, though ambivalently, in the direction of greater openness, liberalization, and political institutionalization.

Justice under the Transition to Democracy

In the following sections, I will consider the goals and the behavior of the most relevant actors involved in dealing with the abuses of the Chilean military regime. The focus will be not only on the courts but also on the broader actions taken by Chile's two democratic governments under Aylwin and Frei, as well as by Congress and by the military. As we shall find, the return to democracy between 1989 and 1995 was largely characterized by a series of pressures and counter-pressures. At times, these forces favored the pursuit of truth and the imposition of criminal sanctions for past offenses, but at other times, they allowed for more or less impunity.

It is helpful to begin our consideration of these issues by examining the political conditions that existed at the starting point of Chile's transition to democracy.[9] After the failure to remove Pinochet from power during the popular protests that began in 1983, Chile's opposition parties viewed the 1988 plebiscite as their great chance to defeat the military regime. However, they also had to recognize the constraints imposed by the constitution of 1980.[10] In particular, although Pinochet was defeated in 1988, the constitution allowed him to remain in power until March 11, 1990.

During this transitional period, several efforts were made to amend the constitution, but they were not enough to alter the well-structured provisions the old regime had put in place to ensure that the new democratic forces would be prevented from making radical changes to the existing social and political order. Among these, for example, was the provision that nine out of forty-five members of the Senate were not to be elected but designated—by the Supreme Court and various branches of the military, among others—in such a way that their alliance with right-wing parties was virtually guaranteed. During subsequent years, this provision limited any attempt to amend the constitution or to change the laws that required qualified majorities in order to be modified. Finally, would-be reformers also found their hands tied by the existence of an independent body, the Constitutional Tribunal, which was charged with the task of preventing Congress from considering legislation that might violate the constitution. Six of its seven members were close to the military regime and its ideology.[11]

Nonetheless, from the very beginning of the presidential campaign of 1989, it was evident that human rights violations would become a key issue in the transition. The representatives of the democratic coalition recognized that they would face severe opposition to any effort on their part to repeal, void, or invalidate the rules under which they had come to power. But at the same time, they were convinced that some laws and statutes had to be amended in the interest of bringing about justice. Thus, Aylwin's campaign program initially declared that the democratic coalition would bring to trial anyone who had committed particularly atrocious abuses under the old regime. Moreover, the program stated that the amnesty decree law of 1978 could no longer be an impediment to the disclosure of the truth, the investigation of facts, and the establishment of criminal responsibility. To this end, the program specifically pledged "to promote the derogation or nullification of the amnesty law."[12]

The reaction of the right-wing parties and of some military officers to these declarations was both quick and forceful, with many arguing that such a position threatened the process of Chile's transition to democracy.[13] Pinochet himself was even more direct, announcing that if even one of his men were touched, the rule of law would end.[14] For these reasons, immediately following Aylwin's election in December 1989, the democratic forces had to ask themselves whether they had the wherewithal to reverse the record of impunity that we have described above. The governing coalition itself was divided on the matter. For some members of the new government, Pinochet's threats were reason enough not to force a situation that could risk the peaceful transition to democracy. For others, in contrast, the administration had a moral obligation to seek to redress past human rights violations; these individuals insisted that the consolidation of

Chilean democracy was unthinkable without some form of justice. Aylwin himself was among this second group.

However, the new government had to recognize the limits to its power. After all, Pinochet was still commander in chief of the army. There was insufficient support in Congress to remove the amnesty law; there was no way to change the composition of the Supreme Court; and there was neither the will nor the necessary conditions to create the special courts that would have been required to deal with many human rights cases. In addition, the members of the new political majority soon recognized that the courts, and not they, would be the main actors on this issue; and it was unlikely that the judges involved would easily alter any of their previous decisions without major changes in the laws. Finally, to amend the most important laws left by Pinochet, large majorities would have been required in Congress. These majorities were simply not available.

Accordingly, nearly everyone in the government could agree that the pursuit of justice in any complete sense was not only impossible but probably not even desirable under the prevailing circumstances. Aylwin himself assumed a stance which he would maintain consistently throughout his presidency, calling for a compromise between the virtues of morality and prudence. This position was epitomized by a statement that he frequently found himself repeating: "Full disclosure of the truth, and justice to the extent possible."[15] In the end, the question was how much and to what extent justice was possible. For Aylwin and for many, although not all, of his supporters, there was never any doubt about their readiness to use political power in a prudent way to obtain justice to the fullest extent possible. But despite their moral convictions, Aylwin and his supporters were not prepared to break the rules under which they had been elected and were ruling the country. Abandoning their own source of legitimacy would have endangered the process of moving towards and consolidating democracy.[16] Hence, for much of the time that Aylwin was in office, his presidency was characterized by a series of forward and backward movements, in which the judiciary handled human rights cases in different ways.

In the following sections, I will outline how the Aylwin administration attempted to deal with these issues, the policies it developed, and especially their impact on the Chilean judiciary. Most important,

I will highlight the complex interplay of judicial and political decisions that took place during these years of transition. As we shall see,
Aylwin's successor, Eduardo Frei, would face similar problems at a
later date.

The Commission on Truth and Reconciliation

In the politically constrained environment of the early 1990s, Chile's
new democratic government determined that its basic moral obligation was to prevent future human rights violations from occurring, to
offer reparations and rehabilitation to the victims of injustice, and to
bring about societal reconciliation. It was understood that such a
process had to start with the official disclosure of the truth about past
human rights violations. Accordingly, on April 25, 1990, the government formed the Commission on Truth and Reconciliation.

Article 1 of the decree that created the Chilean commission
spelled out its function as follows: "[To] help to clarify in a comprehensive manner the truth about the most serious human rights violations committed in recent years in our country (and elsewhere if they
were related to the Chilean government or to national political life),
in order to help bring about the reconciliation of all Chileans. . . ."[17]
After nine months of *in camera* work, the commission produced a
Final Report—the so-called Rettig Report, after the body's chair, Raúl
Rettig—that tried, in a solemn and serious manner, to establish the
truth about events that had been denied and neglected by the state
for so many years.

Like similar so-called truth commissions in other countries, the
authors of the Chilean report tried to serve a cause—the pursuit of
retrospective justice—that is more effectively undertaken by the
courts. However, in many ways this attempt appears to have succeeded. Since nobody has, as yet, managed to challenge its findings,
the report may be considered an authoritative and commonly accepted version of the facts. Additionally, it helped to diminish the
sense of impunity that accompanied many of the crimes of the
Chilean dictatorship. But most important, the report should be seen
as the starting point in a process aimed at restoring the dignity and
good names of the victims of the military regime and easing the lives

of their relatives. While the pursuit of criminal sanctions is normally regarded as the best way of expressing and reinforcing society's repudiation of past human rights abuses, we must still consider the full disclosure of the truth as a respectable, second-best option. For it, too, demonstrates a moral revulsion for human rights violations. Moreover, by enabling a society to remember the facts, it aids in healing wounds and helping a people come to terms with its past.[18]

Nonetheless, one of the undeniable shortcomings of the Commission on Truth and Reconciliation was its inability to determine the fate and whereabouts of many of the missing and disappeared. As a result of this shortcoming, the issue of retrospective justice was immediately returned to the courts, which, as we have seen, are responsible under Chilean law for all matters of criminal investigation. For Chilean society as a whole, but especially for the relatives of the victims, this would remain an open wound.

The Amnesty Law and the Courts

The Aylwin government faced a second challenge in contending with the limitations upon the courts implied by the amnesty law of 1978. In 1992, a group of representatives tried to push a bill through parliament that would have annulled the effects of this law. However, the bill was considered controversial even among the governing coalition, and it was eventually rejected. Given the Senate's ties to the Chilean right-wing, few politicians believed that the amnesty law could ever be modified. Hence, the law remained in effect, leaving the battle about its validity and its consequences to the courts.

At first, some lawyers sought to contest the law by arguing that it was inconsistent with international law. But after the Supreme Court upheld the validity of the law, their claims could not be taken any further.[19] Still, as we have seen with other Chilean institutions, the Court's rulings were never completely consistent. A good example is the case of the illegal detention and later disappearance of a teenager named Juan Cheuquepan Levimilla in 1974.[20] The case had already been closed and reopened several times before the lower court of Lautaro reached its verdict to convict the perpetrators responsible for the kidnapping of the juvenile. But making the case even more unusual, the Supreme Court (and also the Appellate Court of Temuco) chose to dismiss requests to quash the decision.[21] Yet despite the importance of this case, it remains the only instance where the perpetrators of a crime clearly covered by the amnesty law have been brought to justice. By the mid-1990s, most similar cases had been closed. While no one can exclude the possibility that the Supreme Court might revisit the tougher stance it evinced in the Cheuquepan ruling, this would be a surprise for most observers.

In contrast, the most frequent and probably the most relevant discussion regarding the application of the amnesty law was about the problem of deciding at what stage in their investigations the courts should grant amnesty. Sharp disagreements still prevail over this question, and the Supreme Court has been predictably erratic in its rulings. Numerous cases have been closed, reopened, and then closed again as a result of this uncertainty. For their part, the majority of judges have chosen to take an imprecise middle ground concerning the level of investigations that should be completed before the decision is made to close a case. In fact, only a few judges seem to believe that cases should be fully clarified, and responsible individuals clearly identified, before amnesty is granted.

Nonetheless, the practical effects of investigations conducted during the Aylwin presidency have still exercised an undeniable impact upon the quality of the legal culture that has developed in Chile. First, the amnesty debates themselves at least formally raised the all-important question of the judiciary's responsibility to investigate the truth. Second, in the case of some of the missing, the courts' investigations have also meant the discovery of their fates and whereabouts. And finally, the courts' involvement in such cases has led to the subpoena and testimony of active military officers implicated in human rights violations. It is hard to overstate the significance of this final effect. Although the military has not been reluctant to show its restlessness on occasions when retired or active officers have been called to testify before the courts, these investigations have helped to raise public expectations of the law.

In all of these respects, the struggle over the amnesty law has therefore not been a battle over retrospective justice in the conventional sense of convicting the guilty. Rather, it has been a struggle over the public disclosure of the truth, a battle that has frequently centered on the fate and whereabouts of the victims of the military dictatorship. In this sense, Chile's quest for justice may have taken on a broader and even more sophisticated dimension than would ever have been the case had the campaign been limited to criminal punishment alone.

Legislative and Other Efforts to Influence Judicial Outcomes

Aside from the few, failed attempts that were made to nullify the amnesty law, Aylwin's coalition government also supported several legislative efforts to influence the outcome of judicial trials. These efforts met with some success as long as the government confined itself to limiting the jurisdiction of military judges over civilians accused of political or security offenses. They were much less successful in limiting the wide powers enjoyed by the military courts to deal with criminal offenses committed by military personnel on active duty.[22]

The result of this mixed record was that in the majority of cases, the government's efforts to obtain justice were stymied. Once a civilian court had advanced its investigation far enough to establish that a crime had been committed by active members of the armed forces, the case had to be passed on to a military court, either just before or immediately after an indictment was handed down. In these instances, the outcome was preordained. When the case reached the military courts, it would only be a matter of days before the amnesty law was applied. In such circumstances, the most civilian judges could do was to attempt to conduct the fullest investigation possible before actually bringing charges. This minimalist strategy meant that they could at least establish the truth about possible violations and perhaps even determine the whereabouts of the missing.[23]

Among other legislative strategies pursued during this period, the Aylwin government attempted to introduce a number of bills aimed at bringing about changes in the judicial system itself, as well as in the culture and procedures of the Chilean legal system. Some of these initiatives were passed by the legislature. But those that would have had the most direct and immediate impact on human rights questions were rejected. Among these drafts was one in particular that sought to augment the number of Supreme Court judges from seventeen to twenty-one, a move that would have had a major influence on the political character of the Court.[24] When this initiative was rejected, all the administration could do was to hope that time would catch up with the conservative judges remaining on the court. (In fact, this has transpired. Since the bill's failure, time has had its influence on the Court's renewal, and Aylwin and Frei have together appointed seven of the seventeen sitting judges).[25]

In view of these limitations, the governmental coalition was compelled to seek other, less formal means of putting pressure on the judiciary, both to ensure further investigations about the fate of the missing and, at least in cases not covered by the amnesty law, to keep alive the possibility of criminal prosecutions of the guilty. One type of political pressure took the form of public statements, some highly critical, that were designed to raise awareness about the work that still needed to be done in addressing past human rights violations. For example, the Commission on Truth and Reconciliation took the courts to task for their shortcomings in pursuing justice. "During the period in question," the Rettig Report's authors noted,

> the judicial branch did not respond vigorously enough to human rights violations. The country was surprised to see the courts take such a stance, for it was accustomed to regard the judiciary as a staunch defender of the rule of law. Consequently, this posture taken by the judicial branch during military rule was largely, if unintentionally, responsible for aggravating the process of systematic human rights violations, both directly insofar as persons who were arrested and whose cases reached the courts were left unprotected, and indirectly insofar as that stance offered the agents of repression a growing assurance that they would enjoy impunity for their criminal actions, no matter what outrages they might commit. As a result, the people of this nation still do not have confidence that the judicial branch as an institution is committed to defending their fundamental rights.[26]

In his presentation of the commission's findings on March 4, 1991, President Aylwin made clear his own feelings on the subject. "[J]ustice demands as well," he stated, "[that we are able] to know the fate or whereabouts of those missing, and to determine personal responsibilities." Aylwin added, "I hope the judiciary can fulfill its mandate and exhaust these investigations, which—I believe—cannot be limited by the amnesty law."[27] The president reaffirmed this stance in a letter which he enclosed with the report and then sent to the Supreme Court. He urged the judiciary to activate the investigation of all cases dealing with human rights abuses and expressed the hope that the amnesty law should no longer be an obstacle to public knowledge about the cases allegedly covered by it.

Aylwin did not stop at this initiative. Shortly thereafter, he made a public statement in which he observed that many judges "had lacked moral courage" in dealing with the abuses and crimes of Chile's past. In its defense, the Supreme Court responded to Aylwin with even stronger language. In the ensuing battle between the two centers of power, one could say there was a period when the courts were on public trial.[28] Admittedly, it remains unclear how or whether this episode influenced the outcome of actual cases. But it certainly created tension between the presidency and the Court, ironically making it even more difficult to pass judicial reforms in Congress.

Despite Aylwin's stand and the findings of the Commission on Truth and Reconciliation, one should not think that all the political leaders of the governing coalition necessarily subscribed to the same positions. For example, there remained important differences among Chile's democratic politicians about what still had to be done with cases prior to 1978. Some politicians continued to think it was politically imprudent to generate turbulence over matters that would probably never reach the stage of criminal conviction and about whose veracity the Commission on Truth and Reconciliation had already reported. Conversely, others continued to demand full judicial investigations in the interest of acknowledging the truth.

Since the end of Aylwin's government, the majority of these debates have subsided. Nevertheless, I believe that both Aylwin's public statements and the gradual infusion of the Supreme Court with new members have helped to legitimate the proposition that diverse interpretations of key laws are possible. In contrast to the formerly monolithic approach taken by the Supreme Court, this shift has also ensured that lower court judges can act with greater independence and feel freer to choose different approaches to the law.

In any event, the most important political pressure on the judiciary during this period did not come from Aylwin's presidency but rather from Congress, although the message itself was somewhat complicated. In December 1992, the Chamber of Deputies accused three justices of the Supreme Court of "gross neglect of duty," and began an impeachment procedure against them. The major charge raised by the Chamber was that the justices had failed to resolve a human rights case that had been awaiting judgment for over five months, even though there were individuals in jail waiting for their decision. A second accusation concerned the decision to transfer the case from a civilian to a military court (both were claiming jurisdiction), an act that was perceived by a majority of members of the House of Representatives to be so partisan and arbitrary that it amounted to a denial of justice.[29]

The Chilean Senate rejected this second accusation, arguing that a judge could not be dismissed as a result of his interpretation of the law; there were no grounds for ruling that the justices had arbitrarily sent the case to the military court. Yet on the issue of delay, three representatives of one of the Senate's right-wing parties surprisingly crossed party lines and voted in favor of removing one of the three judges accused of having delayed sentencing. It subsequently became apparent that the real reason for their decision to uphold the charges against the judge had little to do with the formal charges against him but was instead based upon some never-specified accusations of corruption. Nonetheless, the significance of this decision was manifest to all. In an impeachment proceeding without precedent in the previous 125 years of Chilean history, a member of the Supreme Court had been dismissed from office. Even if it was not evident that human rights issues per se had influenced the result, they had been an undeniable part of the formal charges.[30]

Counterpressures from the Military

Whether due to the above changes in Chile's political atmosphere, changes made in the laws, the impact of the Rettig Report, the partial renewal of the judiciary, or various political pressures, by the beginning of 1993 many judges were beginning to show greater vigor in addressing human rights cases involving the pre-1978 period. By this time, one could sense a more positive and professional approach to such investigations on the part of the "Investigaciones," the Chilean civil police force. In addition, even the testimony of former DINA (secret police) agents began to play a role in enabling the courts to identify possible perpetrators and to prepare subpoenas to facilitate their testimony. Active officers were among those subpoenaed.

The army's reaction to this shifting climate was not long in coming. *Americas Watch* has captured its response in the following words:

> On May 28, while President Aylwin was on a state visit to Scandinavia, unusual troop movements were reported in the vicinity of the armed forces headquarters in Santiago, where the Council of Generals was holding an emergency meeting, presided over by General Pinochet. Soldiers in full camouflage combat gear, and some carrying bazookas and others heavy equipment, were posted on guard duty outside the building, while armored vehicles from other army units cruised the streets.[31]

Undoubtedly, the most important single reason for this display of military power was the issuance of an arrest warrant for an active, high-ranking officer, Colonel Fernando Laureani, who had been identified by some victims as the perpetrator of numerous human rights crimes. But more generally, there were also rumors that the army was intent upon pressing Congress to institute a law that would put an end to all subsequent investigation of human rights cases in the pre-1978 period. In each case that was considered already covered by the amnesty law, the military alleged that merely by requiring the testimony of active officers, the courts were guilty of subjecting the armed forces to a public trial in the media.

In Aylwin's absence, the fact that the leaders of the governing coalition showed a wide variety of responses to this action made it clear that there was strong disagreement within the regime over the best way of dealing with this situation. Some of the coalition's leaders declared that the military's action proved that it was time to put an end to all further judicial action on the cases covered by the amnesty law. However, upon his return, Aylwin immediately began to look for a way out of the crisis. Rejecting the military's show of force, he initiated a sustained period of consultations. His final position must be regarded as an attempt to placate the interests of all sides.

Without the army's cooperation, Aylwin recognized, the most likely prospect was that the trials might continue indefinitely, albeit with no results. Relatives would never be able to ascertain the fate of the missing, and to its disadvantage, the military would nonetheless continue to experience pressure from the courts. Thus, Aylwin proposed to introduce a bill to speed up the investigation of cases still covered by the amnesty law. According to his proposal, witnesses and defendants who were able to offer the courts precise data or information that would help to clarify unsolved crimes would be assured that their statements would not appear in the public record. They would even be allowed to present their testimony outside of official court buildings.

This proposal was clearly a formula that privileged the pursuit of truth at the cost of justice. But it was also a testimony to the continuing difficulty of wrestling with the Chilean past. The proposal aroused immediate disagreement within the governing coalition, and as a result, it was finally withdrawn in September 1993. Thus, despite Aylwin's desire to find a meeting ground for all sides, there was still no consensus as to the correct balance between morality and prudence or the extent to which justice was realizable.

The Frei Government:
The Political Effects of a Judicial Decision

The election of President Eduardo Frei, who took office in March 1994, was made possible by the same governing coalition as before, *Concertación de Partidos por la Democracia*. However, although the issue of past human rights violations remained very much an unsettled problem, it was not in the forefront of the new administration's political agenda. The Frei governmental program was largely focused on socioeconomic priorities, regarding human rights issues as basically a problem for the judiciary. In this sense, it assumed that the transition to democracy had been completed, and that it was high time for Chile to look forward.

In this spirit, the courts continued to hear their cases, many of which were reaching their final stages as the new government came to power. But nothing could have prepared the government for the public reaction to the ruling in the so-called Letelier/Moffitt, or Contreras, case, which was handed down just prior to Frei's ascent to the presidency. For in this case, the first that actually led to the conviction of high-ranking Chilean representatives of the old regime, the impact of the ruling was so great that the new administration was forced to postpone some of its economic plans and, whether it wanted to or not, throw itself once again into the difficult matter of dealing with the past.

The case dealt with the 1976 assassination of two individuals in Washington, D.C., Allende's foreign affairs minister, Orlando Letelier, and a U.S. citizen, Ronni Moffitt. From the first, the trial was notable because the murders had been expressly excluded from the amnesty law of 1978. After many years of unsuccessful inquiries by the military courts, and due to a special law, the investigation was finally entrusted to a Supreme Court justice, Adolfo Bañados, who was charged with the task of resolving it. (Bañados, the investigating judge of the Lonquén case, had become Aylwin's first appointee to the Supreme Court.) In November 1993, the judge delivered his verdict, sentencing retired general Manuel Contreras to seven years imprisonment and Brigadier Pedro Espinoza to six years for their role in the killings. Contreras had been the notorious director of the DINA, during the years when the most extensive political repression in the country had taken place, while Espinoza had been the organization's chief of operations.

According to Chilean law, the judge's ruling could be appealed to a chamber of the Supreme Court. This case was so sensational that when Contreras's sentence was appealed and argued before the Court in January 1995, Chilean television covered all the oral arguments, recording an unusually high number of viewers. The leaders of the governing coalition's political parties were all in attendance at the proceedings, and even some generals chose to be present in the courtroom, generating a climate of popular expectation unique in Chilean judicial history. On May 30, 1995, the Supreme Court upheld the Bañados decision, and Contreras and Espinoza, both of whom had been out on bail, were finally sent to prison. However, it was the process of actually getting them to jail that said the most about the tense atmosphere that descended upon the country.

Both Contreras and Espinoza eventually ended up in a special prison, Punta Peuco, that was specifically built to house former officers of the armed forces and public officials.[32] But on the evening the decision was released by the Supreme Court, Contreras informed the press from his farm in Fresia that he was "not going to any prison." In fact, military personnel stayed with him the whole time. When Contreras thought the police were coming to detain him, he then traveled to a military area, where he remained for a full day before returning to his farm.

One month after Brigadier Espinoza's arrival at the prison, and before Contreras was captured, a group of army officers wearing civilian clothing met outside Punta Peuco to express their indignation over the imprisonment of military officers. This incident provoked a stormy reaction among Chilean politicians and the media, and the government subsequently demanded a complete reporting of the facts from the army. Since this time, the incident has come to be known as the "picnic in Punta Peuco."

Meanwhile, Contreras himself was taken by active-duty soldiers to a naval hospital in southern Chile, where he underwent several surgical operations. Afterwards, his team of lawyers tried to prevent his incarceration by claiming that the medical facilities at Punta Peuco were insufficient to provide him with adequate medical support. They also requested that Contreras be allowed to serve his sentence at home. In the end, however, all these legal actions came to naught. Finally, on October 21, 1995, Contreras was sent to prison.

Predictably, Chilean public opinion was divided throughout the period between May 30 and October 21. To many Chileans, the army seemed to have been acting with undue autonomy, since there was no apparent reason to delay Contreras's incarceration. It also seemed as though he was being treated as a special citizen, enjoying a unique form of immunity. But whatever one's perspective on the controversy, this was undoubtedly the single most important human rights case in the country's history. With Contreras's incarceration, the most powerful individual from the early years of the dictatorship—after Pinochet himself—had been made to pay for his crimes.

Subsequently, the attention given the Contreras case created a sharp change in the government's political agenda. Whereas the administration's first strategy had been to leave the human rights issue to the judiciary, now even Chile's right-wing parties were quick to propose a bill on the human rights situation. Due to the public commotion and military unrest, the government was forced to recognize that the handling of past offenses could not be simply relegated to the courts. It was also an urgent political problem.

After several weeks of intense discussion among the ruling parties, the government took the initiative and proposed a bill to Congress that was intended to resolve the human rights question once and for all, by amending several provisions of the constitution and by restoring the president's prerogative to retire the chiefs of the armed forces.[33] In a public speech on August 22, 1995, Frei himself affirmed that the matter of reconciliation in Chile was an unsettled issue. The country had gone through difficult times in recent months, he noted, in part because of the delicate problem of human rights. For many, his words were interpreted as an implicit recognition of the fact that Chile's transition to democracy was still not over.

In particular, the government's bill sought to clarify the judiciary's role in handling remaining cases of missing persons. For example, it granted to perpetrators who were willing to collaborate in providing a full disclosure of the truth the assurance that they would not be indicted, detained, or even have their names disclosed. Also, the bill emphasized that cases would not be closed until the fate of all of the missing was ascertained. In the period leading up to the bill's introduction, there was a lively debate about its final form, especially within the Socialist Party. But notwithstanding some initial criticism, the presidential proposal was backed by all of the governing parties.

Nevertheless, even with these signs of progress, the bill could not escape the continuing challenge of consensus-building in Chilean politics. In October 1995, the government accepted significant revisions in the bill's structure when Renovación Nacional, the largest party in the opposition, decided to give its conditional support to the measure. The new draft was immediately criticized from various quarters, by human rights lawyers, various NGOs, spokespersons for the victims, Amnesty International, the Socialist Party, and individual members of other parties.[34] Whereas the original law had sought to ride a fine line between observing the basic provisions of the amnesty law while, at the same time, mandating the full disclosure of the truth in return for these guarantees, the second draft largely abandoned the emphasis on disclosure. To its critics, the new bill seemed only to maintain those provisions that benefited the perpetrators. Due to these criticisms, therefore, it did not seem likely—at least, not at the time of the writing of this essay—that Congress would approve the bill. For very different reasons, both the Socialist Party representatives and their right-wing counterparts let it be known that they would not support the measure, and once again the government found itself immersed in controversy.

Despite this setback, however, Chilean courts were already registering incremental progress in dealing with unresolved human rights cases. This was particularly true of incidents involving the post-1978 period. For example, on March 31, 1994, fifteen former members of the police and one civilian were finally convicted for their parts in the Degollados case that we have considered earlier in this essay. Of these, three policemen—one captain, one colonel, and one corporal—were sentenced to life in prison, while the rest of the convicted received terms ranging from forty-one days to eighteen years. All of the perpetrators receiving the longer sentences, with the exception of the civilian, Miguel Estay Reyno, remain in the same special prison where Contreras is incarcerated.

Making these convictions additionally notable was the fact that the presiding judge subsequently reported these crimes to the military court, suggesting that high officers in the Chilean police may have been guilty of the crime of obstruction of justice. Among the officers that he named were the former director of the police, César Mendoza Durán, and the individual currently holding the same position, Rodolfo Stange. The judge's report was an immediate source of controversy, and on April 5, 1994, the Frei government demanded that the chief of police turn in his resignation. Yet not only did Stange refuse to bow to this order and reject the accusations made against him, but the government itself came under severe criticism for asking for the director's resignation when he had yet to be charged with a crime. In the end, the Minister of the Interior, Germán Correa, was forced to step down as a result of the administration's gaffe, Stange remained in office, and a military court eventually dismissed all remaining charges in the case.

Still, the mood of Chile's courts had changed, and convictions continued to be handed down. On December 12, 1995, a military court sentenced a former captain of the police and member of the Department of Police Communications (DICOMCAR), Héctor Díaz Anderson, to a term of three years and one day in Punta Peuco. The court's investigations determined that Díaz had been chiefly responsible for the torture and death of a socialist student, Carlos Godoy Echegoyen, in a police barracks on February 22, 1985. Similar sentences were passed down in another case which has come to be known as "Quemados," or "the burned." On July 2, 1986, a student, Carmen Gloria Quintana, and a photographer, Rodrigo Rojas Denegri, had received severe burns as a result of their detention by police after a public protest. Rojas later died as a result of his wounds, and Quintana continued to suffer from her injuries. Although the court ruled that a group of soldiers had accidently caused the burns in obscure circumstance, it sentenced a former army captain, Pedro Fernández Ditus, to six hundred days of imprisonment in Punta Peuco for his part in the injuries. On the same day that Ditus entered the prison, January 17, 1996, he was joined by a former army major, Carlos Herrera Jiménez, and a noncommissioned officer of the police, Armando Cabrera Aguilar, who had been convicted for their role in the death of Mario Fernández López in a secret police quarters in 1986. Herrera was sentenced to ten years and Cabrera to six. Even as they began their sentences, both were indicted in another case involving the murder of two trade-union leaders, Tucapel Jiménez and Juan Alegría.

Epilogue

In early February 1995, just days before Contreras's conviction, a former second-in-command of the Chilean army, Jorge Ballerino Standford, now retired, is said to have reminded his countrymen that the Chilean army was "victorious" in building a new social, economic, and political order in his country. In some respects, one could not deny the claim. Ballerino Standford also added, in the cryptic words quoted in the title of this essay, that "no victorious army" had ever been indicted by a criminal court.[35] In the most general sense, as we have seen, this has been an accurate depiction of the Chilean situation. Nonetheless, even if there has been no way to extend the arm of justice to all of those in the Chilean military responsible for human rights abuses under the junta, at least a small group of its members has been forced to serve jail terms for their crimes.

Admittedly, these sentences have covered only a very small percentage of the many crimes committed under the dictatorship. The majority of remaining cases have now been closed. Furthermore, even in those few cases that remain open—especially those involving missing people—there is not much chance for new convictions. At best, one can only hope that the remaining investigations will aid in finally determining the fate and whereabouts of the missing.

Still, a very curious thing about Chilean efforts to wrestle with the past is that they have frequently led the country's most prominent political actors in directions they did not always expect. Thus, on some occasions, when politicians were ready to abandon all further efforts to seek justice, unresolved issues somehow managed to reassert themselves. This experience shows that it is not that easy to brush moral issues aside, even in a time of avowed pragmatism, when Chilean leaders are eager to champion the virtues of concessions and compromise. When democratic reformers failed in their initial efforts to restructure the Chilean courts in 1990, they were compelled to reckon with the past in another, seemingly less threatening way by creating the National Commission on Truth and Reconciliation. This effort to reach the truth then put indirect pressure on the courts, which gradually led to a revised attitude on the part of the judiciary regarding human rights issues. In turn, the courts chose to expand their investigations and to open new cases on unresolved human rights violations. All these developments combined to influence the pace of Chile's transition to democracy.

Based upon Frei's efforts in 1995 to clarify the judiciary's role in cases involving missing persons and on the continuing debates on this subject in Congress, it is clear that this transition is far from over. At the end of the day, it may be that the most Chileans could hope for in their reckoning with the abuses of the Pinochet dictatorship was a partial truth, a partial justice, and a partial healing of old wounds. Perhaps this is the dynamic one should expect of a democracy that was consolidated upon rules left behind by an army that was never defeated on the battlefield but only by a plebiscite.

NOTES

1. These figures are based upon both the records of the National Commission on Truth and Reconciliation (CNVR) and the National Commission on Reparation and Reconciliation (NCRR).

2. Comisión Nacional de Verdad y Reconciliación, *Informe de la Comisión Nacional de Verdad y Reconciliación* (Santiago, Chile: La Nación, Ediciones del Ornitorrinco, 1991). For the English translation of the report, on which the citations in this article are based, see *Report of the Chilean National Commission on Truth and Reconciliation*, trans. Phillip E. Berryman (Notre Dame, Ind.: University of Notre Dame Press, 1993), p. 123.

3. The figures compiled by the National Commission on Truth and Reconciliation show that the highest numbers of human rights violations were committed during the period of time covered by the amnesty law. For instance, 1,261 persons were killed or detained and then "disappeared" in Chile in 1973; 309 in 1974; 119 in 1975; 139 in 1976; and 25 in 1977. It is reasonable to conclude that other kinds of violations that were not presented to the commission, such as torture, cruel treatment, and illegal detention, followed a similar pattern.

4. A more detailed analysis of the role played by the courts during this period may be found in various other sources, such as reports by the United Nations, the Vicaría de la Solidaridad, the National Commission on Truth and Reconciliation, and Amnesty International. See also Jorge Correa Sutil, "The Judiciary and the Political System in Chile: The Dilemmas of Judicial Independence During the Transition to Democracy," in *Transition to Democracy in Latin America: The Role of the Judiciary*, ed. Irwin Stotzky (Boulder, Colo.: Westview, 1993), pp. 89–106.

5. Vicaría de la Solidaridad was the successor organization to the Comité por la Paz, the first human rights organization to be created in Chile, just after the coup of 1973. Comité por la Paz was sponsored by a wide combination of churches and finally closed under governmental pressure. The Vicaría was created by Catholic Cardinal Raúl Silva Henriquez immediately thereafter, with the avowed purpose of promoting human rights work and helping to collect information about government abuses. Among its best-known publications were the book *¿Dónde Están?* and the magazine *Solidaridad*. The Vicaría was a major source of information for United Nations and Amnesty International reports on the human rights situation in Chile.

6. Regarding the prevention of human rights abuses, the first "Recurso de Amparo," or habeas corpus, accepted by a court occurred in the case of Carlos Humberto Contreras, who was detained in front of witnesses on September 3, 1976 by members of the Dirección de Inteligencia Nacional (or DINA, the National Intelligence Office) and never returned home. After a quick investigation, the court ordered the Ministry of Interior "to release this person immediately in order to restore the rule of law and guarantee the due protection of the detainee." However, the order was never honored. This case and the later Lonquén case were isolated events occurring before the shift toward a more active judiciary.

7. The Degollados case began when three beheaded bodies were found near Santiago on March 30, 1985. The bodies were those of Santiago Nattino, Manuel Guerrero, and José Manuel Parada. Nattino had been detained on the afternoon of March 28, while Guerrero and Parada were detained together on the following morning, March 29. All three individuals were well-known people and active members of the Communist Party. Guerrero was a leader of the Teachers Association, and Parada an employee of the Vicaría de la Solidaridad. Because of public outrage over their fate, the Supreme Court appointed Judge José Canovas to head the judicial investigation of the matter. The investigation proved that the same criminal group had detained and killed the three men, and that their murders had been politically motivated. Some evidence also indicated that this case had been tied to an attack upon the communications office of the Teachers Association which took place on March 29, 1985. In this assault, five persons were kidnapped and tortured before they were finally released. From this point on, both cases were investigated together by the same judge.

8. Prominent examples of such publications are *Los zarpazos del puma* (Santiago, Chile: CESOC, Ediciones Chile America, 1989) by Patricia Verdugo; *Lonquén* by Máximo Pacheco Gomez (Santiago, Chile: Editorial Aconcagua, 1983); and *Chile, la memoria prohibida: Las violaciónes a los derechos humanos* (Santiago, Chile: Pehuen, 1989) by Eugenio Ahumada, all best-sellers in the mid-1980s.

9. For a more detailed analysis of these conditions, see Jorge Correa Sutil, "Dealing With Past Human Rights Violations: The Chilean Case After Dictatorship," *Notre Dame Law Review* 67, no. 5 (1992): 1458.

10. "In order to compete in that plebiscite," I have argued previously, "the democratic political parties had to accept the Constitution of 1980, and they had to promise that they would only change it according to its own rules. This Constitution established the calling of the plebiscite and regulated what should happen after the plebiscite. In order to win the plebiscite, the democratic forces had to be very prudent. A large part of the population feared that the return to democracy could bring disorder and chaos, threatening the peace and economic progress that the country was experiencing. Because their vote could be decisive, the democratic parties had to promise full respect for the Pinochet institutional framework and that they would only change the framework through its own mechanisms." Ibid., pp. 1458–1459.

11. See Timothy Scully and Alejandro Ferreiro, "Chile Recovers its Democratic Past: Democratization by Installment," *Journal of Legislation* 18, no. 2 (1992): 325–328.

12. "Government Program of the Coalition of Parties for Democracy" (1989). Translation by the author.

13. See, for example, the interview of the commander in chief of the Air Force, Fernando Matthei, which appeared in the newspaper *El Mercurio*, October 22, 1989. As he told the press, "I hope that everyone has good sense and that they behave in the future in such a way as to permit the country to look forward and build a new country. It is very difficult to walk forward safely when you are looking backward. Probably you will fall on something. I do not think this is a good [approach]."

14. In the newspaper *Las Últimas Noticias*, October 14, 1989, Pinochet informed the press, "Nobody will touch me. The day that one of my men is touched, the rule of law will end. I have said this once and I will not repeat it ever again. But it should be known that this is going to be like this. [There should be] clarity about this."

15. Transcription of Patricio Aylwin's inaugural speech, March 12, 1990, in a booklet printed by Secretaría de Cultura y Prensa, Ministerio Secretaría General de Gobierno.

16. For a more detailed analysis of this process, see Correa Sutil, "Dealing With Past Human Rights Violations," n. 9.

17. Presidential Decree No. 355, Executive Branch, Ministry of Justice, Undersecretary of Interior, published in the "Diario Oficial de Chile" on May 9, 1990. This decree appears in *Report of the Chilean National Commission*, p. 6.

18. For broader discussions on the extent to which such commissions may perform important roles in times of transition, see José Zalaquett, "Confronting Human Rights Violations Committed by Former Governments: Principles Applicable and Political Constraints" in *State Crimes: Punishment or Pardon*, Papers and Conference Report (Queenstown, Md.: Aspen Institute, 1989). Similar reflections may be found from the South African perspective in two books, *The Healing of a Nation*, ed. Alex Boraine and Janet Levy (Rondebosch, Cape Town, South Africa: Justice in Transition, 1995), and *Dealing with the Past: Truth and Reconciliation in South Africa*, ed. Alex Boraine, Janet Levy, and Ronel Scheffer (Cape Town, South Africa: IDASA, 1994). A complete, comparative survey of justice in times of transition may be found in Neil Kritz, ed., *Transitional Justice* (Washington, D.C.: United States Institute of Peace Press, 1995), 3 vols.

19. The process was controversial. In two judgments released by a chamber of the Appellate Court of Santiago, it was decided not to apply the amnesty law or the limitations on prosecution that it imposes on the grounds that the international law of human rights should prevail over domestic legislation. In the first judgment, which was released on September 26, 1994, the Appellate Court chose not to uphold a lower court's dismissal of a case against Osvaldo Romo, who was acused of the illegal detention, torture, and

murder of Lumi Videla, leader of the Movimiento de Izquierda Revolu-
cionaria (MIR). Lumi Videla had been detained by security forces on September 21, 1974 and then taken to a detention camp where she was tortured
to death. On November 3, 1974, her body was thrown into the Italian Embassy in Santiago. In its decision, the Appellate Court stated: "[that] the
Geneva Conventions of 1949, which are applicable to this case, determine
that the crimes investigated are neither subject to a statute of limitations nor
to amnesty. . ." (translation of an original document in author's possession).
In the second decision, the Appellate Court applied the same reasoning to
question the applicability of the amnesty law in human rights cases. This
case involved the kidnapping of Barbara Uribe and Francisco Van Jurick,
who had both been detained on July 10, 1974 by security forces and then disappeared. The court argued that kidnapping should be considered a crime
that continues to be committed until one can either prove that the victim has
been released or death has occurred. As a continuing crime, amnesty cannot
be granted because there is no evidence that it has ceased within the period
covered by the amnesty law. The court stated that the Geneva Convention of
1949 was in force in Chile during at least the first years after the coup; therefore, the crimes included in those conventions were not subject to any limitation of action or to amnesty. Despite the novelty of these decisions, both were
later reversed by the Supreme Court, which upheld the validity of the
amnesty law of 1978.

   20. On June 11, 1974, this indigenous student was detained by a group
of police and civilians. Cheuquepan was beaten and transferred to a police
barracks in Perquenco. He never returned home.

   21. On February 18, 1991, the case was reopened after the Rettig Commission released important additional information to the Court of Lautaro.
This information was enough to determine the names of the perpetrators
and the fate and whereabouts of Cheuquepan. Although the lower court
nevertheless decided to close the case in November 1991, the Appellate
Court of Temuco ordered it reopened. Finally, the perpetrators were sentenced by the lower court. This decision was upheld by the Appellate Court,
and the Supreme Court dismissed a request by the perpetrators to quash the
decision. The Supreme Court justified its decision to deny the request (which
had been based upon the refusal of the lower court to apply the amnesty law
of 1978) by declaring that the appeal had been improperly presented. The
Court said nothing about the substantive issue of the validity or applicability
of the amnesty law to this case.

   22. See, for example, the proposed Law 19.047, 1991. This law, named
after Francisco Cumplido, Minister of Justice under Aylwin, is known as
"Cumplido's Law." It had many features: (1) On the power of military
courts, the law sought to grant civil courts the competence to investigate and
punish crimes committed by both military personnel and civilians. (2) The
law also sought to amend the composition of the Martial Court, which is the
superior court of military jurisdiction. (3) The use of confessions, as evidence
to prove a crime, was limited. Confessions were to be dismissed in those

cases when they were obtained through torture or cruel treatment, or as a result of a period of extended isolation. (4) Additionally, the law called for the adequate treatment of those known as "presos politicos" (those imprisoned for political crimes) and for the full respect of their rights. (5) In order to avoid confusion, the law made a clear distinction between crimes against the state, military crimes, and terrorism. (6) The law also tried to eliminate penal sanctions for a group of crimes, for which punishments were too high in comparison with other crimes. (7) Finally, the law abrogated a series of other laws: for example, one that declared certain political parties illegal; another that permitted authorities to limit the entry of certain persons to the territory of Chile; and another that punished certain crimes against the state and that allowed the security forces to determine the rights of the detained.

23. For example, Judge Dobra Luksic of a lower court in Santiago identified, as detained and disappeared, many human remains that had been buried shortly after September 1973 in Patio 29. (Patio 29 is a section of Cementario General de Santiago, where unknown persons are currently buried.) Judge Germán Hermosilla located some of the remains of other victims who were detained and disappeared in Paine.

24. Presented on the grounds of efficiency, this increase in the Court's size would have permitted Aylwin to name, though with some restrictions, four new justices. The overall bill included many different proposals. Even though it was dropped after a period of congressional debate, one of the most important proposals was the idea of creating a National Counsel of the Judiciary, following the Italian postwar model. Among the proposals finally approved were major changes in the law governing judicial careers.

25. According to the Chilean judicial career system, the president only has a choice among five names submitted by the Supreme Court itself. Thus, one should not assume that all seven judges would necessarily share Aylwin or Frei's values and views on human rights issues.

26. See *Report of the Chilean National Commission*, pp. 118–119.

27. *El Mercurio*, March 5, 1991.

28. On May 13, 1991, the Supreme Court responded to the commission's criticism of the Chilean court system regarding its behavior during the dictatorship. First, the Court declared that it did not accept criticism made by an entity not entitled to do so. The Court added that the commission, in its attempt to spread an absurd criticism, did not hesitate to call into question its own competence. The Court concluded that the commission's judgment against the judiciary was passionate, hasty, and tendentious. See *El Mercurio*, May 16, 1991.

29. This case was known as the Chanfreau case, after the victim's name.

30. According to the Chilean constitution, Supreme Court judges may be removed from their positions if they are found guilty of gross neglect of duty by the Senate, and only after the Chamber of Deputies has charged them.

31. *Americas Watch* 6, no. 6 (May 1994).

32. Espinoza was the first to enter this jail, and Contreras the second.

Aside from Contreras and Espinoza, another eleven former members of the armed forces have been convicted for their crimes. The former members of the police include Colonel Guillermo González Betancourt (Degollados case, life imprisonment), Corporal Alejandro Sáez Mardones (Degollados case, life imprisonment), Sergeant José Fuentes Castro (Degollados case, life imprisonment), Sergeant Claudio Salazar Fuentes (Degollados case, life imprisonment), Captain Patricio Zamora (Degollados case, fifteen years), Major Manuel Muñoz Gamboa (Degollados case, five years and one day), Subofficer Juan Luis Huaiquimilla Cañoepan (Degollados case, five years), Corporal Luis Ernesto Jofré Herrera (Degollados case, five years), Captain Héctor Díaz Anderson (Godoy E. case, three years and one day), Subofficer Armando Cabrera Aguilar (Fernández case, six years). There was also one former member of the army, Major Carlos Herrera Jiménez (Fernández case, ten years).

33.   The government's approach was to push for a draft amending certain provisions of the constitution that it considered undemocratic. It proposed to eliminate nonelected senators (known as designated senators), to incorporate more civilians into the National Security Council, to confine the prerogative to summon the National Security Council to the president, and to change the composition and operations of the Constitutional Court.

34.   This draft expresses the following ideas: Article 1 indicates how judges should conduct the investigation of people missing between September 1973 and March 1978, the period covered by the amnesty law. A judge cannot bring charges, arrest, or indict alleged perpetrators. Both the alleged perpetrators and witnesses enjoy several guarantees: their identities can be kept secret; their testimony is also secret and is to be destroyed at the end of the investigation; their testimony can be taken outside the courtroom. If a judge decides to take testimony from a member of the armed forces or if he needs to visit a military area or demand information from the armed forces, these activities are to be kept secret and are to be carried out by a judge of the appellate court designated by the military court. To speed up these cases, it is proposed that the Supreme Court appoint one or more criminal judges exclusively charged with investigating cases of detained persons and the disappeared. Article 4, which pertains to the general gathering of information about missing persons, includes remarkable guarantees for those who provide information to the courts. They cannot be arrested and they are not required to reveal the source of their information. Their names can be kept secret, and they are required to provide only the information necessary to locate missing persons; it is not mandatory that they provide the names of perpetrators.

35.   *La Nación*, February 3, 1995.

6

Living Well Is the Best Revenge:
The Hungarian Approach to Judging the Past

Gábor Halmai and Kim Lane Scheppele

AS OLD GOVERNMENTS throughout the former Second World fell or negotiated themselves away in the fast-forward days of 1989, the new European governments that replaced them were immediately confronted with a question to which there was no satisfactory answer: What should these new governments do about the past? Millions of the living and many millions more of the dead suffered substantial harm that had never been redressed; for many, the possibility of making lives of which they could be proud had been undermined in decades of political restriction. Calls for revenge, for "lustration," or at least for information about those who had committed these human rights violations could be heard throughout the region. But the new governments answered these calls very differently.

Under pressure from former eastern German dissidents, the German government responded by opening the files and purging the past through publicity and trials. The Czech Republic, with perhaps the harshest approach, required nearly everyone to be checked against the records of the secret police and to be presumed guilty if listed there. People could go to court to reverse the presumption of guilt, and nearly all who did were found to have been listed erroneously, but those whose guilt remained were excluded from almost all aspects of public life. Poland wrestled with the question and in the end did not ask it too loudly in public.[1] Many other countries in the region have not even asked the question yet.

Against this background, the Hungarian solution to the problem is perhaps the most intriguing, for it tries to solve the problem through the strict application of the principle of human rights for all—even and perhaps especially for those who did not respect the human rights of others. Behind this approach is the belief that the best way to deal with those who operated outside the rule of law, as the former state-party officials and functionaries surely did, is to refuse to follow the outlaw state's own inner logic of arbitrariness and disregard for individual self-determination. By operating under a strong human rights approach, Hungary has adopted the view that the best way to deal with the past is to do better now. In other words, for the new Hungarian state, "living well is the best revenge."

In this essay, we will review the debate over and solutions to the question of what to do about the outlaw system of the past in the first five years after the "change of system"[2] in Hungary. The road eventually taken was paved by the newly created Constitutional Court, which generally struck down statutes passed by the first elected parliament; the parliament itself generally voted for punitive means of dealing with the past. Briefly, the Hungarian Parliament wanted to extend the statute of limitations so that ordinary courts could try those who had committed crimes in the past, but the Constitutional Court ruled that this was unconstitutional because it violated the rule of law, with the narrow exception of actions that could be deemed crimes in international law under the Nuremberg principles. The parliament also wanted to lustrate public officials who had been informers for the secret police, and the court limited the ways in which this could be done, so as to preserve the rights of informational self-determination of those who were accused of spying as well as the rights of those spied on. Though the parliament and the Constitutional Court disagreed about precisely what was to be done with those who had committed crimes that were never punished, engaged in surveillance against fellow citizens, or generally maintained the police state under the state-party regime, both the parliament and the court followed established legal procedures in their actions after 1989, and in the end the parliament respected the authority of the court to determine what was and was not constitutional. It was this agreement on legality and its importance that eventually won out, through many different stages over a number of years. It is, however, possible to see now that Hungary neither ignored the past nor allowed that past to morally and legally compromise the present.

Retroactive Justice:
Parliamentary Actions and Constitutional Court Reactions

Hungary's political transformation from a state-party system to a multi-party democratic one was negotiated at the National Roundtable in the summer of 1989. During the Roundtable, leaders of the Hungarian Socialist Workers' Party (for which the Hungarian acronym is MSzMP) met with leaders of the self-appointed opposition groups to plan Hungary's first election and the related changes in its system of government. Different participants in the Roundtable say different things about whether there was ever an agreement not to prosecute those who had been involved in maintaining the state-party system. Some have insisted publicly that there was never a promise to let the old communists go without a reckoning; others say that there was a general promise of amnesty; still others claim that there was an informal amnesty agreement limited to those from the MSzMP who participated in the Roundtable talks. Whatever deal was done in the Roundtable, however, one thing was clear: the elected Hungarian governments since 1990 have never made a general attempt to go after all those who maintained the party state. Instead, efforts at dealing with the past through the criminal law were focused specifically on those who had violated criminal laws in effect in Hungary at the time of their conduct. Even over this limited attempt to come to grips with a state that operated outside the rule of law, however, there were major disagreements and constitutional problems. And the story is still not over.

The first parliamentary election in 1990 produced a fragile government coalition of three mostly conservative, center-right parties: The Hungarian Democratic Forum (the MDF), the Christian Democrats, and the Smallholders Party. The former communists, running as the renamed Hungarian Socialist Party (the MSzP), had suffered a major defeat in the election, and so the new parliament was dominated by those who had been opposed, some quite vocally, to the state-party system. Some of the MPs had served time in prison or been systematically harassed by the former regime. Most of these MPs, however, were among the Alliance of Free Democrats (SzDSz), a political party that was not in the first coalition government and that generally opposed punitive measures to deal with the former state-party officials and functionaries. Over the opposition of the members of the SzDSz, the political party that had arguably been the most affected by political persecution, the center-right coalition government embarked on a program to try to find justice through criminal prosecution of those who had committed crimes in the state-party regime.

The governing coalition, however, was having a hard time governing decisively from the beginning. The three government parties developed substantial disagreements among themselves as their co-tenure went on, and since their majority in the parliament was not overwhelming to begin with, much of the first elected government's term was dominated by a persistent need to make various special deals with the various factions who were threatening to withhold their crucial votes from the government program. It may have been the case that the issue of retroactive justice was "given" to the strong anticommunists within the Hungarian Democratic Forum (MDF) in the parliament in exchange for their cooperation on other bills, but this may never be publicly known for certain. In any event, two members of the MDF's parliamentary fraction, Zsolt Zétényi and Péter Takacs, took on this issue and pushed it through the parliament.

In this atmosphere, a little over a year into its four-year term, the first elected parliament passed a law concerning the prosecution of criminal offenses committed between December 21, 1944 and May 2, 1990. The law provided that the statute of limitations start over again as of May 2, 1990 (the date that the first elected parliament took office) for the crimes of treason, voluntary manslaughter, and infliction of bodily harm resulting in death—but only in those cases where the "state's failure to prosecute said offenses was based on political reasons."[3] The bill was controversial, since its sponsors, Zétényi and Takacs, were members of the MDF but did not clearly have the support of the highest officials of their own party behind them. The debates surrounding this bill showed that there was a tension in the governing coalition between those who wanted to move on without dwelling on the past and those who very much wanted to remember and do something about previous abuses. The most intensely anti-communist members of the new government won the day with this law. As with a number of other laws passed in the first elected government's tenure, disputes within the coalition were patched over temporarily in the parliament, whose members assumed that the Constitutional Court would have the last word on the constitutionality of the agreements.

In this law as it was eventually passed, the parliament aimed only at punishing those crimes that had occurred as defined offenses under the state-party system, specifically in cases where the perpetrators of the crimes had never been prosecuted because they had been closely associated with the state party. The parliament did not try to criminalize actions that had been legal in the old system and it did not allow repeat trials for those who had duly been tried in the past (even if they had been acquitted by politically motivated judges). Either of these approaches clearly would have been legally problematic. Instead, the parliament bill only extended the statute of limitations for previously defined crimes, and then only for those who had not already been prosecuted because their prosecutions had been blocked by the government that just a year before had gone out of power. Given the potential scope of all crimes that could have been prosecuted, the Hungarian Parliament's attempt was quite narrowly drawn.

The President of Hungary, Árpád Göncz, did not sign the bill but instead referred it to the Constitutional Court, which was already up and running. The new Constitutional Court had started its operation on January 1, 1990, fully five months before the first elected parliament went into session. By the time this case arose, the court had already made extensive use of its very broad powers to strike down legislation frequently, and the president could expect a strong response.[4]

The Constitutional Court was itself a creature of the Roundtable and had originally been an idea of the MSzMP Justice Ministry, which had proposed the idea nearly a year before the Roundtable began. Members of the Opposition Roundtable at first were suspicious of the idea, but after a series of constitutional changes were

adopted that made the new constitution, as one Opposition Roundtable representative put it, "worth protecting," then the opposition
went along. The Constitutional Court Act that legally set up the court
was drafted by a subcommittee of the National Roundtable, and it
had been voted into law by the outgoing MSzMP parliament. But the
judges who were appointed to the court represented almost every organized set of political interests that found voice in the first elected
parliament. Five of the judges, representing a variety of factions, had
been agreed to at the Roundtable itself. Five others were elected by
the new parliament after the first national elections were held. In all
three of the governments under which the court has operated (the
MSzMP government in 1990, the MDF government from 1990 until
1994, and now the MSzP/SzDSz government since 1994), the court
has interpreted its powers expansively and has struck down roughly
one challenged law in three.

In the retroactive justice case, Göncz's petition said that "the substance of [constitutional] concern is whether section 1 of the law violates the principles of a constitutional rule-of-law state [*jogállam*]."[5] It
asked whether the law was therefore in violation of Article 57(4) of the
Constitution, which states that "No one shall be declared guilty and
sentenced for an act which was not a criminal offense under Hungarian law at the time when it was committed,"[6] and with Article 2(1) of
the Constitution, according to which the Hungarian Republic is a constitutional rule-of-law state.[7] Göncz's petition went on to question
whether the law did not violate the "historically developed legal doctrine of 'nullum crimen sine lege,' which is internationally recognized
as protecting a human right," and "the basic constitutional principle
that every citizen can have faith in the trustworthiness of the law and
the state." In addition, it raised the issues that the provisions may be
"overly general" and "vague" as well as making an "arbitrary and unreasonable distinction among the perpetrators of the same criminal offense on the basis of the state's reason for prosecution for such
offenses." Given that this petition came from a man who himself had
been sentenced to prison for life after his involvement in the uprising
of 1956, it showed a remarkable ability to think in constitutional/legal
terms about an issue that might well have generated emotional reactions and the desire for personal revenge.

The Constitutional Court in its unanimous decision, 11/1992

(III.5) AB h., struck down the parliament's first attempt at retroactive justice as unconstitutional for most of the reasons that Göncz's petition identified. The court said that the proposed law violated legal security, a principle that should be guaranteed as fundamental in a constitutional rule-of-law state. In addition, the language of the law was vague (because, among other things, "political reasons" had changed so much over the long time frame covered by the law and the crimes themselves had changed definition during that time as well). The basic principles of criminal law—that there shall be no punishment without a crime and no crime without a law—were clearly violated by retroactively changing the statute of limitations; the only sorts of changes in the law that may apply retroactively, the court said, are those changes that work to the benefit of defendants. Citing the constitutional provisions that Hungary is a constitutional rule-of-law state and that there can be no punishment without a valid law in effect at the time, the court declared the law to be unconstitutional and sent it back to the president.

But what is perhaps most interesting is the reasoning that the court used to arrive at these conclusions, because it is the backbone of all future rulings that the court would make on questions of the past. The court used the opportunity of this case to educate the parliament and the government by explaining just what the ideal of the constitutional state means:

> That Hungary is a *Rechtsstaat* is both a statement of fact and a statement of policy. *Rechtsstaat* becomes a reality when the Constitution is truly and unconditionally given effect. For the legal system, the "change of system" [*rendszerváltás*] means . . . that the Constitution of the *Rechtsstaat* must be brought into harmony. . . with the whole system of laws. Not only must the regulations and the operation of the state institutions comport strictly with the Constitution, but also the Constitution's values and its "conceptual culture" must imbue the whole of society. This is the rule of law and this is how the Constitution becomes a reality. . . . For the organs of the State, participation in this process is a constitutional duty.[8]

After setting up a clear role for the Constitution—it must provide the standard against which all other laws and political institutions are judged—the court then addressed the question of the legal status of the pre-1989 laws compared with the post-1989 laws, a question that goes to the heart of the issue of the relation of past and present:

> The "change of system" proceeded on the basis of legality. . . . The politically revolutionary changes adopted by the Constitution and the fundamental laws were all enacted in a procedurally impeccable manner, in full compliance with the old legal system's regulation of the power to legislate, thereby gaining their binding force. . . . With respect to its validity, there is no distinction between "pre-Constitution" and "post-Constitution" law. The legitimacy of the different [political] systems during the past half century is irrelevant from this perspective; that is, from the viewpoint of the constitutionality of laws, it does not comprise[9] a meaningful category. Irrespective of its date of enactment, each and every valid law must comport with the new Constitution. Likewise, constitutional review does not admit two different standards for the review of laws. (136)

Taking a basically positivist view that the validity of a law is determined by its pedigree—that is, by being enacted in a certain way—the court argued that the legal regime of the state-party system and the new democratic Hungary constituted a single continuous legal tradition and that there was no basis for treating the laws of the prior regime any differently than laws of the present one.

Because the legal system is therefore formally a unified whole, the court said, the laws enacted before 1989 have exactly the same legal force and carry exactly the same expectation that they will be predictably applied as those enacted afterwards. The court went on to argue that the certainty and predictability of the law require that "retroactive modification of the law and legal relations is permitted only within very narrow confines" (138). That left open a small window through which to argue that the historical change of political system might be one of these circumstances that would allow the laws of the past regime to be legitimately modified after the fact by the present regime. But the court firmly closed that window.

"A state under the rule of law cannot be created by undermining the rule of law," the court declared. "The certainty of the law based on formal and objective principles is more important than necessarily partial and subjective justice" (138). And the criminal law in particular needs to be certain and not retroactively modified, even in the pursuit of other constitutional goals, because criminal law protections for the defendant are so important that "the presumption of innocence cannot be restricted on account of some other constitutional right" (140). Further,

> [I]n a constitutional state, the violation of rights can only be remedied by upholding the rule of law. The legal system of a *Rechtsstaat* cannot deprive anyone of legal guarantees. These guarantees are basic rights appertaining to all. Wherever the value of the rule of law is entrenched, not even a just demand can justify the disregard of the *Rechtsstaat's* legal guarantees. Justice and moral argument may, of course, motivate penal sanction, but its legal foundation must be constitutional. (141)

Everyone has legal rights in a constitutional rule-of-law state, the court said, and from this it follows that even those who have violated the very principles of a constitutional rule-of-law state itself will be assured these same rights. Given this analysis, the retroactive justice law was clearly unconstitutional because it violated the principle of legal security, which is one of the most important principles in Hungarian constitutional law. Legal security requires that

> the whole of the law, the specific parts and provisions included in the Penal Code, be clear, unambiguous, their impact predictable and their consequences foreseeable by those . . . whom the law address[es]. From the principle of predictability and foreseeability, the criminal law's prohibition of the use of retroactive legislation, especially ex post facto legislation and reasoning by analogy, directly follows. (141)

The statute of limitations must place a temporal restriction on the state's powers to punish, the court continued, because a constitutional state cannot have unlimited punitive powers. Moreover,

> Failure to apprehend [a suspected criminal] or the dereliction of duties by the authorities which exercise the punitive powers of the state is a risk borne by the state. If the statute of limitation had run, immunity from criminal punishment is conferred upon the person as a matter of right. (142)

As prior decisions of the court had declared, any restrictions of fundamental rights guaranteed in the Constitution could only be justified when they were unavoidable, necessary, and proportional to the objective that the state wanted to attain. Criminal law, which has as its purpose the restriction of otherwise constitutionally guaranteed liberty in cases where someone can be shown to have committed a criminal offense, must operate in this manner. But "[n]ot even in an extraordinary situation, state of emergency or grave danger does the Constitution permit the restriction or suspension of the criminal law's constitutional fundamental principles," the court said (143). In addition,

> In a constitutional *Rechtsstaat,* the criminal law is not merely an instrument but it protects and embodies values. . . . Criminal law is the legal basis for the exercise of punitive powers as well as a guarantee of freedom for the protection of individual rights. Though criminal law protects values, as warranty of freedom, it cannot become an instrument for moral purges in the process of protecting moral values. (144)

The Constitutional Court, seeing the drive to extend the statute of limitations as a "moral purge," headed off this effort with an opinion on the principles of constitutionalism and the rule of law.

But this was not the end of the matter.

In February 1993, the parliament tried once again to impose penalties retroactively through three different actions. The same factions that had wanted retroactive justice were still present in the parliament and were still eager, even after the Constitutional Court decision, to see "justice" done. First, the parliament voted in an "authoritative resolution" (which is not a law, but is instead an interpretive guideline to be used in conjunction with understanding duly passed laws) to exempt the period between 1944 and 1989 from the time that could be counted in interpreting the statute of limitations law. This would have much the same effect as the law that the parliament had previously passed on the subject, even though it used different legal means to do so. A clear effort to get around the Constitutional Court's decision, this resolution was appealed to the Constitutional Court by some opposition MPs.[10] Predictably, the court, in its decision 41/1993 (VI.30) AB h., declared this move by the parliament unconstitutional as well. The court said that this resolution was procedurally unconstitutional because it affected fundamental rights of citizens through some means other than a duly enacted statute, and this violated the principle of legal certainty in a different way than that principle had been violated by the prior retroactive justice law. In addition, the resolution was substantively unconstitutional because it was ex post facto legislation of the sort that had been struck down before in the court's earlier decision.

Second, the parliament tried almost at the same time as it passed this resolution to enact another statute, this time amending the Criminal Procedure Act of 1973 to make it obligatory for public prosecutors to level accusations in certain cases, even if the crimes had occurred long enough ago for the statute of limitations to run out. President Göncz once again refused to sign the law and referred it to the Constitutional court for its review, and the court once again, in its decision 42/1993 (VI. 30) AB h., struck down this law for the same reasons that it struck down the first attempt to alter the statute of limitations. Retroactive justice would not be allowed even if it came through an order from the parliament to the public prosecutor's office.

But in a third attempt, the parliament tried something different. In February 1993, it enacted a law "Concerning the Procedures in the Matter of Certain Criminal Offenses During the 1956 October Revolution and Freedom Struggle." Instead of changing the statute of limitations or instructing officers of the government to behave in certain ways, this law relied on the international law principles pertaining to crimes against humanity and war crimes in order to prosecute those who had forcefully put down the 1956 Hungarian popular uprising against the Soviet-backed government. For those activities that might be defined as crimes against humanity or war crimes under the Nuremberg principles, there is no fixed statute of limitations in international law. Going after those crimes, which might be defined as "war crimes," the parliament pointed to international law as the relevant "rule of law regime" to follow.

Here again, the president did not sign the law, but instead referred it to the Constitutional Court for its review, this time asking the court to examine not only the constitutional provisions earlier used in these cases, but also various international human rights conventions. As Göncz pointed out in his petition, such conventions count as domestic Hungarian law under Article 7 of the Constitution, which incorporates all international agreements, so the invocation of international agreements might have provided a different justification for the new laws.

This time, the Constitutional Court struck down the new law only in part. Ruling in its decision 53/1993 (X.13) AB h. that some of the crimes specified in the new law were merely domestic crimes under Hungarian law and not international war crimes or crimes against humanity, the court struck down those parts of the law extending the statute of limitations for these purely domestic crimes on the same grounds as before. But there were two exceptions to the principle that the statute of limitations generally barred late prosecutions, exceptions that the Hungarian Parliament could constitutionally invoke: (1) if there was no statute of limitations in force in Hungarian law at the time of the specific crime, then a crime could be prosecuted long after the fact, or (2) if the crime was a crime against humanity or a war crime and so was covered by international law rules, then prosecutions might also go forward regardless of the statute of limitations provisions of domestic Hungarian law.

As the court noted, Hungary is a signatory to both the Geneva Convention of 1949 for the Protection of War Victims and the New York Convention of 1968 for the Non-Applicability of Statutory Limitations to War Crimes and Crimes against Humanity. It is bound by these agreements as if they were domestic law because Article 7 of the Hungarian Constitution provides that the "legal system of Hungary shall respect the universally accepted rules of international law." But precisely how were these two systems of law, the domestic and the international, to be reconciled, given that the Hungarian Constitutional Court had already determined that the domestic statute of limitations for crimes committed in the past could not be extended? The court took up this question in some detail in its opinion; generally it found that the categories of war crimes and crimes against humanity were thought by the international community to be so grave that they warranted setting up procedures and institutions to handle them independently of the way they were handled in domestic law. A state could choose to mount such prosecutions itself, however, acting "upon the mandate given to it by the community of nations, according to the conditions imposed by international law." This punitive power, that can be exercised either by the international community or by the individual state, "functions differently and within different constraints than that of the individual states; the differences are attributable to the specific characteristics of these prosecuted criminal offenses, especially the danger they contain for the whole of humanity. . . ."[11] And in particular, crimes against humanity and war crimes have no specified statutes of limitations in international law.

Crimes in international law are defined by international conventions and norms, and those actions which count as crimes in international law may not necessarily be the same as those defined by domestic law, said the court. For a crime to be punishable under international legal standards, the crime must be defined as a crime in that body of law even if it is not so defined in the domestic law of a given state. The general maxim that there can be no crime without a law covers not only crimes in the domestic law of particular countries but also crimes in international law as well. The situation may arise, then, when something is defined as a crime in international law even though it is not defined as a crime within the state where it occurred, but this would not prevent a state from prosecuting the crime under international law instead of under domestic law. This invocation of international legal norms by domestic courts, the court noted, is not only not barred, but specifically allowed under the European Convention.

So, could Hungary prosecute those who operated under the protection of the state-party system but who committed war crimes or crimes against humanity, even if the domestic statute of limitations for these crimes had expired? The court answered yes, noting that

> Article 7 of the Constitution mandates that, alongside the domestic law, another legal system—certain rules of international law—must concurrently be given effect. Giving effect to international law concerning these crimes is the condition for the participation in the community of nations, which the Constitution expressly recognizes, mandates its application and harmonization with domestic law, and

the domestic law's interpretation of those obligations in a divergent manner does not alter the state's international obligations. It is isolation from or rejection of international law which is what would be contrary to Article 7 of the Constitution. But what occurs in this case is not the abandonment of the principle of nullum crimen but its limitation to the sphere of domestic law.

Although war crimes are defined in international law, there is no specifically defined statute of limitations in international law to regulate the prosecution of such crimes, the court observed. Therefore, countries could generally use their own domestic statutes of limitations in their domestic courts. But since Hungary had signed the New York Convention, which explicitly refused any statute of limitations restrictions for the prosecution of crimes defined in international law, Hungary had already agreed not to invoke such rules for war crimes and crimes against humanity even in its domestic courts. In these crimes, then, Hungary could not use its own domestic statute of limitations, but had to accept the international convention's rules. Prosecutions for war crimes and for crimes against humanity could proceed, then, even though domestic rules would not allow it.

The court went on to criticize the parliament's interpretation of international law and to instruct the parliament in the way such interpretations had to be made to avoid turning purely domestic crimes into crimes against humanity or war crimes. For example, the court noted, "homicide qualifies as a crime against humanity only if it is committed on a 'massive scale' or as part of a 'large scale regular attack.'" Telling the parliament to go back and modify its law to make it consistent with the court's ruling, the court concluded that there could be prosecutions of some of those who had committed previously unprosecuted horrible deeds under the prior regime, but only if these deeds rose to the level of horror defined by war crimes or crimes against humanity.

One week after the decision of the Constitutional Court, the parliament made some of the corrections demanded by the court and the new law was passed unanimously. The law was promulgated immediately by the president and came into force on October 30, 1993 (Act XC of 1993).

With this new legal framework, the Ministry of Justice investigated fifty episodes of mass shootings that took place during the revolution of 1956 between October 23 and December 28 of that year. The results of the investigation were then given to the Chief Prosecutor, who proceeded to bring charges quite quickly in several of the cases.

The first trial started in June 1994 in the Budapest City Court (the Court of the Capital), which is the court with exclusive jurisdiction to hear these cases. In January 1995, two different chambers within the court passed two different judgments that were each appealed to the Supreme Court. In the first case, the shootings in the city of Salgótarján in December 1956, when government forces shot into unarmed crowds of demonstrators, were held to be "prohibited acts in the case of armed conflict not of an international character" (meaning that they were not war crimes, but could count as crimes against humanity). Two of the twelve defendants were found guilty and sentenced to five years in prison. But in a similar case in another chamber of the Budapest City Court, the court ruled that the shootings were not such prohibited acts within international law, and therefore the domestic statute of limitations was applied to end the procedure. When the cases were appealed to the Supreme Court,[12] most people expected that the Court would make a ruling specifically on the concrete cases before it. But the President of the Supreme Court surprised many by sending a petition together with the Public Prosecutor to the Constitutional Court, asking for an abstract constitutional review of the new law under which the Salgótarján cases were tried.

In the view of the Supreme Court president[13] and the public prosecutor, stated in their petition to the Constitutional Court, the law that allowed prosecution of war crimes was unconstitutional because parliament had not redefined all the relevant international law crimes to comport with the previous decision of the Constitutional Court. In addition, the law was unconstitutionally incomplete because it failed to specify the procedures under which cases could be brought before the ordinary courts of Hungary. While international law provided a clear definition for war crimes and indicated that there should be no statute of limitations for such offenses, the more precise details of criminal procedure to be used in these cases (for example, what sorts of punishments could be legitimately meted out?)

were not in fact concretely specified under international law. Since it was clear that Hungarian criminal procedure did not apply to these cases either (because all criminal matters had statutes of limitations in the Hungarian criminal procedure code), these cases were legally unregulated from a procedural point of view. Therefore the law was unconstitutionally incomplete and could not be used for criminal prosecutions in concrete cases.

In a decision in September 1996, 36/1996 (IX.4) AB h., the Constitutional Court agreed with the Supreme Court president's and the public prosecutor's petition. It ruled that the war crimes law as amended by the parliament was unconstitutional because the parliament had failed to follow completely the directives of the Constitutional Court in the previous retroactive justice case. The new Hungarian statute, in the view of the court, still violated international law by defining war crimes differently from the standard international law interpretation. The court ruled, however, that the ordinary courts of Hungary could directly apply substantive international law without any further amendments from or direction by the parliament because the international covenants and not the Hungarian statute were the relevant laws under which the cases had to be tried. In the view of the court, however, the parliament *did* have to amend the Hungarian criminal procedure code before the ordinary courts could hold more trials, because no international procedural norms bound such war crimes prosecutions and the Hungarian criminal procedure code did not fill in these gaps. Without procedural norms in place, the ordinary courts could not go further in trying suspected war criminals. So, the court found, the Supreme Court president and the public prosecutor were also correct to point out that the new law failed to specify an adequate system of criminal procedure.

As we write, the parliament has not yet acted, but it is expected to comply with the court decision, even though the government has changed since the last law was passed. The new government, dominated as it is by former members of the MSzMP, has no particular incentives to revisit the past, but these leaders have shown themselves willing to comply with the Constitutional Court decisions, even when those decisions go against policies that they very much wanted to adopt. The Supreme Court has not yet decided the appeals, and more cases will no doubt be brought. While the general legal framework is clear at the constitutional level, the specific degree of culpability in individual cases has not yet been determined.

Spies and Files: The Problem of Lustration

Crimes of the past were handled through a scrupulous application of principles of human rights, and problems generated by the ongoing presence of spies and files were handled in exactly the same way. In Hungary, as in other countries emerging from surveillance states, those who injured others by collecting, storing, and sometimes using private information had to be reckoned with. But as the Constitutional Court stated in its critical decision on the matter in December 1994, 60/1994 (XII.24) AB h., it doesn't do to repeat the mistakes of the past. Now, everyone has rights at stake in this matter, even the spies.

The secret police files that the new elected governments inherited had posed a serious question since the demise of the state-party system. What should the state do not only about the files but also about the spies whose reports had constituted the files? Unlike the issue about prosecution for past crimes, where there was widespread public agreement about the heinous quality of the actions and only the methods to be used to address this were in doubt, the underlying moral blameworthiness of the spies was not so clear. Could someone be punished for caving in to blackmail and writing reports because he or she had been threatened? Could the information in the files themselves be trusted? In the days after the state party had negotiated itself out of existence but before power was actually transferred to an elected government, reports had circulated that many files had been altered and some files destroyed. Most believed, however, that new names could not be added to the files. But could the new government proceed now to use the files to implicate those whose names were still included as informers? And what of those who had been spied on? Did they have the right to see their own files? The cluster of questions and the difficulty of answering them contributed to a rather long delay before the parliament got around to trying to find a solution.

The parliament passed a law early in 1994, toward the end of the first elected government's term of office, which included a compromise solution to the spies issue. It neither ignored the demand that something be done about former informants who might be in public office nor authorized a sweeping purge of people with such pasts. Instead, the law set up panels of three judges whose job it would be to go through the secret police files of all of those who currently held a certain set of public offices (including the president, government ministers, members of parliament, constitutional judges, ordinary court judges, some journalists, people who held high posts in state universities or state-owned companies, as well as a specified list of other high government officials). Each of these people would have to undergo background checks in which their files would be scrutinized to see whether they had a lustratable role[14] in the ongoing operation of the previous surveillance state. If so, then the panel would notify the person of the evidence and give him or her a chance to resign from public office. Only if the person chose to stay on would the panel publicize the information. If the person contested the information found in the files, then prior to disclosure, he or she could appeal to a court which would then conduct a review of evidence *in camera* and make a judgment in the specific case. If the person accepted a judgment against him or her and chose to resign, then the information would still remain secret.

After the law had already gone into effect and the review of the first set of members of parliament was already underway, the law was challenged by a petition to the Hungarian Constitutional Court. The court ruled in its decision 60/1994 (XII. 24) AB h. that although the general framework of the law was largely constitutional because it respected the crucial right of informational self-determination of spies, there were still constitutional problems with the law because it failed to respect the equivalent rights of informational self-determination of those who were spied on as well as failing to appropriately limit the scope of lustration to those whose activities were clearly of public relevance.

The lustration decision was delicate *politically*, since the lustration process had already begun. Also, because the second set of elections brought back into power the reform wing of the MSzMP, now under the banner of the Socialist Party (MSzP), many of the government officials being lustrated had held important positions in the state-party regime and it was already known that they had had access to the reports on surveillance activities. Such access constituted a lustratable offense.[15] It also was delicate *constitutionally*, because the decision represented the clash of two constitutional principles: the rights of informational self-determination of individuals (in this case, the spies) and the rights of public access to legitimately public data by everyone (including those who were spied on). Both principles have explicit constitutional protection: (1) informational self-determination is authorized by Article 59 of the Hungarian Constitution, which guarantees the right to the protection of private secrets and personal data, and (2) the right of access to public information is authorized under Article 61, which guarantees the free expression of opinion and the right "to acquire and disseminate data which is in the public interest." Before the lustration case, both principles had been upheld in strong form by the court in a series of other cases that involved, most importantly, the universal personal identification number (the use of which became unconstitutional under the right of informational self-determination) and access to the Communist Party archives (which was guaranteed under the right of access to information of public interest). The lustration case, however, pitted the two principles against each other because the information to be protected in the name of personal privacy was exactly that information that might be thought to be in the public interest.

The 1994 law requiring background checks on a list of influential persons set up a system that provided for the continuing secrecy of the files.[16] The three-judge panels created by the law were given special powers and immunities to look into the secret files and determine which of the listed individuals had been agents or informers under the state-party regime. This process was to be conducted entirely in secret, without public hearings and indeed without the persons to be lustrated being informed of the investigation until after it had been concluded, when, as already noted, they would be given the choice of resigning, contesting the determination in court, or staying in office and having the information made public.

The files themselves had been created under a series of laws, including a 1987 decree of the Presidential Council with the force of a law on state secrets. This decree classified as a potential state secret any information that would be dangerous to the Hungarian state or to any other political, economic, or defense interest. It allowed the speaker of the parliament, the prime minister, the president of the Supreme Court, the attorney general, leaders of state organs, or leaders of social organizations[17] to classify information as a secret if, in the view of any of them, the information endangered anything in this diffuse range of interests. [18] And though the regime that had enacted the regulation had since fallen away, the old state secret decree was still on the books and the files created in this way were still being maintained as state secrets at the time the lustration case arose. (The parliament has since enacted a new state secrets law that changes the way state secrets are classified.)

Taking the whole range of issues, from the constitutionality of the lustration process to the continued secrecy of the security apparatus files, the Constitutional Court attempted to balance a range of interests. First, the court held that the maintenance of this vast store of secret records was incompatible with the maintenance of a state under the rule of law, since such records would never have been constitutionally compiled in the first place in a rule-of-law state. But the fact that the records now existed posed other problems, including the freedom of access to information in the files both by an interested public and by individuals whose names appeared in the files either as subjects or as the agents. Disclosing the files to an interested public also would mean disclosing information of great personal importance to the individuals mentioned. Since individuals have a personal right of self-determination under the Hungarian Constitution, what is left of the claim of public freedom of access to information in determining what can be disclosed from the security apparatus files?

To resolve these questions, the court made an important distinction. It held that public persons have a smaller sphere of personal privacy than other individuals in a democratic state. As a result, more information about such public persons may be disclosed from the security files than would be permitted in the case of persons not holding influential positions, so conflicts between privacy and freedom of information should be resolved differently for the two groups. With this, the court placed the problem back in the hands of the parliament as a "political issue," with the instructions that the parliament is free neither to destroy all the records nor to maintain the absolute secrecy of them, since much of what they contain is information of public interest.

The court also found that the parliament had more remedial work to do on other parts of the law before it could pass constitutional muster. The specific list of persons to be lustrated needed to be changed because it was unconstitutionally arbitrary. In particular, the court found that the category of journalists who were lustratable was both too broad—by including those who produced music and entertainment programs in the public television as well as those who, more relevantly, produced news—and also too narrow—by excluding some clearly influential journalists who produced news for the private electronic media. By lustrating all journalists who worked for the public media and excluding all those who worked for the private media, the law failed to tailor its procedures to fit the situations where having such a past would be relevant to the present. Either all journalists who have as part of their job influencing public opinion— that is, those who are the leaders in news production—must be lustrated or none may be, the court held. Parliament could choose either course. The court did not, however, find the extension of the lustration process to journalists in the private media to be a violation either of the freedom of the press or a violation of the informational self-determination of journalists. Instead, all those who, in the words of the 1994 law, "participate in the shaping of the public will" are acceptable candidates for lustration, as long as all those in the category are similarly included. Extending lustration to officials of universities and colleges and to the top executives of full or majority state-owned businesses was declared unconstitutional, however, since these persons "neither exercise authority nor participate in public affairs," according to the court. A separate provision allowing members of the clergy to be lustrated was struck down for procedural reasons because the procedures to be applied to the clergy did not include as many safeguards as those applied to others.

Another unconstitutional omission[19] in the law, according to the Constitutional Court, concerned the rights of "victims," those people who had been spied on and whose personal information was also contained in the files. Noting that those individuals had rights as well—particularly rights of access to the files as well as rights to destroy the files that were kept on them—the court left to the parliament the task of ensuring these rights in a manner consistent with the equal rights of those who might have been implicated as agents by the records and who are not currently public persons. The parliament was given nine months to rework the law to take all of these various rights and obligations into account.

After the Constitutional Court's lustration decision, the process that was already underway to check public officials slowed down dramatically. The parliament had to rewrite the law, but not the part that pertained to themselves or other high government officials like the president, ministers, or judges. Only the parts having to do with journalists and other groups more peripheral to state decision-making were affected, so the lustration process for the first group did not have to stop because the scope of the second group was being revised. But around the time that the court issued its decision, news appeared in the press that two of the three judges on the panel that was doing the lustration themselves had "lustratable" pasts. These judges had been judges under the state-party system and had passed sentences on people convicted in the show trials of the 1950s. Judges who passed these sentences knowing that the judicial proceedings had been conducted without rule-of-law guarantees were supposed to have their pasts disclosed, and it was a bit awkward, to say the least, that two of the three judges reviewing the secret files for evidence of the suspect activity of others themselves had such pasts.

But the parliament, in designing the lustration process, had set up the review panels so that they could not be easily tampered with by the parliament or by the government, whose members would themselves be under review. That meant that there was no easy way to get rid of these judges who were now known to have these pasts, and the judges themselves refused to resign. Eventually the parliament was able to fire these two compromised judges and hire new ones to carry on the process.

In the meantime, the parliament tried to rewrite the affected parts of the law to comply with the court's decision. Though drafts of a new lustration law went into circulation within the time frame specified in the court's decision, in the end it took longer than anyone expected (and longer than the court technically allowed) to get a new law in place. The new lustration law, LXII/1996, was approved by the parliament on July 3, 1996 amidst controversy that it did not go far enough to root out of public office those who had tainted pasts. Since the government had changed in the meantime from one dominated by center-right former opposition members to one in which a party dominated by the former MSzMP officials was in the lead, the narrowed scope of the new law was perhaps understandable. But here again, the parliament did work out a way to carry on lustrations within the strictures of the Constitutional Court decision.

The new law specifies that only those public officials who have to take an oath before the parliament or the president of the republic or who are elected by the parliament are to be subjected to the lustration process. This takes care of the problem outlined by the court of an excessive scope of lustratable officials. In addition, the law narrows the scope of lustratable offenses. While the previous law made almost any appearance in the secret police files a lustratable offense, the current regulation requires that a person formally worked for the secret police, either by holding a position within the organization, by submitting reports informing on people, or by collecting a salary for other work done. It is no longer sufficient to demonstrate that someone merely signed a statement indicating their willingness to spy.

One controversy surrounding the law which was never resolved had to do with the scope of police agencies covered by the law. The current law deals only with the III/III, or domestic surveillance unit of the Hungarian secret police. But there were other units also, units that engaged in spying on Hungarians living abroad, or on foreigners living in Hungary, or on those who served in the military, and those secret police units are not covered by the law, despite a public protest by a number of leading figures insisting that the lustration law cover all spying activities.

The new law did, however, create a "Historical Office," which will have the responsibility to take control of all of the secret police files and to make them accessible to citizens who are mentioned in those files. Individuals will eventually be able to apply to this office in order to see their files, and such access must be granted, as long as the privacy and informational self-determination of others is not compromised. The Historical Office's purpose is to put into effect the prior decisions of the Constitutional Court.

In the meantime, the lustration of parliament members is proceeding as we write. If someone is found to have worked for the secret police under the terms of the new law, then this person is given the choice to step down and maintain the secrecy of the information or remain in office, in which case the information is published.

The Future of the Past in East-Central Europe

When we compare the route that Hungary has taken in dealing with the past with those of other countries in the region, we can see that Hungary has taken a distinctive middle course. We leave aside the former GDR, which has the dual peculiarities of being absorbed into the former West Germany and of being now part of a state that was stung by criticism of its incomplete denazification and so has resolved to cleanse undesirable pasts more thoroughly. But in comparing the Czech Republic, Poland, and Hungary, whose independent democratic governments have confronted the same questions, we can observe that each country has taken a consistent approach to the varied issues that are raised by having a past from which the present wants to distance itself. Roughly speaking, the Czech Republic has taken the most extreme course, Poland has taken the least extreme course, and Hungary has charted a course in between.

We can see these differences even more clearly by adding one more issue to the ones which we have already explored in some depth in this essay. That is the issue of property claims now being made by people whose property had been nationalized in the days of the state-party system. While we will not go into the details of this program in Hungary,[20] we can say briefly that in almost all cases (the one exception being the former property of churches, which they were allowed to recover), property was left in the hands of those who held it at the end of the state-party regime, and state-backed compensation coupons were issued to those who could demonstrate that they lost property as the result of state seizure in the past. The Constitutional Court was also heavily involved in this issue, and through declaring various attempts by the parliament unconstitutional, was able to require a system that compensated not only those whose property had been seized since 1949, but also those (primarily Jews) whose property had been seized in the previous regime. In the compensation cases, as with the retroactive justice and files cases, the Hungarian solution generally has been not to punish those who maintained the state-party system or benefited from its operation, but instead to use devices like publicity and compensation to right past wrongs.

In contrast, the Czech approach to all of these issues has been more punitive. Not only does the Czech Republic have a very harsh lustration law, but it has also required an accounting of all property with the goal of giving it back to those who possessed it before the advent of the communist regime. The Czech Republic has taken the view that it wants to cleanse itself of the people, institutions, and social arrangements of the past, and to do so in the most complete way possible. Poland, on the other hand, has not lustrated, not reprivatized, and not dealt with the question of the spies and the files. Instead, with the exception of giving the churches their property back, Poland has chosen to move on with the past in its midst without trying to correct injustices from the prior regime.

Hungary shared with Poland a negotiated transfer of power; in both countries, roundtable discussions had occurred in the summer of 1989 that led to an agreement about how the state-party system was to hand over control of the state to a government yet to be elected. It is perhaps significant that in neither Hungary nor Poland has lustration of former communists or revenge against the secret police gotten very far. Perhaps the reason can be found in Adam Michnik's observation that "If I didn't tell [General Czeslaw] Kiszczak at the Roundtable that he would be judged if I came to power, it would be deeply wrong of me to demand it now."[21] In Hungary, there might have been an explicit deal that the leaders of the state-party government would not be prosecuted. But even if an agreement had not explicitly been made, it might be hard for the leaders of new governments to persecute those who persecuted them if these previous leaders gave the new leaders control of the government after extensive face-to-face meetings. In general, negotiated transitions will probably not have heavily punitive processes for coping with past wrongs.

But there is still a difference in the way in which different negotiated transfers of power have dealt with these questions. While Poland did not set up truth commissions, have trials, and open the files, Hungary did attempt to do something more like this. Though the parliament did not try to bring to justice those who had managed the state-party system directly, it did try to prosecute people who had committed unpunished crimes under the past regime and to publicize information about those who had been informers. The Constitutional Court moderated and directed these efforts so that human rights considerations were paramount. Poland has tried to move on without comment; Hungary has tried to bring consideration of the past under rule-of-law principles, creating a "rule-of-law revolution." [22]

Hungary's "middle way" has largely consisted of bringing all attempts to deal with the past under a very strong rule-of-law philosophy, through the intervention of the Constitutional Court. This court has consistently implied that revenge is not a proper motivation in a rule-of-law state, and that the new state must proceed according to proper laws, proper procedures, and a proper sense of fair play, even if those with whom they are dealing did not themselves feel bound by these norms.

This extremely legal, some might say legalistic, approach to dealing with the past has characterized many other "transition" issues with which Hungary has been faced. Unlike any of the other countries going through the change from a state-party regime to a democratic, pluralistic one in the former Soviet world, Hungary has considered many of these issues to be not matters of popular democracy, but instead matters of constitutional law. The Hungarian Constitutional Court has ruled on virtually every major transition law, from retroactive justice to reprivatization to private property to social rights, and has declared roughly one law in three unconstitutional since 1990. The court was able to do this in part because the Roundtable process did in fact produce a substantially new constitution, while the Czech Republic did not get its new constitution until much later and Poland has not yet gotten a full new document, having only its "Little Constitution" to show for all the political changes. Wielding the new constitution, the Hungarian Constitutional Court was able to establish itself as the guardian of the transition.

Those who are familiar with debates over the countermajoritarian difficulty, in which courts are seen as antidemocratic because they overturn laws that democratically elected legislatures have passed, might cringe at this power of the Hungarian Constitutional Court. But, though the court repeatedly says in its decisions that public opinion plays no role in what it does, the court consistently has the highest popular approval ratings of any of the major branches of government. Comparing the Constitutional Court, the parliament, and the government—the three effective policymakers in Hungary—the Constitutional Court is always by far the most popular. (See Figure 1.)

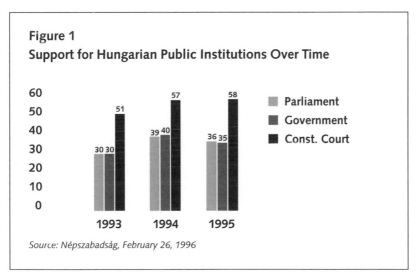

Figure 1
Support for Hungarian Public Institutions Over Time

Source: *Népszabadság, February 26, 1996*

As the figure shows, during the time that these debates were going on over retroactive justice between the parliament and the court, it was the court that retained the most popular support even though the court was striking down the laws that the elected parliament passed. One might ask then: Which is the most democratically accountable branch?

This broad question says a great deal about the way in which the transition has proceeded in Hungary. The constitutional approach to policy questions is clearly something that characterizes a broad spectrum of areas, and not just the subjects about the past. Perhaps, then, the Hungarian approach to dealing with the past may be best described by our title: Living well is the best revenge. If the new democratic polity is to fully repudiate the antidemocratic one of the recent past, then the best way to do so, in the Hungarian view, is to refuse to be tempted by having the power to use power against its enemies. What is invoked is a *constitutional* power rather than a purely democratic one, for it is not the power of numbers that stands behind the sense that this is a just way to deal with the past. It is the power of rights and their realization in the new political world that provides the moral backbone of the policy. Dealing with the past in a fair and constitutionally valid way means going on to live in a better way, a way that would not have been possible under the prior regime.

NOTES

1. The details of the approaches taken by these three countries are given in Tina Rosenberg, *The Haunted Lands: Facing Europe's Ghosts After Communism* (New York: Random House, 1995). For an evaluation of this work, see Timothy Garton Ash, "Central Europe: The Present Past," from *The New York Review of Books*, July 13, 1995, pp. 21–23. Other chapters in the present volume, by A. James McAdams on East Germany and Andrzej S. Walicki on Poland, also deal with these questions.

2. "Change of system" is the more direct translation of *rendszerváltás*, the Hungarian term used to describe what is conventionally called in English "transition." We use "change of system" because it conveys a different sense than "transition"—implying that there was a definite historical moment when things changed, rather than a more gradual process leading to some undefined place.

3. Section 1(1) of the Law of November 4, 1991, "Right to Prosecute Serious Criminal Offenses Committed Between December 21, 1944 and May 2, 1990 that Had Not Been Prosecuted for Political Reasons." Because, as we will see, the law was never promulgated, it was also never officially published. The quotations from the law can be found in the opinion published by the Hungarian Constitutional Court, 11/1992 (III.5) AB h. The English language translation has been published in *Journal of Constitutional Law in Eastern and Central Europe* 1(1994): 129–157. (Hereafter, the *Journal* will be abbreviated as JCLECE.)

4. In fact, the Hungarian Constitutional Court may be the most powerful high court in the world. The court can be said to be powerful for three

reasons: (1) The court has a very broad jurisdiction to review all legal regulations for consistency with the Constitution and also to judge that the parliament has violated the Constitution by failing to enact laws that it is constitutionally required to adopt. These powers the court uses frequently. (2) The court is constitutionally required to declare regulations unconstitutional if *any* interpretation of the regulation in question can be deemed unconstitutional, even if there are interpretations of the law that also would be constitutional. (3) The court can be petitioned at any stage in the lawmaking or law application process. The prime minister, for example, can ask the court for an abstract interpretation of a constitutional provision before a law is even in first draft, but once a law is enacted anyone can ask for a review. In between, a substantial group within the parliament or the president of the republic can ask the court to review a law before voting on or signing a law. In its first five years of operation, the court has struck down about two hundred statutes and administrative regulations, and of that number about half were new enactments and half were old laws that were judged to be inconsistent with the new constitution (The Constitutional Court of Hungary, English Language booklet distributed by the court, 1994).

5. "Constitutional rule-of-law state" is here a translation of the single Hungarian word *jogállam*, which is also roughly equivalent to *Rechtsstaat* in German. The quotation from the petition comes from the published decision of the Hungarian Constitutional Court, 11/1992 (III.5) AB h., English translation: JCLECE 1(1994): 131–132.

6. Quotations are from the English translation of the Hungarian Constitution prepared by the Hungarian Constitutional Court.

7. The Hungarian Constitution under which these decisions were made resulted from the Roundtable agreements, and was modified by another set of amendments passed by the first elected Parliament in 1990.

8. JCLECE 1(1994): 129, 135. Page references for further citations from this ruling are given in the text.

9. The published decision wrongly uses the word "compromise" instead of "comprise." We have corrected the translation here.

10. One reason why the Constitutional Court has been so active in Hungarian politics is that anyone—that is, anyone—can appeal to the court seeking review of a legal norm. One does not have to be involved in the subject, or have a particular grievance, or even be a Hungarian citizen. There are, in American parlance, no "case or controversy" or "standing" rules at all. While in this case, it happened to be opposition MPs who challenged the law, it could have been anyone who felt that this order of Parliament was unconstitutional. Before a legal norm is enacted, however, only those involved in its creation can petition the court for an opinion in the matter. See decision 16/1991 (IV.20) AB h. for further elaboration of this.

11. Citations are to the unpublished translation of the decision, available from the Hungarian Constitutional Court.

12. A note for those unfamiliar with continental legal systems. In Hungary, as in most other countries with special jurisdiction constitutional

courts, the Supreme Court is the highest court of appeal in the ordinary judicial system, while the Constitutional Court deals only with constitutional questions and not with appeals from the regular courts. The Supreme Court has no power to strike down legislation as unconstitutional, though it is supposed to consider constitutional principles in interpreting laws.

13. The president of Hungary's Supreme Court, Pál Solt, was briefly a justice on the Constitutional Court in 1990 before he was elected to his current post.

14. The law classified the following activities as lustratable: carrying out activities on behalf of state security organs as an official agent or informer, obtaining data from state security agencies to assist in making decisions, or being members of the (fascist) Arrow Cross Party.

15. For example, the prime minister and the speaker of the parliament in the second elected government were both ministers before 1989, and they had standing under the legal regulations of the time as persons who regularly got informational briefings from the secret police. Since this was a "lustratable" issue, at a minimum those two important state officials would have to have their pasts disclosed if they stayed in public office. Since the pasts of the former communists had been an issue discussed in the 1994 campaign and voters overwhelmingly elected them to office anyway, most people did not expect the disclosures to rock the Hungarian political establishment. But the possibility that new information would come out when the files were examined still remained.

16. XXII law of 1994.

17. The law was drafted this way because technically the MSzMP was a social organization and not a state organ. But because of the law's wording, any director of an organization in the civil society was granted the power to classify information as a state secret!

18. V law of 1978.

19. The Court can declare the parliament to be in violation of the Constitution by failing to enact a law that it is required by the Constitution or by a law to enact. See also note 4.

20. Ellen Comisso has published a detailed account of the debates, court decisions, and parliamentary adjustments in the case of compensation for previously seized property. See Ellen Comisso, "Property Rights, Liberalism, and the Transition from 'Actually Existing' Socialism," *East European Politics and Societies* 5 (1991): 162–188.

21. Quoted in Ash's review of Rosenberg, "Central Europe: The Present Past," p. 21.

22. The formulation is from the Court's opinion in the retroactive justice case: "revolution of the rule of law," JCLECE 1 (1994): 138.

7 Transitional Justice and the Political Struggles of Post-Communist Poland

Andrzej S. Walicki

POLAND IS OFTEN SEEN AS A country in which the transition to democracy was achieved in a remarkably mild way, sharply contrasting with the lustration laws and decommunization campaigns of its neighbors in the Czech Republic and eastern Germany. Many Poles, especially those who define themselves as belonging to the right, have severely criticized this "mildness." They regard it as a condemnable lack of resoluteness, stemming from an incomprehensible forgetfulness of past evils and thereby preventing Poland from becoming "truly Polish." From a greater distance the same facts can appear, of course, in a different, more positive light. Thus, a foreigner could describe them in a very different way, as a testimony of moral magnanimity, distinguishing the Poles positively from other nations permeated with a spirit of hatred and revenge.[1]

On closer examination, however, both these estimations seem to have missed the mark. As we shall see, problems of retrospective justice and of using the law as a means of settling accounts with the entire communist past have never been neglected in Poland. On the contrary, after the collapse of the communist regime, they aroused deep passions and exercised a decisive influence on the country's intellectual and political life. The failure of attempts to deal with these problems in a radical way cannot be explained in terms of a condemnable "sovietization," or a praiseworthy "magnanimity." Neither can it be explained by any specific features of Poland's legal culture.

To understand the complex story of the vicissitudes of transitional justice in Poland, it is necessary to place this problem in its appropriate political context and, in turn, to interpret this context in the light of different experiences with the communist regime in Poland.

The use here of the plural—"experiences" instead of "experience"—is of crucial importance, for Poland's current political divisions are deeply rooted in contending memories of the past. It is safe to say that for an average, relatively apolitical Pole, People's Poland was simply a much better place to live than for those Poles who yearned for political freedom and were active in a broadly conceived political opposition. For an overwhelming majority of the population, the "real socialism" of the 1970s was not a political tyranny but rather an increasingly ineffective and corrupt system of clientelistic relationships. It was a system in which the ruling party was no longer an alien body but a three-million-strong non-ideological mass organization, in which party members and non–party members collaborated in different forms of "dirty togetherness," taking advantage of its unwritten rules without feeling personally responsible for their existence.[2] Such a system was perceived as having both good and bad aspects, not as an embodiment of moral evil. It was felt to be domesticated and, in this sense, our own, involving all of us; hence, it could be despised but not completely disowned.

In contrast to this stance, however, Poland's political opposition perceived the system in terms of a Manichean division between "us" and "them." It was so for an obvious reason: its activists, in order to mobilize themselves for the dangerous political struggle, needed such an image of the existing system to provide them and their followers with a feeling of absolute rightfulness in their cause. In other words, they needed a spirit of ideological crusade and a demonized picture of the enemy. As we shall see, this militant self-righteousness did not disappear after the unexpectedly quick and peaceful dismantling of Jaruzelski's regime in 1989. It only changed its function, providing the new political elite with the strong belief that its struggle against communism gave it an absolutely legitimate and indisputable right to rule in postcommunist Poland. In this way (to paraphrase Adam Michnik), "the struggle for liberation" was transformed into a "struggle for power."[3]

In this light, different attitudes towards the beneficiaries of the former regime, as well as towards the entire legacy of People's Poland, can be explained without recourse to such terms as "forgetfulness" or "magnanimity." As we shall see, the attitude of the new political elite toward the former "communists" has, as a rule, been very far from magnanimity. The political atmosphere of postcommunist Poland has been far from free of hatred, and this hatred, unfortunately, reflects not only bad memories of the past but also, increasingly, the multiple frustrations of the new political class.

As for the people at large, they have no stake in political polarization. On the contrary: the anticommunist campaigns of their politicians have made them increasingly skeptical about the personalization of responsibility for the communist system, increasingly aware that the hunting for culpables might become uncontrollable and reach too far, hitting, directly or indirectly, almost every family in Poland. Thus, opinion polls invariably show that the majority of the Polish population wants political stability and national reconciliation. It is fed up with black-and-white images of the past, it does not endorse the wholesale condemnation of People's Poland, which it refuses to see as a period of Russian occupation, and it even tends to justify Jaruzelski's martial law.

From the point of view of the anticommunist crusaders, appealing to patriotic imponderables and absolute moral values, the population's stance is proof of a shameful forgetfulness and tolerance of evil, a sad testimony of "sovietization" of the Polish national character. Yet, it is also possible to view these attitudes in a different light: as the manifestation of a collective common sense, an instinctive national wisdom which so many times has helped the Poles to survive. Without denying the need for national memory (and there is no reason whatsoever to blame the Poles for neglecting it), we should take into account the wise observation of Ernest Renan in his famous essay "Qu'est-ce qu'une nation?" that in order to survive, nations must be capable not only of remembering but of forgetting as well.

Anticommunism as a Tool in the Struggle for Power

It is well known that the way states choose to settle accounts with the nondemocratic past depends on the type of transition to democracy. If this transition follows the Spanish model—that is, if it has been effected without a clean break with the past (a *ruptura*, to use the Spanish term), with an active cooperation of the representative of the antecedent authoritarian regime—the transformation of the structures of power proceeds in an evolutionary way, without purges, in a spirit of national reconciliation.[4] If the change starts with a clean break, however, the forms of constructing democracy are very different. This was the case with Czechoslovakia, where the communist regime refused to reform itself until the very end and, therefore, was forced to disappear in an abrupt way. The revolutionary (although nonviolent) beginning of that state's systemic change enabled, and necessitated, the practice of a wholesale purge of former collaborators and informants, sanctioned by the famous "Law on Lustration" of October 4, 1991. On January 1, 1993, Czechoslovakia was officially split into the Czech Republic and Slovakia; thus the continuity of the state was formally broken and the two countries could see themselves as completely new political units. In the Czech Republic this "new beginning" was followed by a radical break in legal continuity. On July 9, 1993, the Czech parliament adopted a "Law on the Illegality of the Communist Regime," suspending the statute of limitations for crimes committed under this regime and not prosecuted for political reasons.[5]

In contrast, the Round Table talks in Poland (February 6–April 5, 1989) led to the adoption of a "Spanish" solution. For General Jaruzelski and his Minister of Internal Affairs, General Czeslaw Kiszczak, Spain provided an acceptable model of transition to democracy; hence they forced the hesitating Central Committee to endorse the Round Table Agreements, by threatening to resign if the party refused to give up its monopoly on power. The overwhelming victory of Solidarity in the semi-free parliamentary elections of June 4 was totally unexpected by both sides. Nevertheless, it was accepted by the party and inaugurated the process of a peaceful transfer of power, followed by the radically procapitalist reforms (the so-called "shock therapy") of Leszek Balcerowicz. In turn, the former opposition respected its part in the agreements by electing Jaruzelski (though by a majority of only one vote) to the office of President, which symbolized the continuity of the state. It was in this context, in his first speech, that the new, noncommunist prime minister, Tadeusz

Mazowiecki, proclaimed his policy of drawing a "thick line" between past and present. By this, he meant that in conditions of political freedom, everyone should be able to start his life anew, and past loyalties would not be regarded as reasons for discrimination.

This declaration reassured the members of the PUWP (Polish United Workers' Party) of their personal security and thus helped them to accept the irreversibility of their political defeat. In January 1990, the party dissolved itself, and most of its leaders gave up further political careers. Its legal heir called itself Social Democracy of the Republic of Poland (SdRP). Its young leader, Aleksander Kwaśniewski, had been one of the main architects of the Round Table Agreements, and his elevation to the leadership of the SdRP owed much to the support of Michnik; indeed, Kwaśniewski's fascination with Michnik was so great that he allegedly even thought of joining forces with him in a single party.[6] However, the SdRP was not just a new name for the PUWP; it rejected the automatic transfer of membership and, therefore, had only sixty thousand members (the membership of the PUWP was two million). Also, the structure of the party was thoroughly changed, breaking ostentatiously with the principle of "democratic centralism" and warmly encouraging the formation of different factions. In the ideological sphere as well, the new party made the final step in a long process of factual decommunization that had characterized the PUWP's evolution after 1956. In its statutes and programmatic declaration, the party embraced the principles of parliamentary democracy and market economy. National will, as expressed in the free elections, was proclaimed to be the only legitimation of power, and the term "Social democracy" was justified through identification with the *Socialist* International and, no less tellingly, with no reference at all to the traditions of Communism or Marxism.[7]

All these events were hailed in the world as a proof that deep, structural changes could be achieved in a nonconfrontational, evolutionary way. Spain immediately understood the relevance of its own experience and celebrated this fact by inviting Jaruzelski to visit and giving him an extremely warm, truly royal welcome.[8] The Polish side was no less aware of the importance of the Spanish example: Michnik and Kwaśniewski (who later confessed that Spain was his favorite country) repeatedly stressed their conscious commitment to this model.

However, the enthusiasm for the "Spanish road" was not unanimously felt in Poland. Quite a few influential members of the new political class saw the Round Table Agreements and Mazowiecki's "thick line" as a cowardly compromise, a nasty deal between the "reds" and the "pinks," or even as a clever communist manipulation, serving the interests of the "nomenklatura" who wanted to enrich themselves while continuing to rule the country indirectly behind the scenes. From their point of view, the "Czech road" was infinitely better. What Poland urgently needed, they argued, was a "clean break" with the communist past, to eliminate all forms of visible continuity between the new Poland and the hated People's Poland.

Those who subscribed to this viewpoint can be divided into three categories, albeit overlapping as a rule and barely distinguishable in the decisive moments. The first was composed primarily of political primitives for whom evil had to be personified. These individuals were unable to perceive communism as a system of rules, let alone as an ideology, and tended to reduce it instead to a system of personal connections. This type of thinking (related, no doubt, to the clientelistic features of "real socialism" in decline) typified not only anticommunist workers but also several highly-placed politicians. Thus, Adam Glapiński, the cofounder and vice president of the Center Alliance, defined the Polish communist elite of the 1980s as a nonideological group of careerists, bound up by personal relations. A central figure among them was Balcerowicz. True, he left the party after the proclamation of martial law, but he never broke with his colleagues. Yet Balcerowicz was allowed to play the most important part in Poland's transition to market economy. Glapiński saw this as a convincing proof that "communists," and not the legitimate anticommunist elite that emerged from Solidarity, were still ruling Poland and implementing marketizing reforms in such a way as to benefit themselves.[9]

A second category was made up of different sorts of moral fundamentalists for whom any genuine compromise with the "communists" was unacceptable in principle—as a pact with the devil, involving a betrayal of the highest values and an irreparable contamination of national identity.[10] From this point of view the Round Table Agreements were either totally unacceptable, or acceptable only in bad faith—as a temporary truce which had to be broken as soon as possible, since the devil should be killed and not merely placated. Those who embraced this position might otherwise have been very different, intellectually and temperamentally, but they shared a pronounced idealization of prewar Poland and an uncompromising rejection of postwar realities. Hence they saw themselves as "independentists," as people for whom national independence, a prerequisite for the dignity and moral identity of the nation, was more important than the conventional right/left dichotomy. The earliest political expressions of this standpoint had emerged as part of the oppositional movement of the 1970s: Leszek Moczulski's Confederation of Independent Poland (KPN) and the Movement for the Defence of Human Civil Rights (ROPCIO), an organization of nationalist intellectuals who split from the Committee for the Defence of Workers (KOR). The final crystallization of this broadly conceived "independentist camp" (*obóz niepodległościowy*) took place after the collapse of communism, as a reaction to the moderate policies of Mazowiecki's government. Revolutionary changes in neighboring countries, especially Czechoslovakia and the former East Germany, provided "independentist" readers with the argument that Poland, due to its rotten compromise with the communists, had foresworn its leading role in the anticommunist revolution. From this perspective the Round Table Agreements appeared not as a tremendous victory, a revolutionary breakthrough for central Europe, but rather as a shameful, cowardly deal, bordering on a national betrayal.[11]

The third category of embittered critics of Poland's "Spanish road" was neither simpleminded nor committed to a moral fundamentalism. These were ambitious and power-hungry politicians, who saw themselves as representing Solidarity's right and could draw upon at least two reasons for deep personal frustration: the first was their marginalization at the Round Table talks, and the second, the failure of Mazowiecki's government to offer them a satisfactory share of power. The leading figure in this group, Jaroslaw Kaczyński, felt neglected, if not openly despised, by highbrow intellectuals like Bronislaw Geremek and Adam Michnik; at the same time, he saw himself and his group as victims of a nasty maneuver by the communists who, in his view, had deliberately chosen to strike a deal only with the "pinks," i.e., with people who deserved their trust as inveterate left-wingers, or even former party members. Lech Walesa's views were very similar. He could not reconcile himself to the fact that Mazowiecki, whom he had suggested (read: nominated) to the position of prime minister, conducted his own policy, refusing to treat Solidarity's leader as his informal boss. This common resentment created a community of interests between Walesa and Kaczyński's group and led them to proclaim the so-called war at the top. Unscrupulously disregarding democratic procedures, Walesa made Kaczyński editor in chief of *Tygodnik Solidarność* (*Solidarity Weekly*). In this role, Kaczyński became the *spiritus movens* of a well-orchestrated journalistic campaign against Mazowiecki's government, demanding a radical "decommunization," forcing President Jaruzelski to resign, and urging Walesa to run for Poland's highest office.[12] His conception of decommunization demanded that the former functionaries of the PUWP be banned not only from politics, but also from positions of leadership in administration and the economy, reaching down even to factory foremen. He also advocated splitting Solidarity into two parties: his own party, the Center Alliance (PC), was to represent the right, while Mazowiecki's Democratic Union (UD) was assigned the role of speaking for Solidarity's left.[13] The curious aspect of this scheme was the idea that Walesa, who, after all, had been the leader of the greatest working-class movement in postwar Europe, would now lead the right and take care of the interests of the emerging middle class, while leaving his own class to the tutelage of left-wing intellectuals, like Jacek Kuroń, Geremek, and Michnik.

It is instructive to point out that Kaczyński was not greatly concerned with moral principles in politics. He thought in terms of an unrelenting power struggle—of "who-whom," as Lenin once put it. He was fully aware of the decisive differences between Czechoslovakia and Poland. Czech communism after 1968 had been *incomparably harsher* than the Polish variant. In Czechoslovakia an osmosis between the communist elite and the oppositional elite had been impossible, since the regime refused to soften the opposition by a policy of liberalization; to the contrary, the Czech opposition was brutally suppressed, its prominent members deprived of their social status and forced to struggle for physical survival as janitors, stokers, and night-watchmen.[14] However, Jaruzelski's Poland, where the opposition was capable of organizing a powerful moral crusade against communism, and where the government tried to legitimize itself by constantly inviting prominent oppositionists to a "constructive cooperation," offered a sharp contrast to the situation in Czechoslovakia (especially in its Czech part, since repression was milder in Slovakia). It would have been reasonable to conclude that the "Czech way" was justified in Czechoslovakia while Mazowiecki's "thick line" was the proper solution for Poland. But Kaczyński was not very interested in historical justice. Above all, he wanted to oust Mazowiecki from power, and this, he thought, could best be done by accusing his followers of the proverbial "softness on communism." Kaczyński also hoped to use radical decommunization as a means of placating Poland's industrial workers: a broad change of personnel in industrial management through the elimination of the old nomenklatura, he thought, would give them "moral compensation" for the inevitable material losses resulting from accelerated marketization.[15]

In the atmosphere generated by these constant anticommunist campaigns, former party members had no easy life in Poland. True, many of the former nomenklatura were quite successful in using privatization laws to transform themselves into private businessmen. However, this transformation was not hailed as proof of their acceptance of the new rules of the game. To the contrary, their successes (explicable mostly by greater experience and local connections) produced an outcry of populist indignation: Look, the communists are enriching themselves at the expense of workers! What is emerging is a "capitalist communism," not democracy, and the government is doing nothing to prevent this new disaster! Still, despite Mazowiecki's "thick line," one could hardly say that the government was practicing excessive leniency and forgiveness in its relations with the unpopular former members of the PUWP. In an "Open Letter" to Walesa, Józef Kuśmierek, a journalist who had shown great merit in disclosing the economic absurdities of "real socialism," revealed that the scope of dismissals among industrial managers in Poland could be compared only to the Stalinist purges of

1948–1950.[16] These steps were taken primarily in response to populist pressures, despite the fact that the people in question appeared completely de-ideologized, relatively competent, and ready to serve the new government loyally. At times, the SdRP tried to intervene, but generally it did not dare speak too loudly.[17] Jaruzelski understood his task as securing Poland's smooth transition to the new system; hence, loyal to Mazowiecki, he willingly refrained from exercising his presidential prerogatives in such controversial matters. In September 1990, he formally asked the parliament to shorten his tenure and to prepare presidential elections on the basis of direct popular vote.

The result of the election was, on the whole, predictable. Aggressively supported by Kaczyński's demagogy, Walesa defeated Mazowiecki, whose popularity had greatly suffered from social tensions created by Balcerowicz's "shock therapy." Nevertheless, Walesa's success (less than 40 percent of the votes in the first round) was only relative. He was a patriot, sincerely committed to the cause of "westernizing" reforms in Poland. But his political repertoire was limited to a combination of demagogical statements (such as the need to combat communism in a country without genuine communists) and to personal intrigues, all aimed at strengthening his personal power.

Redefining Poland: The Symbolic Uses of the Law and Lustration

In the first act of his presidency Walesa sought to open a new, second chapter in the history of postcommunist Poland by making a highly symbolic gesture—a clean break in continuity with Poland's communist past. Jaruzelski was not invited to take part in Walesa's inauguration ceremony, which took place on December 22. Instead, the president-elect chose to receive the insignia of presidential power from Poland's almost unknown emigré president, Ryszard Kaczorowski. Thus Poland was returned symbolically to 1939, and the Polish People's Republic was reduced to a legal nonentity.

The reaction to Walesa's initiative was mixed. Kaczorowski's presence was widely greeted as a sign of national reconciliation, but the humiliation of Jaruzelski, the first president of postcommunist Poland, was regarded as embarrassing and tactless, and by some as simply unjust. What most people failed to realize, however, was that Walesa's action also implied reducing all forms of intrasystemic activity in People's Poland to a sort of collaboration with an illegal government. It is very unlikely that such an attempt, if properly explained and subject to discussion, would have been supported in a free, national referendum. Furthermore, it is arguable that a decision implying the "delegalization" of the previous form of the Polish state should have been discussed and voted on by the parliament. The same is also true for the officially sanctioned habit of referring to Walesa's Poland as "the Third Republic," i.e., as the direct heir to the prewar "Second Republic."

Walesa's political goals were clear. The delegitimization of People's Poland was, of course, intended to fully isolate the postcommunist forces and to endow the new elite with a virtual monopoly on political legitimacy. This strategy was also in accord with the program of Kaczyński's "presidential party." Nevertheless, it is also true that Walesa did not want to give too much power to his ambitious supporter. He made Kaczyński the head of his group of official advisors (the Presidential Office); however, as his prime minister, he chose Jan Krzysztof Bielecki, the leader of a small liberal party interested above all in promoting economic reforms. For himself, Walesa reserved the role of superarbiter in national affairs, and in this capacity, he spoke in different languages for different occasions. Sometimes, he assumed the pose of the responsible statesman, acknowledging Poland's need for "two legs—right and left" and thereby distancing himself from rightist extremism. On other occasions, he pledged to follow the process of decommunization through to its conclusion, promising frustrated workers that he would stop the enrichment of the former nomenklatura, take everything away from the communist thieves that they had stolen, and release them in their socks alone. These were not very credible promises in view of the fact that Bielecki had no intention of softening Balcerowicz's "shock therapy"; despite being a hard-line anticommunist,[18] he had no choice but to rely on the experience and cooperation of many former nomenklatura members. Meanwhile many workers would have to suffer the consequences not only of internal reforms but also of the sudden collapse of economic relations with the Soviet Union.

The new parliamentary elections on October 27, 1991 followed a period of intense political quarrels and brought about an unexpected success for the postcommunist forces. The Democratic Left Alliance (SLD, a coalition grouped around the SdRP) won 12 percent of the vote; together with the Agrarian Party (PSL, a continuation of the Peasant Party of People's Poland, which won 8.7 percent of the vote), the forces associated with the "old regime" were now the strongest group in the parliament. For Kaczyński, who saw his boss as responsible for "strengthening the left leg," this was too much. He gave up his position as head of the Presidential Office and proceeded to form a coalition of right-wing parties, whose backbone was an alliance of the PC, the KPN, and the ZChN (Christian-Democratic Union). Walesa's candidate for prime minister was Professor Bronislaw Geremek, a prominent politician from Mazowiecki's party, but the right-wing parties successfully boycotted this effort to form a government. Their own candidate was Jan Olszewski, a lawyer with a well-deserved reputation as a defense attorney in Gomulka's and Gierek's political trials and also a close friend of the well-known "independentist," Zdzislaw Najder.[19] On December 6, 1991, Olszewski announced his intention to create a government that would be composed of "moral authorities," and on December 23, after long and difficult negotiations, he assumed the prime minister's office.

To celebrate this victory of "independentism," the KPN then hoped to induce the parliament to proclaim a solemn resolution on "the restoration of the independence of Poland." Yet interestingly, the parliament rejected this measure, and even members of the rightist coalition voted against it. The ZChN objected to it on the grounds that it would cast a shadow on Poland's Catholic hierarchy, which, at least from 1956, had recognized the communist regime and did not treat it as non-Polish. Lech Kaczyński from the PC, Jaroslaw's brother, joined forces with Ryszard Bugaj (leader of the leftist Union of Labor) in sensibly observing that a completely "new beginning" would entail legal chaos and anarchy.[20]

However, the KPN's next initiative was successful: on February 1, the parliament accepted a resolution that it introduced on the illegality of martial law. It was suggestive of the spirit of the occasion that Moczulski allowed himself to translate the abbreviation PUWP as "paid traitors, flunkeys of Russia." Then, on May 28, the parliament passed an even more consequential resolution—on lustration. This resolution affirmed the duty of the Minister of Internal Affairs to provide full information on any candidates for governmental positions—in the parliament, administration, local government, and of course, the administration of justice—who had connections with the secret police in the years 1945–1990.[21]

In theory, the principle that candidates for public offices should not have a compromised past was both reasonable and widely accepted. In Poland, however, the practical implementation of the policy proved extremely inept, morally questionable, and politically dangerous. On June 4, Olszewski's Minister of Internal Affairs, Antoni Macierewicz, provided members of parliament with a long list of persons whose names had been found in the secret archives to be communist informers and agents; yet he did not specify which of these individuals had really performed such functions and how the innocent could defend themselves against defamation. Notably, the list included not only Walesa himself but also the most vociferous advocates of lustration: Moczulski, Najder (then Olszewski's chief advisor), and Wieslaw Chrzanowski (the Speaker of the House and head of Macierewicz's party). Macierewicz did not claim that all these people were guilty: he merely said *ex post* that he wanted to force them to "tell the whole truth" and thereby regain their credibility.[22] But the atmosphere in the parliament, and among the political elite as a whole, was too tense to allow for a close analysis of his intentions. This mood was conveyed by one opinion in *Tygodnik powszechny* (Catholic Weekly), a respectable and influential liberal Catholic organ, contending that the country was on the brink of civil war.[23] According to Michnik (whose opinions might be exaggerated but, nevertheless, reflected the mood), the situation was in danger of becoming totally uncontrollable. The "logic of the guillotine," he noted, would demand the blood of all "traitors," including Olszewski (a "communist lawyer") and even Macierewicz himself.[24] Nonetheless, the fact that *almost everybody* could see themselves as being personally threatened by this circumstance also had a positive side. It created a common desire to put an end to the affair. After a dramatic evening debate, the parliament decided to dismiss Olszewski's government and to ignore

its own decision on the need for lustration. Soon thereafter, on
June 19, Poland's Constitutional Tribunal ruled that the lustration law
contradicted the Polish Constitution.[25]

This was the end of the second chapter in the history of postcommunist Poland. For Polish public opinion shifted visibly against the
fundamentalist right-wing, and Olszewski's supporters were now
called "Olsheviks" (to evoke an association with "Bolsheviks"), or
"the dazed" (*oszolomy*). Deeply shocked by Macierewicz's conduct,
Walesa too distanced himself from the militant anticommunists by
nominating Waldemar Pawlak, a young politician from the PSL, to
the prime minister's office. Pawlak, however, proved unable to win
parliamentary support and the premiership was finally given to
Hanna Suchocka, from Mazowiecki's UD. Suchocka was a person of
moderately right-wing persuasion, but she had also belonged in the
past to the small Democratic Party, which (like the PSL) was a satellite
of the PUWP. The coalition supporting her comprised both the UD
and the ZChN, but excluded, of course, Kaczyński's PC and the KPN.

Suchocka's government faced very difficult tasks. It hoped to
continue Balcerowicz's reforms, but its main aim politically was
to isolate the "postcommunists" completely and thus to secure
the domination of the new political elite, calling itself "the post-
Solidarity camp." It was thought that this end could be achieved
through an increased emphasis on Poland's Catholic identity—
hence, its courting of the ZChN, its legislation on "the respect for the
Christian values" in mass media, and, most importantly, the severe
anti-abortion law of January 7, 1993. Meanwhile Poland witnessed a
steady increase in social unrest, caused by the drastic growth of inequalities and constant lowering of the meager living standards of
both state employees (the so-called budgetary sphere) and industrial workers. Suchocka's government categorically refused to re-
spond to the needs of the budgetary sphere, while right-wing
radicals, including Solidarity, now led by Marian Krzaklewski, tried
to direct their demonstrations and strikes into the usual "anticommunist" channels. After the failure of government talks with
Solidarity, state employees went on strike; on May 21, Warsaw was
paralysed by an impressive shutdown of public transportation. In
this situation, on May 28, parliament gave a vote of no-confidence to

the government. On the following day, Walesa responded by exercising his right to dissolve the parliament.

A legal solution to these problems seemed possible through a new parliament and a new government, and happily, elections were scheduled for the fall. Since only 40 percent of all potential voters had made use of their voting rights in the former election, Poland's bishops officially reminded the faithful that participating in the elections was their civic duty. Similarly, the post-Solidarity parties solemnly declared that they would not enter into a coalition with the postcommunists. Walesa attributed the responsibility for the lowering of workers' living standards to a "red spider's web" of the former nomenklatura members, the "communist capitalists." Influential newspapers and the mass media did everything they could to direct the electorate's attention to the nasty aspects of the communist past. A good occasion for this was provided by the trial of sixteen functionaries of the Stalinist security police, headed by Adam Humer, all of whom were accused of torturing Polish patriots in the years 1946–1952.[26]

In spite of these efforts, the result of the 1993 elections was, once more, deeply disappointing for the new elite. The postcommunist SLD won 20.4 percent of the vote and the agrarians (PSL) 15.4 percent, while Suchocka's UD received less than 10.6 percent and Walesa's BBWR (Non-Party Bloc for the Support of Reforms) only 5.4 percent. In addition, a new electoral law, which established a threshold of 5 percent for parliamentary representation, worked in favor of the SLD and PSL. Together, they won the absolute majority in parliament. Furthermore, the right-of-center parties suffered an almost total defeat. Only the KPN was capable of surmounting the new threshold; the ZChN (despite the barely concealed support of the Church), Kaczyński's PC, and the "Olsheviks" (united under the name "Fatherland") won less than 5 percent of the vote and were therefore eliminated from parliament.

The "postcommunists" owed their success to many factors. They had consistently supported economic reforms but, at the same time, had also distanced themselves from Balcerowicz's indifference to social policy and, sometimes at least, defended the weak. They did not defend communism as a system—and of course, not at all its crimes—but they stressed in the same breath that People's Poland was Poland nonetheless, that people who had worked on its behalf had not wasted their lives, that they had achieved a lot in many fields and deserved respect as good patriots. Thus, they stood for national reconciliation and repeatedly pointed out that all anticommunist rhetoric was divisive, even on the family level, and that its real purpose was to substitute past divisions for the present ones. It was increasingly difficult to dismiss this latter diagnosis as merely serving the interests of the former nomenklatura, since people did not view Poland's new entrepreneurial class of non-communist background as a change for the better—on the contrary, its members were, as a rule, more arrogant and more unscrupulous in enriching themselves than the former apparatchiks. Finally, in the eyes of many people, the SLD deserved credit as a party faithful to the principle of the separation of church and state, resisting the "political Catholicism" that had made such great strides under Suchocka's government.

Having won the election, the postcommunists did not become "dizzy with success." They did not fight for the premiership; despite the differences in economic policy, they agreed to give the prime minister's office to Pawlak, since the Agrarian Party (PSL) was more acceptable from the point of view of "Christian values." And on November 9, at the discussion of Pawlak's inauguration speech, the leader of the victorious party, Aleksander Kwaśniewski, surprised parliament by offering an apology to "all of those who had experienced the injustice and wickedness (*niegodziwość*) of the authorities and the system before 1989."[27]

Nevertheless, the defeated parties rejected this apology as both insufficient and late in coming. They rationalized their exaggerated feelings of insecurity by appealing to fears about the restoration of communism in Poland and alleged threats to the country's independence. Immediately after the elections, Walesa assumed the pose of sole guarantor of the reforms, promising to defend them even by applying "the Yeltsin variant," that is, by means of a bloody clash with parliament. Mazowiecki's UD, now united with Bielecki's liberals and renamed the Union of Freedom (UW), joined forces with its right-wing opponents in raising alarm about the alleged "return of People's Poland."[28] Some of its members (for instance, Donald Tusk) did not refrain from recommending a temporary suspension of democracy. How deeply rooted were these moods is shown by the fact that even Bronislaw Geremek, himself a former PUWP member and a target of constant attacks from the right, spoke in the United States about the merits of "the politics of hatred" and about the advisability of an "enlightened absolutism" in Central Europe (if only enlightened enough!).[29] The anticommunist campaign in the media was intensified, coming very close to a cold civil war. The population at large did not take part, but many intellectuals fell prey to an almost hysterical politicization; some of them indulged in self-righteous arrogance, attributing the result of the democratic elections to the masses' notorious lack of enlightenment, political illiteracy, and "sovietization." Although Walesa's authoritarian leanings were generally disliked, his liberal-minded opponents nevertheless failed to criticize him for unveiled threats addressed to the SLD. Thus, the president was seen on public television saying that Poland was ruled by representatives of a "bandits' option" (*bandycka opcja*) and pledging that he would settle accounts with them as soon as possible.[30]

The political situation was further complicated by Walesa's habit of abusing his presidential right of veto and by Pawlak's insistence on promoting the specific interests of his peasant electorate. The situation improved in March 1995, when a temporary understanding between Walesa and the SLD led to Pawlak's replacement by Józef Oleksy, an able politician from the SLD who was firmly committed to the reforms (although, as time would show, not accepting the role of Walesa's puppet). But soon afterwards, Oleksy's government had to cope with a powerful wave of workers' discontent, organized by Krzaklewski's Solidarity and actively supported by the KPN. On May 26, Warsaw witnessed the greatest workers' demonstration since martial law: ten thousand miners from Silesia and workers from the bankrupt "Ursus" plant near Warsaw violently protested against the "communist government," forcing the police to use physical power. Had there been a single, accidental death, the situation might have become totally uncontrollable. Assisted by KPN activists, the angry demonstrators raised the banner of Solidarity against the new incarnation of its old enemy— "the communists." A Solidarity leaflet entitled "Away with the Red bourgeoisie!" claimed that the nomenklatura was still in power while the workers, instead of becoming masters in their country, had been reduced to "an expropriated, pauperized mass," ruled by a communist oligarchy and the red and "pink" bourgeoisie.[31] Typically, the author of "shock therapy," Leszek Balcerowicz, was not even mentioned, while "Comrade Oleksy" was accused of a brutal assault on "the meager social privileges" of workers. Even more telling was the fact that the UW, now led by Balcerowicz, refrained from taking a clear stand in the conflict. Hence, the "communists" had to defend Poland's "capitalist road" alone, without any assistance from those who otherwise claimed all credit for pushing Poland in this direction.

In the second half of the year, Poland's politicians began to prepare for presidential elections. The SLD took credit for Poland's impressive economic achievements (6 percent annual economic growth[32]) and appealed to the electorate to concentrate on the nation's future, not on past divisions. Nevertheless, it was increasingly clear that the electoral campaign would be dominated by a crude "politics of identity." Adam Michnik and Wlodzimierz Cimoszewicz, an independently-minded politician from the SLD, tried to prevent this by publishing an article in which they called for a common effort to understand the complexities of the past and to interpret it in a spirit of national reconciliation.[33] But this appeal was ridiculed by the right and rejected even by journalists from Michnik's own newspaper. Although initially very unpopular, Walesa confidently presented himself as Poland's only salvation from the return of "communism," while for their part, the right-wing parties failed to agree on a common alternative candidate, and the UW proved rather half-hearted in supporting its own candidate, Jacek Kuroń. As a result, the electoral campaign of the opposition parties was probably destined to degenerate into a purely negative affair, aimed at isolating the "communist" candidate, Aleksander Kwaśniewski. Poland's bishops avoided mentioning him by name but described their acceptable candidate in a way that was close to an exacting instruction of how not to vote.[34] Still, Kwaśniewski won the greatest number of votes (35.1 percent) in the first round of the presidential elections. In the second round on November 19, he had to compete with Walesa, who won 33.1 percent. His victory seemed to be doubtful, since all that was required for his defeat was that all those who had not voted for him simply joined forces against him. Making matters more difficult, on November 9 and 10, the media accused him of failing to inform parliament about his wife's income and of deceiving voters by providing a false description of his education.

Nevertheless, Kwaśniewski proved able to defeat the legendary "hero of Solidarity." He received 51.7 percent of the vote. In response, his opponents promptly organized a collective protest, demanding the invalidation of the election. However, the Supreme Court ruled against this. For his part, Walesa took his last stand against allowing the former communists to take "total control" of the state. On December 19, at 9 P.M., he invited the highest dignitaries of the state to his residence—the speakers of the Lower and Upper House, their deputies, and the presidents of the Supreme Court, the Constitutional Tribunal, and the Administrative Tribunal—where he informed them that Poland's security was under threat since Prime Minister Oleksy had been, and still was, a Russian spy. Yet Walesa's guests refused to authorize an emergency action and the press conference, that had been called to hear their announcement, had to be cancelled.[35] Then, only two days later, on December 21, Minister of Internal Affairs Andrzej Milczanowski repeated these accusations against Oleksy before the parliament; however, despite the natural excitement that ensued, these accusations only led to the creation of a special, preliminary committee to investigate the affair. Oleksy forcefully declared his innocence and refused to resign. Soon thereafter, Kwaśniewski took the oath and became president of Poland.

We now know how the Oleksy affair ended. On April 22, 1996, the military prosecutor who headed the investigation, Col. Slawomir Gorzkiewicz, declared that there was no legal basis to charge the former prime minister. Unfortunately, this will not be enough to keep those who want to believe in Oleksy's guilt from treating him as guilty. Yet it is also true that from the beginning, many honest and well-informed persons suspected that the Oleksy affair was merely a brutal manipulation, designed to play upon anticommunist neuroses in the struggle for political power.[36] Two of Poland's most prominent former dissidents, Jacek Kuroń and Karol Modzelewski, published an open letter accusing the Polish secret police of interfering in politics and using methods unacceptable in a democratic society; their suspicion that the allegations against Oleksy were fabricated were based, among other things, on the fact that they were prepared by the same security officer, Wiktor Fonfara, who had been working on compiling cases against themselves in the early 1980s.[37] But the issue was far too emotional to be treated as a subject of cool and rational analysis. Kuroń and Modzelewski's letter aroused such a wave of self-righteous indignation that Poland's Spokesman for Human Rights, Professor Tadeusz Zielinski, felt it necessary to warn that the verbal aggression in the opposition-controlled mass media created a threat to freedom of expression in Poland.[38]

As we can see, Poland *is not* a country in which the problems of decommunization and lustration have been solved, in accordance with the Spanish model, in a completely peaceful way. On the contrary, these two issues have been very divisive through the entire postcommunist period, and they have repeatedly been used as instruments in the struggle for political power. The specificity of the Polish situation lies in the fact that the hostility towards the old political elite was caused *not by its opposition* to market economy and democracy *but by its successful adaptation* to these new conditions. Thus, the more successful the former communists appear to have been in using the democratic rules of the game and in promoting economic reforms, the louder have been the demands for decommunization, accompanied by more and more radical critiques of both the Round Table Agreements and Mazowiecki's "thick line."

Understandably, the Oleksy affair gave rise once again to calls for lustration. This time, however, history took an ironic twist. The most radical proposal, which would have involved about ten thousand state officials, was submitted to parliament on February 1 by no less an institution than Kwaśniewski's Presidential Office. It proposed the creation of a special Commission of Public Confidence whose aim was to protect the state against former agents and, no less importantly, help innocent people to defend themselves against false accusations. Its head—"the Polish Joachim Gauck"—was to be the Deputy Speaker of the House, Aleksander Malachowski, a prominent former dissident now associated with the Union of Labor (UP) and seen by many people as "the conscience of the Polish Left." He agreed to perform this difficult mission in the interest of national reconciliation. However, despite their long-standing championship of the idea of lustration, the anticommunist militants, this time strongly supported by the centrist UW, promptly rejected Kwaśniewski's initiative. Their reasons were set forth by the *Catholic Weekly* in an article under the title "The Giggle of History."[39] Kwaśniewski's idea of lustration, the author argued, was not bound up with a decommunization program; hence it would merely affect the secret police's numerous "secret collaborators" without, however, touching upon the lives of the former policemen themselves. More importantly, it would not ban from political life the former functionaries of the party under whose rule the security police had been flourishing. In other words, it would be used to compromise people with oppositional backgrounds, without damaging the former communists, now members of the SLD.

Undeniably, there was much sense to this argument. But this only shows why a wholesale lustration had become so difficult in Poland. What remained from the pet idea of the "anticommunist revolution" boiled down to something more commonsensical. The majority of politicians simply called for the screening of candidates for important public office, and only then, to protect them against the possibility of political blackmail.

Settling Accounts with Martial Law

With the context of Polish politics in mind, it is now possible to turn to a detailed analysis of the problem of "historical justice." This vague expression is used here as a convenient label for the differing attempts that have been made in Poland to use legislation and the law to satisfy the demand for moral justice made by the victims of "real socialism" and, at the same time, to provide Poland's new political class with a moral mandate to rule.

For those who became political activists in Solidarity's heroic period, the most important issue was to settle accounts with the immediate past, above all, with Jaruzelski's "martial law." Mazowiecki's government, cohabitating with Jaruzelski's presidency and the "contractual parliament" born out of the Round Table Agreements, was never in a good position to undertake this task. Mazowiecki himself did not wish to engage in the effort for moral reasons, since as he once observed, a moral politician is someone who observes agreements. As a result, the first attempt to pursue retrospective justice was made only after the parliamentary elections of October 1991. On February 1, 1992, the new parliament approved a resolution which proclaimed that martial law had been illegal and demanded the formation of a special committee to investigate its consequences.[40]

The discussion which preceded the vote was very interesting, and it is worthwhile offering a brief summary of it here. On the one hand, Jaruzelski's defenders appealed to the notions of a "higher necessity" and a "lesser evil." These concepts, they pointed out, had been understood by both western statesmen and the successive primates of Poland, Cardinal Wyszyński and Cardinal Glemp. Similarly, an SLD deputy reminded his colleagues of the number of victims of the Soviet invasion of Hungary, and he asked how many Poles would have been killed had Jaruzelski failed to do his heavy duty.[41] Professor Jerzy Wiatr, one of the leaders of the SdRP, indicated that Jaruzelski's intentions were well understood by the people, because even in December 1991, 56 percent of the respondents to an official opinion poll saw martial law as justified while only 29 percent expressed the opposite view. He also recalled that Pilsudski's coup d'état of May 1926 had led to about four hundred deaths (at least four times the total number of victims of martial law), for which no one was ever punished.[42] Finally, Aleksander Kwaśniewski paid tribute to the merits of Solidarity and its historical victory, but he also pleaded that political and moral issues not be mixed with legal justice.[43]

On the other side, the position of the right-wing boiled down to seeing martial law as an unpardonable "crime against the Polish nation." The KPN's leader, Moczulski, repeated once more that the communists were guilty of nothing less than national treason and that history had already passed this verdict.[44] A deputy from the ZChN, Marek Jurek, asked Wiatr to refrain from comparing independent Poland with communist Poland. In the conflict of 1926, he said, people were being killed on both sides, because of their different understanding of what was good for Poland, whereas under martial law the victims were only on one side and the forces of repression could not legitimize their conduct by any higher aims.[45] In this way, a young nationalist fundamentalist proved to be immune to the hermeneutical culture of understanding of the other side. We should note, however, that an older member of the ZChN, Stefan Niesio-lowski, showed an ability to distinguish between different periods in Poland's postwar history, stressing that "real socialism" in decline had differed substantially from the dark period of Stalinism, and that it would be ungrateful and morally dishonest to compare the mild lot of the internees under martial law with the cruel fate of the victims of the first decade of the communist regime in Poland.[46]

Especially interesting was the position of Jacek Taylor, the legal expert of Mazowiecki's UD. He accepted the proposed resolution with a qualification, adding that the settling of accounts with the past should respect the period of limitation and not allow the law to be applied retroactively. The rule of law, he stressed emphatically, did not tolerate retroactive justice and attempts to punish what has ceased to be punishable.[47] In this way, the UD wanted to go beyond the policy of the "thick line" without radically breaking with the essentials of the former agreements. This position, however, did not stand the test of time. After the elections of 1993, Taylor's party moved to the right and he himself came to be known as an ardent advocate of abolishing the limitation period for crimes of the old regime.

The resolution on the illegality of martial law was extremely brief and supported by no legal argumentation whatsoever. Somewhat illogically,[48] it anticipated the findings of the parliamentary Committee on Constitutional Responsibility, whose work had begun in September 1992 and was to last until February 1996. This committee was convened in response to a motion of the KPN (of December 5, 1991) which demanded that the members of Jaruzelski's Military Council of National Salvation (WRON)—i.e., the body which implemented the decision about martial law—as well as the members of the State Council—which endorsed this decision—should stand trial before the Tribunal of the State and be properly punished for their actions.[49] The committee was to investigate the validity of this motion. Although it was a political organ, composed of eighteen members of parliament, its proceedings actually took the form of a lawsuit and became known as "the trial of the authors of martial law."[50]

The first meeting of the committee was mostly formal, but its second session had very dramatic moments. It was preceded by a press conference at which Jaroslaw Kaczyński anticipated the outcome of the inquiry by stating: "General Jaruzelski and his comrades, who introduced martial law, are guilty of betraying the nation and, therefore, should be prosecuted, sentenced to death, and executed."[51] In contrast, the committee chairman, Edward Rzepka, who was motivated by the desire to reduce the possible punishment, accused the defendants of a much lesser crime—of violating an article of the penal code which said that public functionaries who used illegal means for promoting their material or personal interests should be punished by imprisonment up to ten years.[52] Understandably, Jaruzelski reacted to these statements by declaring that, as a front-line officer, he was neither afraid of death nor ready to compromise his dignity. Accordingly, he declared his inability to discuss Rzepka's accusation and asked the committee to reformulate the charge against him.[53] Other defendants took the same line. Jan Szczepański, a member of the State Council and internationally known sociologist, very calmly noted that the accusation of self-enrichment through martial law was too strange to be treated with due seriousness.[54]

Analyzing the rich and numerous reports from the consecutive meetings of the committee would require much more space than is available in this essay. The depositions of the defendants are, as a rule, valuable documents that shed much light on different aspects of the period of agony of "real socialism" in Poland. Hence, they deserve to be better known by the general public and to be more widely used by professional historians. In the present context, however, we may at least offer a brief and necessarily schematic summary of their content. From the point of view of a comparative treatment of the problems of retrospective justice in postauthoritarian societies, it is important to stress that the committee did not discuss concrete cases involving the violation of human rights. If one expects to find in its reports information on extra-judicial killings, "disappearances," and torture, all so widely practiced in such countries as Argentina, Brazil, or Uruguay, one would be utterly disappointed. This can be explained by two obvious reasons. First, the members of the committee were interested, above all, in establishing whether or not the introduction of martial law had been justified. Second, they well knew that for an operation of this scale, martial law was remarkably mild; its instigators had cautiously avoided unnecessarily harsh measures, and it was not at all comparable to the cruel repressions of the Latin American authoritarian regimes. Hence, the more important thing was to define the intentions and aims of the martial law regime. Was it proclaimed in the interests of international communism (in which case it would have been simply "national treason"), or was it possibly a means of protecting Poles against the disaster implied by a Soviet, German, and Czech invasion?

Otherwise refraining from any patriotic rhetoric, Jaruzelski's generals strongly supported the second interpretation. They took it for granted that an invasion by foreign troops would have been the greater disaster, and they had no doubt that this was a very real threat. They described themselves as fully understanding that it was politically impossible to discuss this threat openly, and at the same time, they stressed their deep conviction that in the existing international situation, the only alternative to foreign intervention was to preempt it with an internal, "Polish" solution. Some of them claimed to have known very concrete and truly "terrifying" scenarios of invasion.[55] These statements were confirmed by a German expert on the subject, Professor Manfred Wilke, who provided evidence about East German pressure, as well as concrete preparations, for invasion.[56] In addition, Professor Andrzej Werblan presented detailed documentation that the Soviet, East German, and Czechoslovak leaders, regardless of tactical differences between "moderates" and "hard-liners," saw Poland as overrun by an "unbridled counterrevolution"; they viewed the Polish party as responsible for this, as no longer Leninist, and therefore, deserving no confidence on their part.[57]

For their part, the experts sympathizing with "the post-Solidarity camp," Professor Jerzy Holzer and Professor Krystyna Kersten, did not question these facts—they only stressed that the available documentation was not full and therefore was inconclusive.[58] Several witnesses pointed out that the specificity of the Polish situation consisted in the fact that the leadership of the PUWP explicitly asked the Soviet military and party leaders not to introduce their troops to Poland, and that the latter knew very well that no prominent person in the Polish party would have endorsed plans for intervention; according to Manfred Wilke, this was Brezhenev's most difficult problem.[59] Further, Professor Henryk Jabloński, the former president of the State Council, expressed the view that Polish resistance to outside pressures made this situation especially dangerous; as the most independent country of the Soviet bloc, a country which had deviated so much from the Soviet model, Poland was actively disliked by other members of the Warsaw pact and the price for its resistance would have been terrible.[60] Unlike Honecker, Brezhnev was aware of these problems, and this awareness (plus, of course, Soviet involvement in Afghanistan) greatly tempered his interventionist impulses. Nevertheless, according to Werblan, some members of the Soviet oligarchy would have welcomed any pretext for "helping" Poles, even after the proclamation of martial law. They knew that such "help" was their only chance for a bloody suppression of "counterrevolution" and for terrorizing Poland, at least for a while, into genuine submission.[61]

It is proper to recall in this context that Jaruzelski's intention was precisely the opposite. He did not want to allow for any sort of "settling accounts" with Solidarity activists, regardless of their behavior. Because of this, the decree on martial law was accompanied by the so-called "abolition decree," which formally prohibited prosecuting individuals for any illegal actions undertaken before its proclamation. Nonetheless, it is also true that Jaruzelski did not choose the easiest way of defending himself. He repeatedly stressed that the threat of invasion was *not the only* reason for his action. In his view, excusing himself by devolving responsibility for martial law to the Russians would have been incompatible with his military dignity.[62] The danger of intervention was very real, and clearly perceived in the West, but it was also a function of the internal situation in Poland. The country was plunged into full anarchy, the economy was in a state of disintegration, the disruptions in the delivery of coal and food before the winter months had created a threat to many people's survival, and the growing radicalism within Solidarity and the mounting aggression against the forces of order (resulting, as he stated, in hundreds, or even thousands of acts of physical violence against the police[63]) were all pushing Poland to the edge of civil war.

Martial law, therefore, was a "lesser evil" but *not only* in comparison with the foreign invasion.

Admittedly, this stand did not facilitate the task of Jaruzelski's defenders. Nevertheless, the general's other statements made it no less difficult to classify him as an uncritical advocate of the old regime. Jaruzelski described himself as seeing the need for profound reforms, and wholeheartedly supporting Gorbachev's *perestroika* (whose appearance, however, he could not have predicted in 1981). Thus, he saw it as a bitter paradox that people like himself, the party reformers, who had paved the way for an independent and democratic Poland, now had to face a humiliating trial.[64] In this sense, he did not define himself as an enemy of the new, postcommunist Poland. But he refused to condemn his past, to renounce his loyalty to People's Poland. He continued to think that a socialist Polish state in alliance with the Soviet Union had been Poland's only choice after the war, and not a bad choice at that. Hence, the country was worthy of being served and defended not only out of fear of a Soviet invasion. He deeply felt that he could not betray the millions of Poles who had served People's Poland with the conviction that socialism was not in conflict with patriotism, and that alliance with the USSR was not merely an external necessity. This was the meaning of his farewell speech as Poland's president in which he expressed his regrets for the suffering caused by martial law. "As a soldier," he stated, "I know that the commander, the chief, bears responsibility for everybody and everything. The expression `I apologize' may sound trite, but I cannot find other words. I ask for only one thing—if time has not extinguished one's ill will and anger, let these feelings be directed primarily against myself. Let them not affect all those who in the really-existing conditions worked honestly, hard, and in the best faith for the reconstruction and construction of our fatherland."[65]

Of course, this was hardly enough for the nationalist fundamentalists. They demanded an outright repentance for the entire past, claiming that Christian forgiveness was due only to those sinners who had fully repented for their wrongdoings. And full, unqualified repentance meant for them nothing less than a wholesale rejection of People's Poland. More importantly, this point of view was no longer a trademark of the right. With a few exceptions, the country's new political elite as a whole assumed (as Michnik put it) "that People's Poland should be treated as a form of Soviet occupation, and the PUWP as an organization of traitors and collaborators with a foreign power."[66] This was the main rationalization of the policy of consistently isolating the SLD. The idea of constructive cooperation with the postcommunists seemed to be incompatible with the anticommunist identity of the new Poland.

Michnik rightly observed that this way of thinking suffered a spectacular defeat in the elections of 1993.[67] He even thought that this would put an end to the policy of militant anticommunism and to dividing people in accordance with "genealogical" criteria. This would have been in tune with his repeated calls for national reconciliation and for a "minimum of fraternity" for the former enemies.[68] Realistically, however, this policy had little chance of prevailing, and Michnik, so many times brutally attacked for being "half-red," if not just a renegade, was well aware of it. The politically frustrating results of the 1993 elections would not make the new elite more tolerant and open-minded. Indeed, the very fact that the postcommunists dared to win the elections tended to mobilize the opposition into intensifying its efforts to condemn the entire communist past unequivocally, and especially martial law. As a result, successive anniversaries of martial law were used as occasions for media campaigns leveled not only against postcommunist politicians but also, and above all, against anyone who voted for them, showing thereby their moral relativism and sovietized mentality. To this end, right-wing journalists used the language of abuse, while sophisticated intellectuals indulged in intentionally intimidating displays of moral indignation.[69]

Against this background, in December 1994, the parliamentary opposition made an attempt to anticipate the findings of the Committee on Constitutional Responsibility—and to exercise pressure on its work—by voting for a resolution describing martial law as a "violation of the constitution." Demonstrators outside the parliament (mostly members of Solidarity and the KPN) burned effigies of Jaruzelski and Kwaśniewski, and a mock executioner displayed a sign: "I wait for you, Wojciech!"[70] When the SLD managed to reduce the proposed resolution to a tribute to "the victims of the struggle for freedom," the sophisticated intellectuals, in their turn, rushed to condemn the vote as a "moral crime against the nation."[71] The next anniversary of martial law coincided with the success of the SLD's candidate in the presidential elections and, therefore, called forth an even more powerful paroxysm of hostilities. It culminated in a rightist demonstration organized by the KPN in front of Jaruzelski's house; with torches in hand, the demonstrators castigated the first president of postcommunist Poland as a man who "had raised his hand against the Polish nation" and pledged "not to allow him to die in peace." The direct connection between this event and the presidential elections was pointed out, as something entirely natural, by a publicist of the *Catholic Weekly*, who expressed the view that had the outcome of the elections been different, nobody would have cared to commemorate the anniversary of martial law in this way.[72]

The Committee on Constitutional Responsibility, despite multiple external pressures, continued its work in a relatively calm way. Moreover, Jaruzelski seemed to have partial success in "relativizing" the evil caused by his actions. His comparison of the consequences of martial law—a move approved by 69 percent of the Polish population—with Pilsudski's coup d'état of 1926 was striking. Eight years after 1926, the opposition remained crushed and Poland had 3,755 political prisoners and an extra-legal internment camp at Bereza Kartuska; five years after December 1981, she was a country without political prisoners and three years later witnessed a negotiated transfer of power.[73]

At times, the exchanges between witnesses and defendants before the committee transformed themselves into a sort of national debate in which both sides enjoyed the opportunity to acquire a better understanding of one another. For example, the discussion of Jaruzelski's motivations took the form of a classically Polish controversy over the meaning of patriotism and one's understanding of national duty. Jaruzelski quoted Max Weber's distinction between the "ethics of convictions" (or "absolute ends") and the "ethics of responsibility"—responsibility for one's country and for the fate of its citizens.[74] The legal expert, Professor Arnold Gubiński, paraphrased Roman Dmowski's credo of political realism: "One can be a gambler, one can risk his private property and even his life, but nobody is allowed to expose to risk the fate of his state and nation."[75] Another expert, Professor Andrzej Grabiński, countered these words by saying that from the point of view of this principle, the prewar Polish government should have been tried for choosing to resist Nazi Germany.[76] These exchanges sounded exactly like the traditional Polish discussion about idealism and realism in politics, national honor and national interest, the imperative of rising up against the enemy, and the duty to consider the consequences of one's actions.[77]

The strictly legal substance of the proceedings boiled down to two points. The first dealt with the formal prerogatives of the Polish State Council. At the time parliament was in session, as was true in this case, the State Council had no right to issue decrees. Henryk Jabloński, the former president of the State Council, categorically rejected this interpretation.[78] In a separate article he distinguished between "the state of war" (*stan wojny*), whose proclamation was the exclusive prerogative of the parliament, and "martial law" (*stan wojenny*), defined in another article of the constitution, whose introduction depended on the decision of the State Council.[79] He also stressed that the parliament had immediately endorsed the Council's decision and that no other parliament had reversed this vote. Yet, the committee rejected this interpretation, claiming that the State Council had abused its power. But there remained a practical problem. Had it really been possible to openly discuss the introduction of martial law in parliament? This question, of course, remained unanswered.

The second point of contention dealt with the ultimate justification for martial law, "the state of a higher necessity." Quoting Article 23, §1 of the penal code, Professor Gubiński defined this rationale as follows: "The essence of the state of higher necessity is conduct which sacrifices a legally protected good for the sake of preventing an immediate danger threatening another such good of a comparable value."[80] In defending this position, he also discussed the problem of acting in the name of a higher necessity when the danger that it is intended to prevent does not really exist. In such a case, according to Gubiński, the majority of legal scholars in Poland took the position that even an erroneous judgment about such a danger could not be punished, provided merely that it did not stem from rashness or neglect.[81] From this, it followed that the decision to impose martial law was legally justified even if the Soviets had not really intended to intervene.

Despite these explanations, however, many of the committee's discussions and the popular press continued to focus not on the premises for Jaruzelski's decision but instead upon what became known about the Soviet intentions after the fact. For instance, one of the committee's experts, Andrzej Paczkowski, argued in an interview coinciding with the presidential elections that in the light of newly available documents, it was by no means clear whether Jaruzelski had truly been afraid of a Soviet intervention. If such a threat really existed, he contended, the party would have prepared itself by selecting from its ranks a group to endorse the Soviet decision; the very fact that this was not done, Paczkowski maintained, showed the alleged danger was not taken seriously.[82]

In this way, what Brezhnev himself saw as the main obstacle to intervention—the absence of high-level Polish support for such a measure[83]—was interpreted as testifying that no intervention was ever seriously considered! But in the current context, it is even more important to note the falsity of the general assumption about intervention itself. At the time of the Polish crisis, Soviet intentions were in a process of continuous change, and thus no responsible person in Poland could have claimed to possess sufficient knowledge of them. Not only Jaruzelski but all thinking Poles were aware of the limits of Poland's sovereignty and of the danger of crossing the invisible line about what was ultimately permissible. Even very radical Solidarity activists had been well aware of this danger: Zbigniew Bujak informed the committee about very concrete preparations for such an event.[84] The final choice of a nonviolent, self-limiting revolution was by no means a proof that the union would have remained peaceful; the moods within it were aggressive enough and what restrained them (sometimes not sufficiently, to be sure) was *only* the keen awareness of an external danger. Without this danger, Solidarity leaders would not have deserved their reputation for bravery; the self-limiting character of the Solidarity revolution would have been unjustified and its leadership would have been guilty of an inexplicable timidity and cowardice.

Finally, in February 1996, the parliamentary committee voted for the discontinuance of its work, recommending that the parliament drop its case against "the authors of martial law." The vote was not unanimous. Five members out of eighteen, representing the UW, the KPN, and the Union of Labor, voted against it and announced their intention to defend a "minority resolution" in the parliament, demanding that the people responsible for martial law be put before the Tribunal of the State.[85] The KPN's representative, a respectable lawyer, Andrzej Ostoja-Owsiany, delivered a speech expressing the view that General Jaruzelski should have chosen the way of Romuald Traugutt when facing the Russian danger; Traugutt, the last leader of the insurrection of 1863–1864, had become a martyr and a symbol of a hopeless but heroic struggle. In contrast, the committee's chairman, Professor Wiatr, called this speech "beautiful" and polemicized against it in an extremely polite way, pointing out that Polish history also knew other models of legitimate and respectable patriotic activity.[86] Understandably, Jaruzelski was not satisfied; he would, he declared, prefer to face a formal trial and hear a final verdict. In this, he found support from Stanislaw Podemski, a commentator for the widely-read weekly *Polityka*. The existing parliament, Podemski noted, might endorse a resolution by the committee, but only a decision by the Tribunal of the State would finally remove the problem of how to deal with Jaruzelski's actions from the political agenda.[87] Such a decision, he added, could only be for acquittal, because the benefit of doubt in a court must always be given to the defendant. But, of course, no one could say how long it might take to prepare such a trial or even to bring it to a conclusion.

In this respect, the problem of settling accounts with martial law is still very much alive in Poland, and remains divisive. An influential minority continues to demand a legally binding verdict on the imposition of martial law and at least some form of punishment, if only a symbolic one, of its perpetrators. The deep passions aroused by the issue reflect not only many individuals' intense commitment to the idea of Poland's anticommunist identity but also the increasing political frustration of the new elite. As Jan Rokita, a member of the moderate, liberal-democratic UW, has put it, this frustration reflects "a feeling of deep defeat in the struggle with the legacy of People's Poland."[88]

Settling Accounts with the More Remote Past

In most postauthoritarian countries, the main point of pursuing transitional justice is, of course, the attempt to deal with the many concrete crimes, abuses of power, and violations of human rights that have been committed in the past. As we have seen, the emphasis in Poland is very different: the greatest passions have been aroused not by the cruelties of Jaruzelski's regime (in fact it would have been very difficult to perceive Jaruzelski as a cruel dictator) but instead by the very fact that he dared to use force in resisting the will of the nation. Those who have noisily demanded Jaruzelski's severe punishment, or even his execution, did not see him as a simple criminal or a bloody tyrant. Rather, they have sought to have him condemned and punished as a national traitor.

Nevertheless, the classical problem of what to do with the cases of a criminal violation of *human* rights (i.e., not only *national* rights) has arisen in Poland. It is a particularly burning problem for those Poles who remember the first decade of the communist regime, a time of fratricidal struggles bordering on a civil war and, somewhat later, a period of forcible "stalinization." However, because the new political elites of postcommunist Poland have chosen to concentrate their attention primarily on the most recent past, this situation has led to a neglect of the matter of settling accounts with the more remote periods of the country's history. As a result, the initiative to correct this deficiency has largely been taken by private citizens, and in most cases by former officers of the underground Home Army who were heavily persecuted in the first years after World War II. In January 1993, Michnik's *Gazeta wyborcza* published an open letter devoted to this issue. It was signed by a number of important persons, veterans of the Home Army, such as the famous historian of the holocaust, Wladyslaw Bartoszewski, the president of the Polish Academy of Sciences, Aleksander Gieysztor, the former head of the Polish section of Radio Free Europe, Jan Nowak-Jeziorański (who personally asked

Michnik to publish the letter), and many others. The letter expressed bitter disappointment with the fact that the Stalinist criminals, who had been responsible for sending to death the best patriots from the Home Army (some of them the letter mentioned by name), had not been punished. Accordingly, its authors demanded concrete legislative and organizational efforts to bring the perpetrators to justice and to render due tribute to their victims.[89]

The public reaction to this letter was ambiguous, not so much because of the letter's concrete demands but rather because of its merciless condemnation of the entire postwar period in Polish history. The critics' stand was best summarized by Stefan Bratkowski, a well-known journalist and a former Solidarity activist.[90] He protested against attempts to compare the crimes of Polish Stalinists with those of either Nazi or Soviet genocide; he distinguished between genuine fanatics and agents of foreign powers; and he pointed out that communism in Poland had been much milder than elsewhere, and that Polish communists had their share not only in making Poland "the most comfortable barrack in the bloc" but also in dismantling Stalinism and in paving the way for democracy. Hence, Bratkowski concluded, the only wise choice for Poles was national reconciliation, and not a policy of cold civil war, hatred, and revenge. Adam Michnik supported this conclusion. He opposed the view that hard-line anticommunist rhetoric was good for shaping the collective imagination of the Poles. Yet because he was also against supporting a collective amnesia, he proposed to counteract this tendency by making a magnanimous gesture of amnesty.[91] He even dared to suggest that the Polish Catholic Church, which was rightly proud of having told the German bishops "we forgive and ask for forgiveness," should itself extend this formula to Poland's former communists, thereby becoming the leader in the process of national reconciliation.[92]

At the end of the year, however, the unexpected outcome of Poland's parliamentary elections made the handling of these issues even more difficult. Moral issues had become excessively politicized. For example, Nowak-Jeziorański attributed the result of the elections to the country's softness on postcommunism. In his view, maintaining normal relations with the SLD blurred the distinction between "good" and "evil," between People's Poland and independent

Poland, thus ensuring the partial return of the former communists.[93] While Michnik disagreed with this position, he was becoming increasingly isolated and exposed to vicious attacks from the right. And over the following year, the entire "post-Solidarity camp" moved visibly to the right. Among the moderates from the UD, it became fashionable to engage in retrospective criticism of the Round Table Agreements, to deplore Mazowiecki's "thick line" and of course, to condemn the strange, supposedly procommunist aberrations of Michnik. However, this change of policy did not save the moderate forces from attacks by right-wing radicals; in their eyes, the entire UD remained a "pink" party, responsible for moral confusion and the political setbacks of healthy national forces.

Nevertheless, the problem of "what to do with the crimes of the past" was still very far from finding a workable solution. At the beginning of 1995, *Gazeta wyborcza* tried to shed light on the causes of this state of affairs by publishing two important interviews, one with the First President of the Supreme Court, Professor Adam Strzembosz, and another with Wlodzimierz Cimoszewicz, Deputy Prime Minister and Minister of Justice. Strzembosz, a relatively moderate Catholic conservative, deplored the "lack of political will" to solve the problem; he even spoke of a pseudo-Christian tendency to absolve all sins in a universal forgiveness. Still, he also pointed to some cases of deliberate concealment of the guilty, as a result, for example, of the elimination of names from archival documents. His own proposal to resolve the question can be characterized as a mild way of applying severe principles. Strzembosz suggested that the entire leadership of the PUWP before 1956 should be treated as a criminal organization and that no "liberalism" should be shown in dealing with either such Stalinist criminals or with persons responsible for the casualties of martial law. At the same time, however, he expressed a readiness to accept a blanket "amnesty [*abolicja*] law" (not applicable to murders and crimes against humanity), and regretted that this had not been made a part of the Round Table negotiations. Such an amnesty, he concluded, would be much better than shelving the matter and slowly forgetting about it altogether.[94]

Cimoszewicz, an independent member of the SLD, fully agreed that all criminal violations of human rights under the "old regime" should be properly punished. He refrained from advocating an "abolition" because this was, he said, a moral question and the Minister of Justice should not suggest legislating morality. In addition, he noted that were he in the place of the accused, he would prefer the due process of law and an unambiguous verdict. However, Cimoszewicz refused to endorse the view that Polish courts had deliberately neglected the issue of retrospective justice. Over the preceding four years, the Main Commission for Investigating the Crimes against the Polish Nation had conducted more than 500 inquiries and passed 95 cases to the Office of the State Attorney, which, in turn, had issued 20 indictments. True, only one of these cases—that of Adam Humer (see below)—actually led to a public trial, but the reasons for this circumstance were entirely objective. An overwhelming majority of cases pertained to the remote period of Polish Stalinism; thus, they involved aged and decrepit individuals who were dispersed all over the country and often unable to travel. The more recent cases involving criminal abuses of power by the security police and the citizens' militia had not been sufficiently documented and remain unclear. True, in many instances, the relevant documents had been destroyed, but the courts still needed to have a legal basis for acting. The bloody suppression of Gdańsk's riots in December 1970 had been investigated for four years by the regional court in Gdańsk; in this case the slowness of the proceeding was caused not by the lack of documents but by the excessively voluminous documentation that had been presented (including seventy volumes of acts). General Czeslaw Kiszczak, who was accused of causing the deaths of nine miners in a clash with the army in December 1981, had a heart attack while traveling to the court in Katowice, and for this reason he was unable to cooperate fully with the investigating magistrates. Finally, the courts had to reckon with the fact that the legal basis of prosecution is not the legal consciousness of today but the law of the time in question. From this perspective, many of the activities of the opposition before 1989 were plainly illegal, but the fact they are now highly appreciated does not mean that the defenders of the old regime should not have followed the logic of their own laws.[95]

Cimoszewicz's last remark signals the main problem, the contradiction between the legal positivism of the judges and the legal consciousness of many anticommunist politicians, a consciousness which justified the Solidarity revolution and demanded the punishment of its opponents. It is obvious that the interests of the legal profession in Poland are different from the interests of the country's new political class. The latter is impatient with positivist interpretations of law and ready to appeal to a higher justice, even to natural law. The former wants to remain independent of politics and to preserve its reputation for impartiality. This, of course, can be achieved only by clinging to the letter of the existing law.

Let us turn now to a brief discussion of the main cases of retrospective justice in Poland. The trial of Adam Humer and eleven other functionaries of the Stalinist security police lasted for more than two years and was perceived as a trial of the entire Stalinist system in Poland. Humer was accused of cruelly beating political prisoners (including women) in the years 1944–1954, and of causing the death of one of them (which, however, has not been proved). His conduct during the trial was ostentatiously unrepentant. He clung to his communist convictions, stressed the unavoidability of a merciless struggle for power, and let no one forget the fact that his own father, also a communist, had been killed by members of an anticommunist underground organization. Ultimately, Humer received a sentence of nine years of imprisonment, while his helpers got from two to eight years. However, because of bad health and advanced age, he was allowed to wait out the validation of the verdict at home.[96]

The reaction to this verdict was generally positive. It was seen as severe but just. Indeed, Poles evidently do not need additional arguments to be convinced that Stalinist rule in their country and elsewhere rested on terror, and that terror as such is an unacceptable evil. But precisely because of this fact, it is necessary to point out that Humer's trial was accompanied by a political campaign whose aims must be considered less commendable than a simple "restoration of justice." These campaigns had an underlying political purpose, to obliterate the difference between the Stalinist and post-Stalinist periods by using old, Stalinist crimes as a way of creating a uniformly black picture of the entire forty-five years of People's Poland. For the right-wing radicals, it was a normal routine to propagate such views. But it was unusual to see respectable individuals, like Adam Strzembosz and the liberal-democratic UD senator, Jacek Taylor, trying to convince their listeners that there was no difference between Humer's crimes and the shooting of workers in Gdańsk or Jaruzelski's martial law, and that all these acts were aspects of the same criminal system and deserved to be classified as "crimes against humanity." All this took place on a public television program with the self-explanatory title, "We have learned how to torture from Humer."[97]

As George Orwell once put it, "whoever controls the past, controls the future." Nevertheless, while the political purpose of these campaigns was clear, it seems that their actual effect was rather meager, if not counterproductive. Humer's crimes were repulsive, but still, they looked insignificantly small in comparison with the massive crimes of Russian and German totalitarianism. Torturing people is not an exclusive specialization of the communist regimes. Unfortunately, it also occurred in prewar Poland[98] and, on an incomparably greater scale, under the authoritarian regimes of Latin America, just as it has occurred in all countries undergoing violent revolutionary change. The expression "crimes against humanity," as defined in different United Nations documents,[99] could be applied to Humer, but it was entirely unjustified to extend its meaning to cover the deeds of Jaruzelski and Kiszczak, and not supported by any existing definition of the term.

In August 1995, another "anti-Stalinist" trial was announced. Maria Gurowska, an 80-year-old judge, who in 1952 had sentenced to death General Emil Fieldorf, the Home Army's chief of diversionary activities, was formally accused of judicial murder. Gurowska refused to accept this charge, saying that she had acted in accordance with her conscience; Fieldorf had been unable to change himself and, therefore, had to be "eliminated from society."[100] Legally, this is bound to be a very complicated and instructive case, though we can hope that its outcome will not be influenced by any political pressures.

Naturally, for younger Poles, Stalinism is a remote past. But because the Gdańsk events of December 1970 are a part of their life experience, the beginning of their own oppositional legend, it is understandable that another trial, which began in Gdańsk on March 28, 1996, was a truly vital issue. In this case, twelve defendants—among them, General Jaruzelski, then Minister of Defence, Kazimierz Świtala, former Minister of Internal Affairs, and Stanislaw Kociolek, former Deputy Prime Minister—were accused of ordering police to shoot at protesting workers, which resulted in the killing of forty-four people and wounding of about two hundred. The initial trial was well prepared, but the court took into account the appeal of the counsels for the defence, who argued that the former members of government had to be tried before the Tribunal of the State. As a result, the trial was postponed and, at the time of this writing, very little can be said about it. It is known, however, that the main decisions in this incident were taken by Gomulka himself, in close collaboration with two members of the Politburo, Kociolek and Zenon Kliszko, who is no longer alive. Jaruzelski has consistently denied his responsibility. At the trial's opening session, he stated: "I see in the audience the families of the killed, as well as people who were mutilated, or wounded. I direct to them words of regret and compassion. But I cannot forget about the hundreds of wounded policemen and soldiers. And although I take responsibility for martial law, I am not morally responsible for December 1970."[101]

Of course, we should not anticipate judicial decisions. But the same maxim applies to journalists and politicians as well. They should not accuse independent judges of being afraid of their responsibility, nor should they indulge in putting pressure on the court by comparing the Gdańsk tragedy to the crimes of Nazism. They should also not suggest that the Gdańsk trial should be seen as a Polish equivalent of the Nuremberg trial.[102] Yet, since such comparisons have already been made in the press, it is worthwhile to consider why they are untenable. The protest of the Gdańsk shipyard workers, which was caused by steep and unexpected price increases less than two weeks before Christmas, took the form of uncontrollable riots, accompanied by violence, acts of vandalism, and efforts to storm the Party headquarters. To quote a well-informed British journalist, who sympathized with the workers: "In the fighting, the Party building and the main railway station were burned down. The following day, the rebellion spread to the near-by towns of Slupsk and Elbląg, and there were reports of sympathy strikes elsewhere. The men and women of the Warski Shipyard at Szczecin prepared to strike."[103]

Under these conditions, the communist authorities had reasons for fear, and it is therefore arguable that they acted not out of cruelty but out of fear. True, their conduct was condemnable, but it was not comparable to the savage butcheries organized by the Nazis or the Stalinists. Nor could it be classified as a "crime against humanity." Had it been otherwise, how could we explain the fact that Cardinal Karol Wojtyla, the future Pope John Paul II, condemned not only the government's shooting but also the rioting, violence, acts of vandalism, and robberies? What should we think about his appeal to Poles to support Gomulka's successor, Edward Gierek, in restoring order in the rebellious city?[104] How, too, should we explain the jubilant, if transient, mood of national reconciliation in December 1980, when a monument to the fallen workers was erected in Gdańsk? Finally, how are we to classify violent reactions to social disturbances in prewar Poland? Comparison is not a justification, but it is useful to remember that in November 1923 the price of crushing the workers' riots in Cracow and a few small towns in the vicinity was forty dead and several hundred wounded; and that during the great peasant strike in August 1937, the police wounded hundreds of people and killed at least forty-one.[105]

Similar things can be said about Kiszczak's trial in Katowice. At the time of this writing, the trial had not yet concluded [Kiszczak would later be acquitted of all charges in August 1996]. However, it has been widely publicized that in May 1995, Michnik spoke at the trial as a witness for the defense. He testified that Kiszczak, with whom he maintained personal relations after the Round Table, had always maintained that the killing of nine miners in December 1981 was done in contravention to his orders. He also quoted a very positive opinion about Kiszczak by a high-ranking dignitary of the Church.

Apart from Father Jerzy Popieluszko—the well-known oppositional priest whose brutal killing by security police at the end of 1984 was intended to wreck Jaruzelski's policy of reconciliation, and whose murderers were subject to public trial and sentenced the following year—the most important victim of political conflicts after martial law was Grzegorz Przemyk, son of an oppositional writer, Barbara Sadowska, who was beaten to death by "unknown perpetra-

tors" in May 1983. At this date, the trial of the two policemen suspected in his death is unfinished and remains inconclusive. However, it is a sign of the complexity of the case and the need to avoid
premature judgments that the policemen are defended by Stanislaw
Szczuka, a lawyer with an oppositional record and a reputation as a
hard-line anticommunist who is, at the same time, convinced of his
clients' innocence.

In short, the controversial issue in Poland is not whether politically motivated crimes of the past should, or should not, be punished. No political group advocates a wholesale amnesty. The real
problem has to do with the political uses of these crimes. Is it warranted to compare them to the crimes of genocidal, totalitarian
regimes? Is it justified to obliterate the difference between Poland before and after 1956? And is it morally and politically permissible to
use retrospective justice as a way of stirring up hatred against postcommunists, mobilizing right-wing radicals, and trying to deepen
the divisions of the past and make them unbridgeable? Is it reasonable to deplore the fact that there was no Polish equivalent of the
Nuremberg trial, and that Polish political life has not been subject to
systematic decommunization, modelled on the denazification of
postwar Germany?

Unfortunately, these sorts of complaints and demands are typical
not only of "anticommunist bolsheviks." They also turn up in the re-
spectably moderate, liberal-democratic press. Furthermore, the reaction against such practices seems to be increasingly bold and visible.
Thus, Jerzy Jedlicki, a respected historian and one of the authoritative spokesmen for post-Solidarity moderates, reacted sharply to demands for a radical acceleration of the cause of settling accounts with
the past which appeared in the columns of the *Catholic Weekly*.[106]
There were many objective reasons, he noted, why Polish courts
were sometimes irritatingly slow; only a lynch law could be really
quick. Further, he resolutely protested against all comparisons between the problem of decommunization in Poland and the problem
of denazification in Germany: "Such comparisons, trivializing
Auschwitz and Treblinka, are, in my view impermissible. In this
question I have behind me a majority of the enlightened public opinion in Europe."[107]

Concluding Remarks

The outcome of the presidential elections of 1995 was a great shock to many Polish intellectuals and to the entire post-Solidarity political elite in Poland. Reactions to the event were often very emotional and uncontrolled. A rabidly anticommunist writer, Jacek Trznadel, divided his compatriots into "genuine" and "nominal" Poles, suggesting that Aleksander Kwaśniewski owed his election only to the latter.[108] A sophisticated classicist poet, Jaroslaw Marek Rymkiewicz, described in vulgar terms what a dog should do with the unworthy Polish society.[109] A Catholic publicist called the results of the elections "the fourth and greatest national defeat in Polish history." Other writers declared themselves humiliated and deeply ashamed, feeling nothing in common with Kwaśniewski's electorate.[110] Many people used the occasion to repeat the view that the main cause of all political disasters was the failure to implement a policy of lustration and decommunization.

It cannot be denied that lustration has failed completely in Poland. It does not seem that it has a chance of being successfully implemented in the foreseeable future. Antoni Macierewicz, the author of the failed policy under Olszewski's government, has himself faced a trial, behind closed doors, for his irresponsible disclosure of state secrets.[111] In this light, Jerzy Giedroyc, the editor of the emigré monthly *Kultura*, has concluded that the best thing one can to do to avoid a possible repeat performance of this initiative is to burn the relevant documents under the supervision of the Spokesman For Human Rights.[112]

However, the question of decommunization is still very much alive on the right wing of the political spectrum. It is, of course, too late to imitate the Czech model, but the growing dissatisfaction and anger of industrial workers threatened by unemployment and relative impoverishment has created a fertile ground in Poland for demagogic demands to settle matters with the "old thieves from the nomenklatura." Such demands have been repeatedly voiced both by Solidarity, whose members seem to think that capitalist entrepreneurs, in order to be acceptable, must have a "correct" political genealogy, and by Walesa, who has threatened to take away what has been plundered. Today, the idea of expropriating those "communist capitalists" who have enriched themselves by making use of their old connections, is voiced by Jan Olszewski's Movement For the Reconstruction of Poland, the only party on the right whose social support has been on the increase. (In 1996 it attracted 16 percent of the voters). In a recently published interview, Olszewski extended the threat of expropriation to foreign investors, warning against fences who might try to sell stolen property.[113]

While it is hard for this writer to believe that this program has any chance of realization, its very existence shows that the greatest threat to the stability of market economy and rule of law in Poland may now be represented by the radical right. By contrast, the SdRP (and SLD as a whole) has earned the reputation of being a force of stabilization in Poland, genuinely committed to the new rules of the game. Bronislaw Łagowski, one of the most consistent conservative liberals in Poland, has tried to explain this fact to the rationally-thinking politicians of the right. "The so-called post-communists," he has written, "are continuing the policy of the post-Solidarity governments with only one modification—they are more cautious in concrete questions. If the continuity of reforms inaugurated in 1989 is threatened, this is so because of those who have started the struggle for a 'universal affranchisement' [i.e., those who have called for the redistribution of property to everyone]. . . . Solidarity's project of a revolution in property relations is a negation of the reforms implemented in the years 1989–93. The main opponent of this project, and of the entire paradigm of collective farms on which it is based, is the SdRP."[114]

A problem that will continue to divide Poland is that of General Jaruzelski and martial law. The present parliament will certainly approve discontinuing the inquiries of the Committee for Constitutional Responsibility, but such a decision is likely to be immediately questioned as politically motivated. The "anticommunist opposition" will not cease to struggle for Jaruzelski's indictment, since only a wholesale condemnation of the recent past can provide it with a clear mandate to rule. Many people think that magnanimity is good, perhaps, in the moment of triumph, but this will not be true at the time of the electoral successes of postcommunist forces. In other words, Jaruzelski should be made to pay for Kwaśniewski's victory. He should suffer constant attacks and humiliation, accompanied by threats, even if no court has sentenced him to endure such punishments, and even if the overwhelming majority of the Poles do not believe that he deserves such an ordeal.

Thus, the Polish record is really a very sad story, and there is still no good solution in view. At the beginning of 1993, Andrzej Micewski, a well-known Catholic journalist, proposed to deal with the matter by issuing an "amnesty [*abolicja*] decree."[115] At the time, this would have been a magnanimous gesture and also amounted to a political victory for the new elite, which seemed firmly in power. In the current period, however, an abolition might be regarded not as a gesture of good will but as a belated and forced concession. In addition, the post-Solidarity camp has fallen into a genuinely mean-spirited mood; it even wanted to deprive Jaruzelski, the first president of new Poland, of his presidential pension, while offering such a pension to Kaczorowski, the symbolic president in exile. As Jerzy Giedroyc commented, "This is simply indecent—especially since it was the deputies of Solidarity who elected Jaruzelski to presidential office."[116]

The final problem—the problem of past crimes—is, as we have seen, simple in theory but difficult in practice. Almost everyone agrees that all crimes should be punished, but—and here the difficulties begin—with the due process of law, on the basis of solid evidence. An even more important obstacle to the resolution of such cases has to do with the political and moral context in which justice is pursued. First, retrospective justice should not be used for political purposes, let alone to arouse resentment and hatred. Second, in judging the past, a sense of proportion must be preserved. The repressions under Jaruzelski's regime should not be compared to Stalinist terror, and Polish Stalinism, even at its worst, should be clearly distinguished from Soviet Stalinism and Nazism. The much abused argument that the very distinction between the "greater" and "lesser" evil stems from an unacceptable moral relativism, is demagogic and untenable. After all, moral absolutism entails, as a rule, a belief in an objective *hierarchization* of values, that is to say, the ability to make distinctions between greater and lesser goods and evils.

Having said this, let us stress that morality is not law, that it cannot be legislated, and that moral absolutism supported by the state is utterly incompatible with the rule of law and democracy. Adam Michnik, the most consistent advocate of a humanitarian and magnanimous way of dealing with the difficult past, has proclaimed the primacy of freedom over justice. Some demands for justice, he has maintained, should be abandoned as the price required for the peaceful dismantling of dictatorship, for democratic compromise and national reconciliation.[117] This observation is quite correct, but I would phrase it in a somewhat different although fully compatible way. Retrospective justice would be much simpler if its legal aspects were separated from demanding the so-called "restoration of moral justice." If some people's feelings of justice cannot be satisfied without an unequivocal condemnation of the communist past and without drawing a Manichean line between "good" and "evil," this is merely their private problem. Liberal-democratic states must remain neutral in such matters, because to do otherwise would contradict their guiding principles, freedom of conscience and justice as fairness.[118] A democracy's legislative and judicial organs cannot be expected to determine a binding truth about the past. Thus, they must not try to render justice to true patriots and to teach lessons to those who are supposedly not worthy of this name. The problem of political justice should not be confused with the problem of the highest good. The essential task of political justice is to define the fair terms of social cooperation between people of different world-views, different moral convictions, different life experiences, and of course different opinions about the recent national past.

NOTES

This article is based upon events in Poland up to the end of May 1996.

  1. Philip Earl Steele, "Wielkoduszność—skaza na wielkości?" *Życie Warszawy*, December 30, 1995–January 1, 1996.
  2. For an excellent analysis of Polish "real socialism" of the 1970s as a clientelistic system, see J. Tarkowski, *Patroni i klienci (Socjologia świata polityki, t.2)* (Warsaw: Instytut Studiów Politycznych PAN, 1994). The expression "dirty togetherness" has been coined by Adam Podgórecki. See

A. Podgórecki and M. Loś, *Multi-dimensional Sociology* (London: Routledge and Kegan Paul, 1979).

3. See A. Michnik, "Polskie Kredowe Kolo," in the collection *Książka dla Jacka. W sześćdziesiątą rocznicę urodzin Jacka Kuronia* (Warsaw: Fundacja Nowej, 1995), p. 122.

4. See E. Malefakis, "Spain and Its Francoist Heritage," in Neil J. Kritz, ed., *Transitional Justice: How Emerging Democracies Reckon With Former Regimes*, vol. 2, *Country Studies* (Washington, D.C.: United States Institute of Peace Press, 1995), pp. 321–322.

5. See ibid., pp. 533–535 ("Czechoslovakia. Editor's Introduction").

6. See the conversation with J. Kaczyński, in J. Kurski and P. Semka, eds., *Lewy czerwcowy* (Warsaw: Editions Spotkania, 1992), pp. 15–16.

7. See "Deklaracja Socjaldemokracji Rzeczypospolitej Polskiej," *Trybuna*, no. 4, 1990, p. 4; and "Statut Socjaldemokracji RP," accepted by the founding Congress on January 28, 1990, ibid., pp. 4–5.

8. For a vivid description of Jaruzelski's visit to Spain in June 1990, see W. Górnicki, *Teraz już można* (Warsaw: Wyd. Dolnośląskie, 1994), pp. 32–51. In the following year Jaruzelski, no longer president of Poland, came to Spain once more, this time to participate, together with Michnik, in the international seminar at Antonio Pelayo University in Santander. He was met there by the Queen of Spain, a sign of special respect from the royal family.

9. See the conversation with Glapiński in Kurski and Semka, *Lewy czerwcowy*, pp. 107–111.

10. The word "communists" is put here in inverted commas because the PUWP had undergone, after 1956, a long process of decommunization and in the 1970s could no longer be regarded as communist in any acceptable meaning of the term. This was quite clear to Poland's socialist neighbors: the lack of a genuinely "Marxist-Leninist" (i.e., communist) group within the PUWP was for them one of the main arguments against their direct intervention in the Polish crisis of 1980–1981. For the concept of internal decommunization, see chapter 6 ("The Dismantling of Stalinism: Detotalitarization and Decommunization") of my book *Marxism and the Leap to the Kingdom of Freedom: The Rise and Fall of the Communist Utopia* (Stanford: Stanford University Press, 1995).

11. It is interesting to note, however, that many "independentists," despite their manifest intolerance of all forms of collaboration with communism, had previously been active in the ranks of the PUWP. Moczulski himself was once a party member, actively supporting General Moczar's nationalist faction in 1968. I do not think, by the way, that this fact is enough to discredit him; it shows only that his type of patriotism was not rigidly inflexible and fully incompatible with membership in the PUWP. On the whole, the position of broadly conceived "independentism" is deeply rooted in certain Polish traditions. The moral fundamentalism bound up with it stems from an absolutization of certain authentic values. Hence it is sometimes represented by people with creative intellects and unquestionable moral integrity. A good example of this is the famous poet Zbigniew Herbert.

12. For a detailed presentation of this campaign, see my article "From

Stalinism to Post-Communist Pluralism: The Case of Poland," *New Left Review* 185 (January/February 1991): 108–112.

13. See M. Zalewski, "Let Solidarity Break in Two," *Newsweek*, July 16, 1990, p. 6.

14. See the conversation with Kaczyński in Kurski and Semka, *Lewy czerwcowy*, pp. 21–25.

15. This rather cynical plan has been outlined in Kaczyński's interview with *Le Figaro*, July 31, 1990.

16. See "W kraju," *Polityka*, April 17, 1990, p. 2.

17. For ironical remarks on these half-hearted attempts, see J. Sądecki, "Aparat w odwrocie," *Tygodnik Solidarność*, March 30, 1990, pp. 1 and 17.

18. He deeply wounded and antagonized many people in Poland by stating that "real socialism" was a greater disaster to Poland than the Nazi occupation.

19. In 1976 Najder founded the underground group *Alliance for Independence*. Unlike KPN, it was not a party but limited itself to publishing materials to help Polish intellectuals prepare themselves for possible independence. After martial law, he became the head of the Polish Section of Radio Free Europe. For this reason, a Polish military court accused him of national betrayal and sentenced him in absentia to the death penalty.

20. See Sejmu RP, Kadencja I: Sprawozdanie stenograficzne z posiedzenia Sejmu RP w dn. 30–31. I i 1.II 1992. Projekt ustawy o restytucji niepodległości.

21. See *Monitor Polski*, no. 16, June 11, 1992, p. 181.

22. See the interview with Macierewicz in Kurski and Semka, *Lewy czerwcowy*, p. 245.

23. J. Gowin, "Polska niemota," *Tygodnik powszechny*, June 28, 1992, p. 1.

24. A. Michnik, J. Tischner, and J. Żakowski, *Między panem a plebanem* (Cracow: Znak, 1995), p. 588.

25. For the text of this verdict, see J. Snopkiewicz, ed., *Teczki, czyli widma bezpieki. "Czarny scenariusz" czerwcowego przewrotu* (Warsaw: BGW, 1992), p. 114. This book contains a comprehensive analysis of the political context of Macierewicz's "lustration affair."

26. The trial began on September 6, that is, just two weeks before the elections.

27. Quoted from the chronicle of events June 4, 1989–December 28, 1995 in *Res Publica Nowa*, no. 2, 1996, p. 17.

28. For a good summary of such views, see E. Wnuk-Lipiński, "Recydywa PRL—z naszą pomocą," *Gazeta wyborcza*, July 5, 1994, pp. 10–11. Fear of "the return of People's Poland" was also expressed by the Primate of Poland, Józef Glemp. See "Czy PRL trwa?" *Gazeta wyborcza*, March 16, 1995, p. 3.

29. See B. Geremek, "Parliamentarism in Central Europe" (a speech delivered at the University of Chicago Law School on December 1, 1994), *East European Constitutional Review* 4, no. 3 (Summer 1995): 43–48. What is peculiar is the fact that Geremek refers to the PUWP as "the Communist Party," or the CP, as if this were its official name, and more importantly, as if the

PUWP of the 1980s could be regarded as a genuine communist party (which was patently untrue). Even worse is the widespread habit of applying the term "communist" to the SLD, despite its clearly noncommunist statute and program. Such a practice deserves to be seen as a dishonest political manipulation. See, for instance, Roszkowski's handbook of modern Polish history, where we read that SLD means "the communists." (W. Roszkowski, *Historia Polski 1914–1991* [Warsaw: PWN, 1992], p. 415).

30. I heard Walesa saying this in the television program "Linia specjalna" (Special line) on November 20, 1994. He said explicitly that only fear of a civil war prevented him from settling accounts (*rozliczenie*) with the communist bandits.

31. This leaflet, entitled *Precz z czerwoną burżuazją*! and also containing eleven demands of the Masovian branch of Solidarity, is in my possession.

32. The UW, of course, claimed this merit for Balcerowicz, i.e., for Mazowiecki's government. It could not deny, however, that the SLD, on the whole, continued Balcerowicz's reforms and defended them against its agrarian ally.

33. A. Michnik and W. Cimoszewicz, "O prawdę i pojednanie," *Gazeta wyborcza*, September 9–10, 1995.

34. It is fair to note that in the last moment the bishops changed their tone and issued a pastoral letter on "The need for dialogue and tolerance." (See E. Nowakowska, "Zmiana tonu," *Polityka*, October 28, 1995, p. 13). As might have been expected, the influence of this letter on the attitudes of the local clergy was rather limited.

35. For an account of these dramatic events, see R. Walenciak, "Ostatni hak Walęsy," *Przegląd Tygodniowy*, January 3, 1996, p. 4.

36. See, for instance, A. Drawicz, "Nie liczy się przeszłość," *Gazeta wyborcza*, March 9–10, 1996, pp. 12–13. Cf. also J. Giedroyc, "Notatki redaktora," *Kultura*, January 1996.

37. See Jane Perlez, "Dissidents Say Secret Police Still Make Trouble in Poland," *New York Times*, January 23, 1996, p. A5.

38. He was shown saying this on television after the daily "News," on February 9. See M. Nowicki, "Kalendarium wolności," *Res Publica nowa*, no. 4, 1996, p. 29.

39. W. Pięciak, "Chichot historii," *Tygodnik powszechny*, February 18, 1996, p. 3.

40. For the text of this resolution, see *Monitor Polski*, no. 5, Feb. 19, 1992, pp. 77–78.

41. See "Sprawozdanie stenograficzne z 7 posiedzenia Sejmu w du. 1 lutego 1992," p. 174 (the speech of T. Iwiński).

42. Ibid., p. 162.

43. Ibid., pp. 199–200.

44. Ibid., p. 202.

45. Ibid., p. 198.

46. Ibid., pp. 163–164.

47. Ibid., pp. 160–161.

48. This was pointed out in Jaruzelski's letter of January 21, 1992, to the

Speaker of the House, Professor Wieslaw Chrzanowski (ZChN), and S. Podemski's article in *Polityka* of February 1, 1992. Both texts are available in A. Karaś, ed., *Sąd nad autorami stanu wojennego* (Warsaw: BGW, 1993), pp. 11–13.

49. See *Sąd nad autorami*, pp. 7–8.

50. Ibid., p. 223 (the words of Jaruzelski's advocate, K. Łojewski).

51. J. Kaczyński in *Nowy Świat*, October 24–25, 1992. Quoted from *Sąd nad autorami*, p. 323.

52. *Sąd nad autorami*, pp. 33, 39.

53. Ibid., p. 41.

54. Ibid., p. 47.

55. See General E. Molczyk in *Biuletyn Kancelarii Sejmu*, no. 1608/II Kad., Meeting of the Committee on Constitutional Responsibility, June 6, 1995, p. 10.

56. Manfred Wilke, in *Biuletyn*, no. 1455/II Kad., Meeting of the Committee on Constitutional Responsibility, April 7, 1995, pp. 8–13.

57. A. Werblan, in *Biuletyn*, no. 461/II Kad., Meeting of the Committee on Constitutional Responsibility, April 19–20, 1994, pp. 26–33. Before martial law, Werblan, a former member of the Polish Politburo, represented the reformist wing of the party.

58. See Holzer and Kersten, ibid.

59. See M. Wilke in *Biuletyn*, no. 1455/II Kad., Meeting of the Committee on Constitutional Responsibility, April 7, 1995, p. 9.

60. H. Jabloński, in *Sąd nad autorami*, p. 133.

61. A. Werblan, in *Biuletyn*, no. 461/II Kad., Meeting of the Committee on Constitutional Responsibility, April 19–20, 1994, p. 32.

62. W. Jaruzelski, ibid., pp. 3, 44. See also Jaruzelski's earlier statements of November 24, 1992 and of March 10, 1993 (*Sąd nad autorami*, pp. 78 and 204). On March 10, 1993, he said: "I knew very well the Imperial status of the Soviet Union. But I will not swim with the current. I have always been convinced that good, friendly relations with our eastern neighbor are important for Poland. I will not repaint myself into a scoffer and an enemy of the Russians. I knew very well the realities of these time, I took them into account as a politician and as a general. I knew there were limits of risk that we should not overstep." Tina Rosenberg claims that Mieczyslaw Rakowski, Jaruzelski's friend and the last general secretary of the PUWP, told her that "Jaruzelski would have called martial law, Soviet threat or no." (T. Rosenberg, *The Haunted Land: Facing Europe's Ghosts After Communism* [New York: Random House, 1995], p. 217). She also says that Gomulka bluffed Khrushchev in 1956 but that Jaruzelski lacked the will to bluff Brezhnev (ibid.). This observation ignores a fundamental difference: Gomulka could have bluffed the Russians without endangering Polish socialism, but in 1981 the Polish socialist system really was under threat and Jaruzelski did not want its collapse, both for internal and for external reasons.

63. *Sąd nad autorami*, p. 264. Curiously enough, the question of violence against the police has not been subject to further investigation.

64. Ibid., p. 207.

65. W. Jaruzelski, *Stan wojenny-dlaczego?* (Warsaw: BGW, 1992), p. viii. This book bears the motto, "Nobody can be a judge of himself" (*nemo judex in causa sua*).

66. A. Michnik, "Im gorzej, tym gorzej," *Gazeta wyborcza*, September 25–26, 1993, pp. 10–11.

67. Ibid.

68. On the eve of the elections of 1993, the formula "a minimum of fraternity" was also endorsed by B. Geremek. See "Odrobina braterstwa," Adam Michnik's interview with Prof. B. Geremek, *Gazeta wyborcza*, September 16, 1993, p. 12.

69. On the whole, attempts to fan hostile feelings against Jaruzelski conspicuously failed. In the spring of 1994, 52 percent of the population saw him as a better president than Walesa (with only 24 percent holding the opposite view), and 71 percent thought that he should not be punished for martial law (the opposite view was held by only 15 percent). See J. J. Wiatr, *Co nam zostalo z tych lat?* (Toruń: Adam Marszalek, 1995), p. 11. Nevertheless, in October 1994 at a presentation of Jaruzelski's book on martial law, an individual named Helski threw a large stone at Jaruzelski's face, seriously damaging his cranium and one of his eyes. Jaruzelski expressed forgiveness for this act and said he did not want Helski to be prosecuted. The right-wing press, however, did not refrain from celebrating Helski's deed as an act of justice. Its mood was well expressed in a rhyme: "Beware Jaruzelski of a platoon of Helskis!"

70. See "Wybaczymy po wyroku," *Gazeta wyborcza*, December 17–18, 1994, p. 1.

71. See, for instance, A. Szczypiorski, "Galop mastodontów," *Gazeta wyborcza*, December 19, 1994, p. 5.

72. A. Szostkiewicz, "Kto może spać spokojnie?" *Tygodnik Powszechny*, December 24–31, 1995, p. 3.

73. *Sąd nad autorami*, pp. 80–81. People were sent to Bereza Kartuska without due legal procedure, and many of them were beaten and subject to different forms of humiliation.

74. Ibid., p. 252.

75. See *Biuletyn*, no. 990/I Kad., Meeting of the Committee on Constitutional Responsibility, January 6, 1993, p. 12. (For unexplained reasons the report of this meeting has not been included in *Sąd nad autorami*, although the book ends with the report of March 9–10, 1993). Gubiński did not refer to Dmowski but the source of the quoted words is unmistakable. In his *Polityka polska i odbudowanie państwa* (1925), Dmowski said: "Everybody can risk his private property and sacrifice his own life. Sometimes it is a moral duty. But no individual, no organization, and no generation can expose to danger the very existence of Poland. . . . The man who exposes to risk the existence of his nation resembles a gambler who plays with someone else's money." (R. Dmowski, *Wybór pism* [New York: Instytut Romana Dmowskiego, 1988], 2: 67).

76. Ibid., p. 14.

77. See A. Bromke, *Poland's Politics: Idealism versus Realism* (Cambridge, Mass.: Harvard University Press, 1967). For an updated treatment of this problematic, see A. Walicki, "The Three Traditions of Polish Patriotism," in S. Gomulka and A. Polonsky, eds., *Polish Paradoxes* (London: Routledge, 1990), pp. 21–40.

78. H. Jabłoński in *Sąd nad autorami*, p. 111.

79. H. Jabłoński, "Uwagi o genezie stanu wojennego," *Dziś*, no. 12, 1994, pp. 108–110.

80. *Biuletyn*, no. 990/I Kad., Meeting of the Committee on Constitutional Responsibility, January 6, 1993, pp. 9–10.

81. Ibid., p. 11.

82. "Kontrrewolucyjny zamach stanu." An interview with A. Paczkowski, *Tygodnik powszechny*, November 19, 1995, pp. 1 and 7. The use of archival documents in political struggle was characterized by Max Weber as signifying "a lack of dignity." This was pointed out by B. Łagowski ("Adresowane do prawicy," *Tygodnik powszechny*, March 24, 1996, p. 5), who quoted the following sentences from Weber's "Politics as a Vocation": "Every new document that comes to light after decades revives the undignified lamentations, the hatred and scorn, instead of allowing the war to be buried, at least morally. Instead of being concerned about what the politician is interested in, the future and the responsibility towards the future, this ethic is concerned about politically sterile questions of past guilt, which are not to be settled politically. To act in this way is politically guilty, if such guilt exists at all." Quoted from H. H. Gerth and C. Wright Mills, eds., *From Max Weber* (New York: Oxford University Press, 1958), p. 118.

83. See note 59 above.

84. Z. Bujak in *Biuletyn*, no. 1266/II Kad., Meeting of the Committee on Constitutional Responsibility, February 14, 1995, pp. 31–32.

85. See "Umorzenie postępowania," *Polityka*, February 24, 1996, p. 12. One member of the committee abstained from voting.

86. I have the text of Wiatr's speech (fifteen pages), thanks to the author's courtesy.

87. S. Podemski, "Stan wojenny bez Trybunalu," *Polityka*, February 24, 1996, p. 13.

88. "Widmo powolnej śmierci." An interview with Jan Rokita, *Polityka*, March 2, 1996, pp. 24–25.

89. "O sprawiedliwość i prawdę," *Gazeta wyborcza*, January 28, 1993, p. 4.

90. S. Bratkowski, "O mądrość narodową Polaków," *Gazeta wyborcza*, February 2, 1993, pp. 12–13.

91. A. Michnik, "Im gorzej, tym gorzej," *Gazeta wyborcza*, September 25–26, 1993, pp. 10–11.

92. See A. Michnik, J. Tischner, and J. Żakowski, *Między Panem a Plebanem* (Krakow: Znak, 1995), p. 560.

93. As summarized by Michnik in "Im gorzej, tym gorzej."

94. "Prawo pod sukno." Jaroslaw Kurski's interview with Professor Adam Strzembosz, *Gazeta wyborcza*, January 9, 1995, pp. 14–15.

95. "Gorzka bezradność." Jaroslaw Kurski's interview with Wlodzimierz Cimoszewicz, *Gazeta wyborcza*, January 10, 1995, pp. 12–13.

96. See P. Lipiński, "Dziewięć lat dla Humera," *Gazeta wyborcza*, March 9–10, 1996, p. 1, and S. Podemski, "Sprawiedliwość przybywa za późno," *Polityka*, March 16, 1996, p. 15.

97. "Uczyliśmy się torturować od Humera," a television program of March 28, 1995, followed by a discussion between A. Strzembosz, J. Taylor, and others.

98. For instance, seven political prisoners were beaten to death in Janów Lubelski in 1930. Or consider the cases of physical violence in the pacification of Ukrainian villages. See J. Buszko, *Historia Polski 1864–1948* (Warsaw: PWN, 1980), pp. 325–327.

99. The term "crimes against humanity" was defined in an agreement between France, the United Kingdom, the United States, and the Soviet Union for the persecution and punishment of the major war criminals, signed August 8, 1945 in London. It was also used in 1974 by the so-called Bertrand Russell Tribunal, which applied it to the torture of the authoritarian regimes in Latin America. See E. J. Osmańczyk, *Encyclopedia of the United Nations and International Agreements* (Philadelphia, London: Taylor and Francis, 1985), p. 179 ("Crimes against humanity") and p. 808 ("Tortures and the UN Declaration 1975"). It was never used to describe using arms for the suppression of riots.

100. See "Zabójstwo sądowe," *Życie Warszawy*, August 12, 1995, p. 1.

101. See "Tydzień w kraju," *Polityka*, April 6, 1996, p. 12.

102. See "Polska Norymberga," *Tygodnik powszechny*, December 24–31, 1995, p. 8.

103. N. Ascherson, *The Polish August* (Harmondsworth, England: Penguin, 1981), p. 101.

104. See "Gdy Gierek zastąpil Gomulkę." Documents published by A. Garlicki, *Polityka*, February 3, 1996, pp. 68–69.

105. See Buszko, *Historia Polski 1864–1948*, pp. 281, 382.

106. The author of this article was A. Szostkiewicz. See note 72 above.

107. J. Jedlicki, "O znieważonym poczuciu sprawiedliwości (Letter to A. Szostkiewicz)," *Tygodnik powszechny*, January 21, 1996, p. 5.

108. Trznadel's essay "Nominalni Polacy" appeared in *Tygodnik Solidarność*. See "Polityka i obyczaje" in *Polityka*, February 24, 1996, p. 88.

109. Quoted from Smecz, "Z ukosa," *Kultura*, March 1996, pp. 75–76 (originally published in *Tygodnik Solidarność*).

110. See the summary of such opinions by W. Zaluska, "Po wielkim szoku," *Gazeta wyborcza*, January 2, 1996, p. 11. The first of the above quoted opinions belongs to S. Janczak ("Przegrane wybory," *Slowo-Dziennik katolicki*, no. 237, 1995), the second—to B. Pociej ("Nasz dramat," *Tygodnik Solidarność*, no. 50, 1995).

111. For brief information about the political manifestations accompanying the opening of this trial, see "Polityka i obyczaje," *Polityka*, April 6, 1996, p. 96. The court decided to discontinue the trial because the parliament failed to provide an act of indictment of Macierewicz.

112. See the interview with Giedroyc, in M. Łukasiewicz and E. Sawicka, eds., *Co zrobiliśmy z naszą wolnością?* (Warsaw: Presspublica, 1995), pp. 87–88.

113. See "Wszyscy zawiniliśmy." J. Kurski's interview with Jan Olszewski, *Gazeta wyborcza*, April 20–21, 1996, pp. 12–13. It is worthwhile to add that the Congress of the Right, organized by the KPN in May 1995, defined the current foreign investments in Poland as "the economic partition of Poland." See A. Nowakowska, "Wspólnota wladzy," *Gazeta wyborcza*, May 22, 1995, p. 3.

114. B. Łagowski, "Adresowane do prawicy."

115. See A. Micewski, "Jestem za abolicją," *Trybuna*, April 19, 1993. Quoted from *Sąd nad autorami*, pp. 368–371.

116. J. Giedroyc, "Notatki redaktora," *Kultura*, March 1996, p. 102. The final decision was to offer a presidential pension to Walesa, Jaruzelski, and Kaczorowski. The opposition, including the moderates, voted against granting a pension to Jaruzelski. To his credit, Tadeusz Mazowiecki did not take part in the voting. Jaruzelski refused to accept the pension, saying that he had retirement pay as a general. He agreed, however, to accept money for a small bureau to take care of his archives.

117. A. Michnik, J. Tischner, J. Żakowski, *Między Panem a Plebanem*, p. 596.

118. See J. Rawls, *Political Liberalism* (New York: Columbia University Press, 1993), p. xxv.

8

Communism on Trial:
The East German Past and the German Future

A. James McAdams

COMPARED TO THE MAJORITY of cases in which modern democracies have sought to use legal means to wrestle with the offenses of past dictators, the Federal Republic of Germany (FRG) seems to have enjoyed unprecedented advantages in coming to terms with the crimes and abuses of the former German Democratic Republic (GDR). After all, when Germany was reunified in October 1990, its leaders confronted a completely defeated regime. Thus, they did not have to worry about the kinds of concerns that have made the pursuit of transitional justice in other settings so precarious and complicated. Unlike the negotiated transitions of Argentina and Chile, for example, there were no contending military elites in the wings waiting to reassert themselves should their country's democratically-elected leaders appear to go too far in their reckoning with past crimes. By the same token, in its central European context, the German government could draw upon unquestionable institutional advantages in comparison with formerly communist states, such as Poland, Hungary, and Czechoslovakia. Unlike the latter cases, in which democratic norms and a liberal legal culture had to be reconstructed virtually from the ground up, German policymakers could count upon the unique circumstances of national unification to guide them. Not least among their strengths was, of course, forty-plus years of experience with the traditions of the German *Rechtsstaat* (roughly, "state under law") in the West.

As a result, the FRG offers a record of transitional justice that will likely remain unmatched in the postcommunist era. In the first half-decade after unification, German courts conducted trials for crimes and human rights violations in the GDR that covered the gamut of logical offenders—from the ranks of the old regime's least-known representatives (e.g., the borderguards at the Berlin Wall) all the way up to the most prominent officials of the ruling Socialist Unity Party (SED), among them former party chief Erich Honecker. Nonetheless, even in these advantageous circumstances, it would be a mistake to believe that the Federal Republic's leaders were always able to follow a straightforward or easy path in their pursuit of justice. Nor should we assume that they managed to avoid mistakes along the way. The fact that at least one-half of the FRG was already a fully established democratic state when Germany was reunified meant that the country's leaders had to deal with differing, and sometimes fiercely opposed, constituencies in their efforts to wrestle with eastern Germany's communist past.

On the one hand, policymakers in Bonn had to contend with the manifest skepticism evinced by many of the GDR's former dissidents. For these individuals, the Federal Republic already had a moral obligation to make up for the well-known shortcomings in Germany's post–World War II reckoning with the crimes of Nazism. Further, they argued that if the FRG's leaders were truly intent upon taking the eastern German revolution of 1989 seriously, they had to prove their sincerity by making the pursuit of justice a priority. For some of these critics, there were aspects of the Federal government's approach to unification which suggested that Bonn's attention to legal niceties, rules of procedure, and due process, was far too slow and cumbersome to meet their expectations. "We expected justice," eastern German dissident Bärbel Bohley would later observe in a famous complaint about the rigidity of the German legal system, "but we got the *Rechtsstaat* instead."[1]

On the other hand, an opposing group of critics attacked the German government for even considering the idea of post-unification trials. Such undertakings, they argued, would be tantamount to revisiting the judicial arbitrariness of the Nuremberg tribunals and pandering to a "victor's justice." Moreover, they felt that the credibility of the German legal order would be undermined in the process. Particularly in the early years of unification, there seemed to be ample evidence to support the view that German authorities were almost too eager to bring *somebody* to trial. One thinks, for example, of the 1991 proceedings against trades-union boss Harry Tisch, who was tried and convicted solely for the minor offense of having misused union funds, or of the investigations and first trial of secret police chief, Erich Mielke, that were based solely on his alleged complicity in the murder of two policemen in 1931. In other cases in the early 1990s, German courts prosecuted East German intelligence officers (including the notorious master-spy Markus Wolf) for the unlikely crime of having committed *treason* against the FRG, only to find their convictions overturned by the Federal Constitutional Court in 1995.[2]

If one were to rely solely upon popular accounts about the post-GDR trials, it would be tempting to conclude that this latter model of justice became the norm for German courts in the years between 1990 and 1996, and that the FRG's efforts to take seriously past crimes were therefore flawed from the outset. Yet, as we shall find in this chapter, such a conclusion would be misguided. True, German jurists were embroiled in an important debate about the costs and consequences of using judicial means to prosecute crimes and human rights violations in the former GDR. Nonetheless, as I shall contend, by 1992 the courts had arrived at a way of justifying their actions that was both consistent with the rigors of the *Rechtsstaat* and attentive to public demands for retribution. By itself, this was a noteworthy achievement. However, as I shall also suggest at the end of this essay, one should not think that the Germans had thereby found the elusive means to square the circle—to attain the reconciliation of the backward-looking demands for justice and the forward-looking realities of governance that has eluded so many other democratic regimes. In fact, the FRG's experiment with retrospective justice remains at best a precarious and unfinished exercise.

The Demand for Justice

In the initial euphoria attending the GDR's fall, the use of the courts to pursue transitional justice did not seem to be a problem to the majority of Germans, East or West. In both parts of the formerly divided nation, one encountered a widespread conviction that Germany was once again being called to confront and overcome—in common parlance, *aufarbeiten*—the legacy of totalitarianism. According to this view, Honecker and his associates were not merely guilty of having committed specific criminal offenses during their time in office. As the leaders of the SED, they were responsible for setting into motion and then maintaining what many Germans felt was a distinctively unjust political order, an *Unrechtsstaat* ("state without law"). This was a state in which—to quote Karl Jaspers' well-known judgment about the Nazi regime—the entire legal system had been nothing more than "a means for pacifying the masses of its people and forcing them into submission."[3]

Admittedly, those who sought to prosecute the East German elite on these grounds did not always agree about how far one could go in likening the Honecker regime to the system of injustice propagated by Hitler. For some observers, such as Rudolf Wassermann, a former Higher Regional Court president and an outspoken proponent of a judicial reckoning with the GDR past, the similarities between the two systems were "disturbing." "The campaign of destruction against 'Marxists' and 'alien peoples,'" Wassermann has written,

> had its parallels in the communist struggle against the bourgeoisie as a 'class enemy.' The one group disregarded human rights from the standpoint of race while the other did it from the class standpoint. The oppression in [East Germany] was even more tangible than under national socialism, because communist rule had no legitimacy at all and people had to be forced to go along, while almost to its end, the national socialist system was based upon the broad consent of much of its population.[4]

In contrast, other critics of the East German regime were less inclined to equate the SED's rule with that of the National Socialist German Workers' Party. They noted the different origins of the two dictatorships and the greater extent of the crimes committed under the Nazis.[5]

Nevertheless, both groups could agree on one point that was central to the characterization of the GDR as an *Unrechtsstaat*. Precisely because of the distorted nature of the East German legal system, no one—from Honecker down to the lowliest borderguards—should be able to excuse or justify manifestly criminal behavior by claiming that they were operating within the law of their land. To allow them to hide their crimes behind the elaborate web of legal fictions that had been created to give the GDR its veneer of legitimacy would make a mockery of the idea of law as it was understood in the West. It would be tantamount, as legal theorist Eckhard Jesse has underscored, to "factually affirming" the abuses of the old East German order.[6]

In fact, within the body of German jurisprudence, there seemed to be an excellent precedent for dealing with the protests of innocence that could be expected from the GDR's representatives at their trials. In cases when former Nazi officials had sought to excuse their crimes by claiming fidelity to the law of the Third Reich, West German courts frequently appealed to a natural law standard set by one of the Federal Republic's preeminent legal philosophers, Gustav Radbruch. In a formulation still associated with his name, Radbruch argued that the courts could not be bound solely by the strictures of the positive law in reaching their judgments. In circumstances where a conflict existed between the codified law and a higher conception of justice, and the contradiction between the two assumed, in Radbruch's carefully chosen words, an "intolerable dimension," it was not only suitable but imperative that the law be declared "unjust" (*unrichtiges Recht*) and subordinated to the cause of morality.[7]

Nonetheless, there were two problems with using such suprapositive standards to justify the SED trials. The first problem was political. In the heated context of national unification, the FRG's leaders, Chancellor Helmut Kohl and Minister of Justice Klaus Kinkel, were intent upon avoiding the impression that the legal mores of the Federal Republic were being imposed upon the defeated leadership of the GDR. By itself, this was no easy task. Up to 1989, the West German government had maintained a relatively cordial, if not always amicable, relationship with the SED regime; Honecker himself had been welcomed with some fanfare for an official state visit to the FRG only two years before the opening of the Wall. Thus, Kohl and Kinkel were understandably at pains to stress that they were "strictly against" any politicization of the proceedings against the East German head of state. "We do not hold political trials," the chancellor announced.[8]

However, Germany's leaders were also concerned about an even more delicate issue. This was the impact that the appeal to a higher— but still relatively amorphous—conception of justice might have upon the FRG's self-understanding as a *Rechtsstaat*. As citizens of the newly-unified German state, Honecker and everyone else who had been associated with the GDR government were entitled to all of the protections of the Basic Law.[9] They enjoyed the presumption of innocence. They could be punished only in proportion to the severity of their crimes. And most important in this context, they had the right to have known *in advance* whether their actions constituted criminal offenses. As the Basic Law itself specified, in a formulation commonly known by its Latin equivalent, *nulla poena sine lege*, "an act [could] be punished only if it was an offense against the law before the act was committed" (Article 103, § 2).[10] The architects of German unity were so attentive to this prohibition on ex post facto lawmaking that they deliberately incorporated the principle into the Unification Treaty of 1990. The accord expressly stipulated that crimes committed before the date of national unification could be adjudicated only according to the East German penal code.[11]

This was no mean guarantee. On the one hand, it protected German policymakers from Honecker's and others' claims that the FRG was behaving in the same capricious and arbitrary fashion as that of which it was accusing the GDR. Adherence to *nulla poena sine lege* meant that Germany's courts would act squarely within the letter of the Basic Law.[12] But on the other hand, this protection had the rather paradoxical consequence of shaping the way one viewed the GDR as a historical entity. Unavoidably, once the decision had been made to hold East German officials accountable for specific violations of their country's laws, one had to begin thinking of the GDR as something much more complex than the undifferentiated *Unrechtsstaat*.

Klaus Kinkel admitted as much in a major address in February

1992, when he warned against giving any of the individuals on trial the opportunity to treat their crimes as "the independent activities of systems, apparatuses, and organized collectivities [*Großgruppen*]." "Even in a dictatorship," Kinkel emphasized, "the individual's room for maneuver is just not as small as the perpetrators would like us to believe."[13] Apparently, the justice minister was fully aware of the implications of this statement. If there was room for individual choice in the old GDR, there must also have been standards of behavior, legal and otherwise, that the country's leaders simply decided to ignore. Again Kinkel: "Even the criminal code of the GDR treated manslaughter (*Totschlag*), bodily harm, [false] imprisonment, and violations of the peace as punishable offenses. In numerous ways, the GDR's rulers disregarded and infringed upon their laws, and thus they can be prosecuted today according to the criminal code of the GDR."[14]

By late 1992, when the FRG's courts finally turned to the cases against Honecker and his co-leaders, the majority of German judges seem to have come around to Kinkel's differentiated understanding of the legal culture of the GDR. However, this way of thinking about the former communist state was by no means automatic. Even before Honecker was brought to trial, Kinkel and his supporters still needed to overcome the reservations of many judicial authorities who felt that the GDR could only be judged according to a special standard of justice. This tension was nowhere more apparent than in the first of several trials of former East German borderguards that began in 1991.

Seeking Justice Within the Law

In retrospect, it seems logical that Honecker's trial would be preceded by the trials of those individuals who could be directly tied to the killings at the Berlin Wall and along the inter-German border.[15] If one could not hold them responsible for their crimes, it was likely to be even harder to prosecute the individuals above them. (Though as we shall see later, this reasoning also made it all the more imperative that those higher authorities be punished as well.) Yet, as the first of the borderguard trials showed, some judges refused to believe that GDR law should play any role at all in resolving this uncertainty.

Only later, after the courts had revisited the issue, did a general understanding begin to emerge about the criteria to be used in adjudicating these cases.

The first borderguard trial began on September 2, 1991, and eventually led to the conviction of two soldiers for killing twenty-year-old Chris Gueffroy (the so-called "last victim" of the Wall) on February 5, 1989. From the first day of the proceedings, however, the trial was marked by controversy. The credibility of the presiding judge, Theodor Seidel, was impaired because he had once belonged to an organization that smuggled refugees out of East Germany, and he did not try to hide his political biases at the trial. Making matters even worse, Seidel was never able to insulate his court from the frenzied attention of the media. But for our purposes, the most problematic aspect of the trial lay in the way Seidel went about finding the defendants guilty of their crimes.

In their defense, as one might have predicted, the former guards appealed to the argument already made famous at Nuremberg. They admitted to using their weapons against persons who had sought to flee the GDR, but they contended that they were simply carrying out their duty as soldiers and acting well within the law of their country. On one level, these claims were not without foundation. The East German penal code (§ 213) made it a criminal offense to seek to leave the GDR without official permission. Furthermore, the border troops seem to have enjoyed some latitude in enforcing this statute. The Revised Border Law of 1982 expressly stated that "the use of physical force [was] allowable when other means were not sufficient to prevent serious consequences for the security and order of the border territory" (Section 26.1). Also, the law permitted the use of firearms "to prevent the imminent commission of a crime" (Section 27.2).[16]

Given these provisions, one might have expected Seidel to base his judgment against the defendants upon their erroneous interpretation of the law or, at least, upon the fact that the appeal to superior orders had ultimately failed to win the judges' sympathy at Nuremberg. Yet, interestingly, the judge acted as if the existence or nonexistence of previous statutes or precedents was irrelevant to the case. The real issue was what kind of state the GDR had been. Explicitly citing the Radbruch principle, Seidel emphasized that one could not respect the laws of a regime whose leaders enjoyed "no form of legitimation" (*durch nichts legitimiert waren*). In his view, the legal standards of the GDR stood—again he used Radbruch's terminology—in "crass contradiction to the generally recognized foundations of the rule of law."[17] Therefore, the guards' claims that they were merely following orders in taking the lives of innocent human beings were not compelling. "Even in the former GDR," Seidel concluded, "justice and humanity were understood and treated as ideals." Hence, the soldiers must have recognized the immorality of their actions: "shooting with the intent-to-kill those who merely wanted to leave the territory of the former GDR was an offense against basic norms of ethics and human association."[18]

From a strictly moral standpoint, Seidel's observations cannot be dismissed out of hand. As the judge stressed in his ruling, the defendants themselves had shown in their testimony that they had known what they were doing was wrong. They admitted that they had routinely done everything they could to maintain the secrecy of shootings, such as Gueffroy's, after the fact. Also, demonstrating that they could have acted differently, they had refrained from using their weapons against would-be border crossers on occasions (e.g., official holidays) when such actions would have embarrassed their government.[19]

But, was acting immorally the same thing as breaking the law? This was the decisive question for the more famous trials to come. For on this count, quite a number of German scholars *and* several appeals courts parted ways with Seidel. There was widespread agreement about the guards' moral culpability, but many experts felt that Seidel's invocation of a higher law ran right up against the prohibitions within the Basic Law and the Unification Treaty on ex post facto lawmaking.[20] This was the unmistakable message that was conveyed at the second of the borderguard trials, which began on December 18, 1991, and became the precedent for all subsequent proceedings. In this instance, two soldiers were charged in the 1984 shooting death of an individual who had sought to escape over the Wall into West Berlin. Both defendants were found guilty, but this time, in contrast to Seidel's more free-wheeling reasoning, the court was at pains to demonstrate that justice could be pursued only within the bounds of East German law.

In her ruling of February 5, 1992, Judge Ingeborg Tepperwein explicitly turned to the Border Law of 1982 to show that each of the defendants had exceeded his authority in shooting to kill. Tepperwein conceded that the GDR's criminal code gave the soldiers the right to use forceful measures of some kind to prevent illegal border crossings. However, she noted that the East German code was similar to the law of the Federal Republic in one crucial respect: it required that the means employed to prevent a crime be proportionate to the crime being committed. In this instance, the judge argued, "the flight of a single, unarmed person from whom there was evidently no apparent danger for other persons or things" could not be considered a violation serious enough to justify the use of deadly force. Moreover, Tepperwein added, GDR Border Law specified that the guards seek to "preserve human life if possible" (Section 27.5). Therefore, she concluded that one could reasonably have expected the soldiers to chose only the "mildest means" available—for example, "a single, deliberate shot at the legs"—to fulfill their obligations.[21]

In her nearly exclusive emphasis upon codified East German law, Tepperwein was not only setting an important precedent. Her ruling was noteworthy for the tone which it set. Despite finding both defendants guilty, the judge suspended their sentences after reading her decision. Like Seidel, Tepperwein acknowledged that "superior orders" could not be used to excuse or to justify criminal behavior. Nevertheless, she emphasized that the two soldiers were operating in conditions that militated against completely independent action on their part. "Not selfishness or criminal energy" had led to their crime, Tepperwein contended, but "circumstances over which they had no influence, such as the political and military confrontation in divided Germany [and] the special conditions of the former GDR."[22] Thus, it was appropriate that their punishment be administered accordingly. As sensible as this nuanced view of the East German past might have appeared at the time, it did give rise to a tantalizing question. If the borderguards were not completely responsible for their actions, who then should also be held accountable?

A "Trial of the Century"

It may be only a coincidence that Germany's high appeals court, the Bundesgerichtshof (Federal Court of Justice), voted to uphold Tepperwein's verdict in the second borderguard trial on November 3, 1992. This ruling came a mere nine days before Erich Honecker's trial was set to begin in Berlin.[23] Coincidence or not, the proximity of the two cases provided a fitting rejoinder to critics who had been claiming that only the least of the offenders were being made to pay for the crimes of the East German past. Earlier in the year, on May 12, 1992, the Berlin Prosecutor General's office had released a nearly eight-hundred-page indictment which charged Honecker and five other defendants with the crime of "collective manslaughter."[24] The indictment maintained that Honecker and former secret police chief Erich Mielke, minister-president Willi Stoph, defense minister Heinz Keßler and his chief-of-staff Fritz Streletz, and Suhl district party secretary Hans Albrecht, as members of the GDR's secretive National Defense Council, had enjoyed "unlimited influence" in determining how their state's border was fortified. They had been responsible for all of the decisions, from the selection of soldiers to the deployment of weapons and exploding mines, which ensured that the border regime ran "like clockwork." Hence, the indictment held, they, and not the guards on the periphery of the chain of command, should be considered the "key figures in everything that happened."[25]

These charges were a far cry from the guilt by association that one might have tied to an *Unrechtsstaat*. The indictment provided a detailed outline of the procedures of the National Defense Council and painstaking descriptions of sixty-eight of the hundreds of killings that had taken place on the inter-German border between 1961 and 1989. In addition, the document's authors acted like court historians in meticulously linking each of the defendants to his crimes. On August 12, 1961, the indictment demonstrated, Honecker himself, in the presence of Mielke and Stoph, had given the order that had led to the construction of the Berlin Wall.[26] This decision had then led to numerous follow-up meetings—on September 20, 1961; November 29, 1961; April 6, 1962; June 13, 1963; October 23, 1969; July 14, 1972, and so forth, in abundant historical detail—in which all of the defendants had eventually taken part in "further steps to increase the security of the border." At one particularly notable meeting of the National Defense Council, on May 3, 1974, Honecker had supposedly endorsed the "unhampered use" of firearms to prevent escapes and called upon his co-leaders to "praise those comrades who used their weapons successfully."[27]

Of course, at no time can the Prosecutor General's office have underestimated the difficulty of trying the GDR's leaders for these offenses.[28] With the exception of Admiral Dönitz, Honecker was, as commentators liked to point out, the first German head of state to be put on trial in over eight hundred years. Indeed, during the first half of 1992, no one could even be sure whether the chief defendant would be present in the courtroom to hear the charges against him. With national unification, Honecker had fled to Moscow, where he had found refuge in the embassy of the Republic of Chile; his return to Germany literally required the fall of the Soviet Union and heavy diplomatic pressure on the part of the Kohl government. Nor was Honecker's presence in Berlin—he was ironically held in the same Moabit prison where he had once been confined by the Nazis— bound to make the proceedings any easier. As the "trial of the century" began, the world-wide media attention and high emotions that converged upon the German capital guaranteed that Kohl's and Kinkel's hopes of avoiding a political spectacle would be tested.

From the standpoint of the defense, therefore, conditions were ideal for suggesting that a miscarriage of justice was at hand. In his one and only statement to the court, on December 3, 1992, Honecker gave one of the more spirited speeches of his career—amazing in view of his past oratorical standards—in which he portrayed himself and his colleagues as the victims of a cruel twist of historical fate. It was not, he insisted sarcastically, "'criminal' individuals, such as I and my comrades," who bore responsibility for the wall in Berlin and the deaths at the border. Rather, the roots of this tragedy lay in a world-historical conflict that had begun with Hitler's rise in 1933 and culminated in the formation of two opposing German states after World War II and the hysteria of the Cold War. Now, the wrongs of the past were about to be repeated with his own conviction. "One would have to be blind or consciously close one's eyes to the events of the past," Honecker lectured his accusers, "to fail to recognize that this trial is a political trial of the victors over the defeated, [or] to fail to recognize that it amounts to a politically motivated misrepresentation of history."[29]

As we shall see, these would not prove to be insuperable objections for the courts. But, there was a more serious complication for those seeking to prosecute the East German leadership, and a fact that nobody could deny about the majority of the defendants—their advanced age. Within the Basic Law, there is arguably no more important guarantee than its opening promise (Article 1, § 1) to protect "human dignity."[30] Given the rapidly deteriorating health of many of the defendants, German prosecutors were aware that a long and exhausting trial would amount to a violation of this right. Thus, on November 13, only one day after the trial had begun in Berlin, the court temporarily suspended all proceedings against Willi Stoph, since the former prime minister was experiencing heart trouble. Only a few days later, similar steps were taken in the trial of Erich Mielke, on the grounds that the one-time police chief, also in failing health, was simultaneously being tried for the murders about which we have commented earlier.[31]

In both of these cases, it is noteworthy that there was little if any public opposition to the court's actions. When the attorneys for the defense requested that the same protections of German law be applied to Honecker, however, the public reaction was quite the opposite. Perhaps it was the fact that Honecker, more than any other figure, seemed personally to embody the crimes of the GDR government. Also, Honecker's health problems were more serious than those of the other defendants. Since most, although not all, medical experts gave the GDR's former leader less than a year to live because of a cancerous tumor that was spreading in his liver,[32] it was clear that to postpone his case was to ensure that he would never be tried.

For weeks, the contending attorneys engaged in macabre debates about the condition of the defendant's liver. How *much* pain was he experiencing? How *big* was his tumor? How *fast* was it growing? When *would* it kill him? As these battles ensued, the presiding judge, an avowed anticommunist, Hansgeorg Bräutigam, seemed almost fixated upon bringing about Honecker's conviction, regardless of his health or mental state. Nevertheless, on January 12, 1993, Berlin's constitutional appeals court intervened to stop the proceedings.

From the first, the judges on the court had asked themselves what the point of the trial would be were the defendant not around to face possible punishment. Their conclusion was a significant statement about the German conception of the rule of law. If the trial were allowed to become an "end in itself" (*Selbstzweck*), they reasoned, the FRG would be as guilty of violating the human dignity of its citizens as was the GDR. "The individual," as the judges put it, "[would] become a simple object of state measures," and a fundamental distinction between the two political orders would be obscured.[33] As a result, the court chose not only to postpone the trial but also to dismiss all of the charges against Honecker on health grounds.

For many Germans, the decision to free Honecker was an occasion for outrage. The minister-president of Mecklenburg-Vorpommern, Berndt Seite, proclaimed Honecker's subsequent departure for Chile a "slap in the face" of the victims of the Wall. Likewise, Saxony's outspoken environmental minister, Arnold Vaatz, claimed that the judgment reinforced earlier suspicions about the borderguard trials: "One hangs the little guy, but lets the big shot get away."[34] Seeming to lend fuel to his critics' arguments, Honecker himself was quick to proclaim victory upon his arrival in Santiago.

But was this really a victory for Honecker? More to the point, did the constitutional court's decision confirm the cynical view that the *Rechtsstaat* was incapable of responding to its citizens' demands for judicial retribution? Despite the loss of the trial's most prominent participant, it is essential to note that the courts still abided by the standards that had been used in the Prosecutor General's indictment of May 1992. More important than the trial of Honecker himself, the proceedings against the three healthy members of the GDR's National Defense Council continued after his departure. Finally, on September 16, 1993, Keßler, Streletz, and Albrecht were all found guilty of the charges against them, the first two for being "instigators" in the border deaths and the latter for being an accessory.

These convictions present a provocative picture of the trial as it might have been, had Honecker only been sufficiently healthy to endure the proceedings. Throughout the intervening eight months fol-

lowing his departure and leading up to this verdict, the three defendants had sought to maintain, like Honecker before them, that they
were not individually responsible for the shootings at the Wall. The
Soviet Union, it seemed, had been the prime mover behind the construction of the barrier in August 1961; East Germany's leaders had
done nothing more than to act upon their government's sovereign
right, and its obligations to the Warsaw Treaty Organization, to ensure their country's external security. If there had been deaths along
the inter-German border, these incidents were the regrettable consequence of years of hostility between the eastern and western military
blocs.[35]

These claims were not without some historical foundation.
Moscow had played a decisive role in the erection of the Wall, and
the GDR had been at the center of some of the Cold War's greatest
tensions. However, in coming to his judgments against Keßler,
Streletz, and Albrecht, Hans Boß, who replaced Bräutigam as presiding judge on January 7, 1993, refused to be persuaded by these arguments.[36] Applying the same legal standards and emphasis on
preexisting law that Tepperwein had used in the second borderguard
trial, he contended that the members of the National Defense Council had played a key role in deciding how the inter-German border
was secured. They knew, Boß asserted, that the killing of their citizens "was wrong" (Unrecht), since even GDR law recognized the primacy of protecting human life over serving state interests. But, he
added, "[the defendants] chose to put up with this wrong out of political considerations."[37]

Boß conceded that the trial would have been easier had experts
been able to locate the smoking gun that many had hoped to find in
the top-secret protocols of the National Defense Council, that is, an
explicit order (Schießbefehl) requiring the borderguards to shoot to kill.
In any case, the evidence showed that the members of the Council assumed that such extreme measures would be used. They knew, he
noted, that "their actions would lead to deaths on the border. They
consciously accommodated themselves to the possibility of such
deaths."[38] In this sense, there was an identifiable "causal link" between their actions and the soldiers' violations of the GDR penal
code: "Without their decisions and commands, the succeeding chain

of command would never have been set into motion and the actions of the border soldiers which led to the deaths of the victims would never have followed."[39]

In contrast to the turmoil of the trial's early stages when Honecker was in the courtroom, Boß's ruling was notable for the care with which he delivered it. The judge acknowledged the awkwardness of his position as a western German seeking to come to a satisfactory judgment on the East German past. "It would have been better," Boß advised his listeners in his oral statement on September 16, 1993, "if East Germany had tried its own leaders." Unfortunately, this was impossible: "German unification came far too quickly to allow for this."[40] Partly for this reason, Boß chose to take mitigating circumstances into account in sentencing Keßler, Streletz, and Albrecht to milder jail terms than those requested by the prosecution. Without excusing any of the officials' actions, he noted that the defendants were themselves "prisoners of German postwar history and prisoners of their own political convictions." In the absence of the Cold War, the judge reasoned, there would have been no division of Germany, and therefore none of these individuals would presumably have committed the crimes for which they had been convicted.[41]

At this point, the Honecker trial might have come to an end. However, given the controversial nature of the proceedings, Boß chose to postpone the implementation of the three sentences until the Bundesgerichtshof had the opportunity to review his decision. On July 26, 1994, the court delivered its verdict, not only upholding the decision on nearly all counts but also taking his conclusions one step further. Whereas Boß had held that Keßler, Streletz, and Albrecht had only indirectly participated in the killings at the inter-German border (as "instigators" and as an "accessory," respectively), the higher court chose to underscore their individual culpability by labelling them "perpetrators" (Täter). It would be an inadequate reflection of the three individuals' roles as "behind-the-scenes actor[s] at the peak of a hierarchy," the judges contended, "were they only to be treated as participants" while the borderguards were convicted for having "committed the [crimes]."[42] To be sure, in modifying the lower court's decision, the Federal court altered only one of the defendants' sentences; Albrecht was sentenced to serve an additional seven months. But the meaning of the ruling was clear. The three remaining members of the National Defense Council were as responsible for the deaths at the Wall—indeed, the fact they received jail terms suggested even greater culpability—as the soldiers who had acted on their behalf.

Architects of German Unity

For those who had expected nothing to come of the post-GDR trials, this judgment against Honecker's colleagues could not be easily ignored. Some observers may have wished for an even more dramatic statement about the significance of these convictions. Had not a major part of German history also been on trial when Honecker and his associates sat in the docks? Did not the courts have a responsibility to help all Germans, and particularly eastern Germans, to make sense of their country's troubled history? The simple, and correct, response to these questions is that the courts' sole charge, as servants of the *Rechtsstaat*, was to determine the guilt or innocence of the accused. But this is not to say that the German judges made no contribution to the "working out" (*Aufarbeitung*) of their country's past. They may not have recognized it as such.

We have already encountered some examples of what the courts thought about the record of East German communism. Adherence to the strictures of the Basic Law meant that German judges were practically required—at least, from the second borderguard trial onward—to approach the forty-year history of the GDR in more exacting terms than those allowed by the ambiguous concept of the *Unrechtsstaat*. As the Federal Court of Justice reasoned in upholding the convictions in the borderguard trial, representatives of the East German state apparatus could be tried precisely because the GDR was a far more complex entity than the lawless state that had existed under the Nazis. For all of its shortcomings, the codified law had meant something in East Germany. "[U]nlike under the national socialist dictatorship, there was no doctrine in the GDR according to which the simple whims of those who happened to be in power could become law." "Laws," the court insisted, deliberately citing a passage from the East German constitution, "were binding."[43]

As an interpretation of the GDR's past, this statement was enlightening. The court was saying that even in a dictatorship such as the GDR, specific individuals had had a choice in committing the crimes for which they were accused. They could have followed the law, but they had consciously chosen to do wrong. Although this was a provocative corrective from a legal and even historical standpoint, it is also conceivable, in view of the ongoing challenge of German unification, that the judges' stand was significant from a social and political standpoint as well. After all, if some individuals had knowingly violated their country's laws, was it not reasonable to conclude that there were other eastern Germans, even former soldiers, policemen, and politicians, who had just as deliberately chosen to do the right thing? Assuming this premise to be true, might not the post-GDR trials have something to say about the terms according to which the eastern German population should be integrated into the Federal Republic?

Over thirty years ago, Otto Kirchheimer anticipated the courts' social function in a classic work, *Political Justice*. "Successor justice," he wrote, "is both retrospective and prospective. In laying bare the roots of iniquity in the previous regime's conduct, it simultaneously seizes the opportunity to convert the trial into a cornerstone of the new order."[44] At the time he was writing, Kirchheimer was primarily concerned about the abusive ends to which legal procedures could be put by successor regimes, and he warned against allowing the courts to become mere tools in the replacement of one dictatorship with another. This was not a problem with the Federal Republic of Germany. Nevertheless, Kirchheimer's insight about the courts' prospective function rings true when one views the Honecker trial and others like it as possible cornerstones in the construction of a united Germany.

Let us imagine that instead of focusing on specifically punishable crimes under the codified law of the GDR, Germany's courts had followed the model of retributive justice enunciated by Seidel at the first borderguard trial. In this case, arguably, Honecker and his colleagues would have been convicted not so much because of the illegality of their actions but rather by virtue of their participation in an immoral and unjust state apparatus. Such a trial would have had some advantages. In applying Radbruch to the GDR, the courts

would have been able to cut right to the heart of East Germany's status as an *Unrechtsstaat*. Along the way, many of the cumbersome and
tedious aspects of the German legal process—the "pedantry and ju-
ristic nit-picking," to quote Neal Ascherson[45]—would have been
eliminated.

However, if one takes the courts' prospective function seriously,
there was also an undeniable drawback to this approach. This lay in
the implications of the *Unrechtsstaat* for anyone who had ever been
associated with the East German state. In a world in which guilt was
not clearly identified with the violation of specific laws, there was
very little to prevent many eastern Germans from becoming citizens
of the Federal Republic with a nebulous cloud of collective responsibility hanging over them. At its height, the SED alone had over 2.3
million members. If one threw into this equation all of the members
of the country's state bureaucracy, its armed forces, and its police, not
to mention the hundreds of thousands of individuals who had secretly spied on their friends and families for the Ministry of State Security, the list of the guilty might include a third of the East German
population.

Lest this danger seem overly abstract, even many of the GDR's
greatest critics had reservations about how finely the line could be
drawn between guilt and innocence in their former homeland. Consider social activist Jens Reich's bleak assessment of the Honecker
trial. "Every expectation of punishment is fruitless," he wrote in late
1992, as the trial began, "because we were participants. We consented
to everything. We looked away. We held our tongues. We rolled our
eyes. We knew everything better. Many even took part. Only a miser-
able few sought to stop what was happening."[46] Most likely, Reich
did not intend to suggest that the passivity of the GDR's citizens over
forty years of communist dictatorship or their tacit consent in their
government's practices was quite the same thing as their leaders'
much more direct involvement in the killings at the Berlin Wall. Still,
it is not hard to see why his well-meaning image of daily life in the
GDR could convey a misleading message about the eastern German
population. Although the FRG's new citizens were every bit as German as their western counterparts, it seemed to imply that they were
tainted as a result of their ties to a dubious past.

In contrast, so long as they avoided the shoddy procedures of the early stages of the Honecker trial, the courts that prosecuted the SED chief and his associates were offering a potentially more hopeful message about the German future, even if this was not their explicit intention. In insisting upon a strict definition of criminal responsibility, they were making a distinctive claim—not everyone was guilty. This may not seem like an unusual pronouncement. But if one takes into account the historical context of the courts' rulings, there is good reason to think the *presumption* of innocence had a special relevance in eastern Germany. The early 1990s was a time of intense social and economic disruption for the majority of the GDR's former citizens. Once the exhilaration attending the fall of communism had worn off, many felt that they had been unfairly relegated to a second-class status vis-à-vis their western cousins. In particular, public opinion polls revealed widespread skepticism about whether eastern Germans were to be accorded the same legal protections as their relations in the West.[47] In this instance at least, the careful and consistent rulings of judges like Tepperwein and Boß held out the promise that equal standards would be applied to all.

In setting this example, the courts may have also conveyed a salutary message about the purposes of the German *Rechtsstaat*. Even for those who were convicted for their crimes (or those who were sympathetic to their plight), the way the judges reached their verdicts bespoke a legal culture profoundly different from that which had been dominant in the GDR. To see the point, one has only to consider the treatment accorded Honecker. Had only his health been better, the East German leader would in all probability have been found guilty of the same offenses as Keßler, Streletz, and Albrecht. However, precisely because he could not have survived his trial, Honecker—the man, and not the former SED chief—was accorded the protections of the Basic Law's commitment to human dignity. Whereas state interests had frequently defined the administration of justice in the GDR, the mercy and compassion that the courts showed in this instance demonstrated that a different standard prevailed in the Federal Republic. The value of human life outweighed the public clamor for retribution.

Hopeful lessons could also be derived from the courts' readiness to take extenuating circumstances into account in handing down their sentences. It is notable, for example, that out of the scores of borderguard trials conducted between 1991 and 1996, only two soldiers were actually sentenced to serve time in jail, and only because their crimes were unusually heinous. As we have seen, similarly lenient standards were applied in the sentencing of Keßler, Streletz, and Albrecht. For these reasons, one may cautiously side with those legal experts who have observed—as did the former president of the Federal Constitutional Court, Ernst Benda, during the proceedings against Honecker—that the post-GDR trials have the potential to become a positive "learning process" for the FRG's new citizens.[48]

The Risk of Going Too Far

It would be misleading, however, to conclude this essay without noting that there are still significant risks involved in every additional trial that the FRG's courts are called upon to conduct in the name of retrospective justice. In fact, as novel and as instructive as the German trials may seem, we can gain some perspective on their limitations by comparing them with another case of transitional justice that has been addressed earlier in this volume: Argentina. In the Argentine case, those responsible for the prosecution of nine members of the military junta were given the opportunity to conduct their trials in the manner of Nuremberg, imposing sweeping judgments upon individuals who were—by all accounts and particularly in the sense of international law—guilty of numerous types of human rights violations. Yet, much like the Germans, Argentine authorities chose instead to take the problem of retrospective lawmaking to heart and to make their cases against their former dictators on the basis of acts that were criminal at the time they were performed. Just as in the German case, Argentine lawyers collected abundant amounts of evidence to this effect. On these bases, on December 8, 1985, five of the nine military commanders were found guilty of a variety of crimes; the other four were acquitted.[49]

In addition to carefully observing the manner in which these trials were conducted, those in charge of the Argentine proceedings were also attentive to a related problem, which should have been apparent to the Germans as well. It was one thing to hold those at the pinnacle of the chain of command responsible for their actions, but quite another to pursue prosecutions at every other level of the old governing structure, where proof of criminal behavior was necessarily harder to establish and complicity more difficult to measure.[50] On this score, whatever one's judgment about the appropriateness of the trials of the Berlin Wall borderguards, it should be clear from this essay that Germany's courts had already faced a weighty challenge in defining the standards to be applied to the shootings at the inter-German border. Yet on November 30, 1994, the Berlin Prosecutor General's Office demonstrated that it may have lost sight of these difficulties when it indicted an additional seven of Honecker's colleagues.

At first glance, this follow-up trial, which began on January 15, 1996, may have appeared no different than its predecessor. Once again, well-known names from the GDR past were being held to account for crimes committed under the old order. However, this would be to miss the ways in which the prosecutor's office had not only broadened the scope of its investigations to make these indictments possible but arguably begun to overstep the limits of the *Rechtsstaat*. For one thing, the first trial of the GDR leadership had been exclusively based upon membership in the National Defense Council, the agency specifically responsible for the border-control question. But in the second trial, only four of the figures indicted belonged to this body. This time around, the prosecution chose to use the much broader criterion of Politburo membership as the measure of complicity.

Even more significant, the second indictment was based upon a fundamentally different understanding of personal culpability than that which had been used to prosecute Honecker. Only two of the individuals named in the document, Erich Mückenberger and Kurt Hager, were actually charged with "active involvement" (*aktives Tun*)[51] in decisions affecting the border regime, and even then, both men had been responsible for areas (economic policy and cultural affairs) far afield from security questions. In contrast, the other five members of the Politburo were charged not so much for what they did, but remarkably, for what they failed to do. As members of the SED's highest body, the indictment held, they must have known that they had the power in their hands to do more to secure the rights "to life and freedom" of the GDR's citizens. However, they consciously failed to take advantage of this possibility "to work to achieve a humanization of the border regime, and thereby prevent the killing and wounding of escapees."[52]

From a moral standpoint, the accusation may well have been deserved. As one of the defendants, Günter Schabowski, acknowledged in his statement before the court on February 26, 1996, the deaths at the Wall were the logical consequence of his and others' faith in Marxism-Leninism and their "misguided attempt to free humanity of its troubles." In this sense, everyone who had been a part of the SED regime had a moral responsibility for their behavior under the old system. "As a former follower and protagonist of this world view," Schabowski admitted, "I feel guilt and pain at the thought of those killed at the Wall. I ask for the forgiveness of the victims' relations, and I must also [be prepared] to accept when they refuse me. Indeed, were I unable to adopt this view, it would be impossible for me to continue existing."[53]

Yet, moral responsibility is by no means the same thing as criminal liability.[54] Furthermore, it is hard to see how the attempt to bind these two principles together could ever contribute to the healthy respect for the rule of law that we have described in the later stages of the Honecker trial. Quite the contrary, there are a number of ways in which this second indictment of the GDR's leaders seemed to paint a very ambiguous picture of the legal culture of unified Germany. At least by implication, the broadening of charges to include other members of the SED regime suggested that a new basis for criminal prosecutions had been introduced, one's membership in a collectivity. More striking, the document seemed to say that individuals would henceforth be held accountable not only for specific violations of the law, the cardinal principle of the earlier proceedings. Now, they could be tried for what they had not done, for their moral failings—a curious standard in any liberal society.

Why were German prosecutors willing to risk sending such a potentially confusing message about the rule of law to their citizens? To listen to many of the Politburo members on trial (although not Schabowski), one would think that Germany's leaders were merely continuing their campaign of "victor's justice" against their former adversaries in the GDR.[55] However, one can offer an alternate explanation for the prosecutors' behavior that is both more charitable *and* more revealing of their motivations. As we have noted earlier, the convictions in the borderguard cases practically required that those who had given the guards their orders, the members of the National Defense Council, also be held accountable for their actions. In this sense, the decision to expand the list of those indicted from the SED leadership must have seemed to German officials like the logical next step in the pursuit of justice, regardless of the peculiar terms according to which the proceedings were justified. In the familiar words of one prosecutor, Heinrich Kintzi, it would have been a "skewed picture" had German courts only convicted the least important figures and failed to pursue "those who had more responsibility and, correspondingly, also bore much more guilt."[56]

Will such follow-up trials, in fact, call into question the consistency of the German *Rechtsstaat*? Will they prevent the FRG's courts from living up to their prospective potential for bringing eastern and western Germans together again on an equal basis? Because the challenge of German unification is still very much in its early stages, more time will be required to provide satisfactory answers to either of these questions. It should be clear, however, from the cases we have considered in this chapter that, despite the FRG's well-known advantages over many new democracies, the German model of transitional justice has been far from trouble free. In some ways, given the unique demands of unification, the Federal Republic may already have grappled with far more complex legal and political challenges than those that are likely to be encountered by less consolidated democracies in the region.

NOTES

This chapter is a revised and expanded version of an article which appeared as *"The Honecker Trial: The East German Past and the German Future,"* The Review of Politics *58, no. 1 (Winter 1996): 53–80. I am grateful to the* Review's *editors for permission to reprint sections of the original article, as well as for the help and assistance of numerous individuals who have stimulated my thinking on this subject:*

Alex Hahn, Donald Kommers, Hans-Heinrich Mahnke, Juan Méndez, Walter Nicgorski, Patti Ogden, Peter Quint, John Roos, Brad Roth, Gunnar Schuster, John Yoder, and José Zalaquett. I am also grateful to the Institute for Scholarship in the Liberal Arts and the Helen Kellogg Institute for International Studies, both at Notre Dame, and the John D. and Catherine T. MacArthur Foundation for supporting the larger project of which this essay is a part.

1. Cited in Andreas Zielcke, "Der Kälteschock des Rechtsstaates," *Frankfurter Allgemeine Zeitung*, November 9, 1991.

2. For a thoughtful account of these cases in the light of other central European approaches, see Tina Rosenberg, *The Haunted Land: Facing Europe's Ghosts after Communism* (New York: Random House, 1995), chapter 8.

3. Unlike contemporary references to the *Unrechtsstaat*, which frequently draw upon Jaspers' work, Jaspers himself used the more easily translatable term *Verbrecherstaat* ("criminal state"). See *Wohin treibt die Bundesrepublik?* (Munich: Piper reprint, 1988), p. 21.

4. Rudolf Wassermann, "Zur Aufarbeitung des SED Unrechts," *Aus Politik und Zeitgeschichte*, no. 4 (January 22, 1993): 3. Cf. Christa Hoffmann, *Stunden Null? Vergangenheitsbewältigung in Deutschland 1945 und 1989* (Bonn: Bouvier, 1992), pp. 287–302.

5. See the subtle assessment of the GDR as "*im Kern ein Unrechtsstaat*" by Horst Sendler, a former president of the Federal Administrative Court (Verwaltungsgericht), in "Über Rechtsstaat, Unrechtsstaat und anderes—Das Editorial der Herausgeber im Meinungsstreit," *Neue Justiz*, no. 9 (1991): 379–381. Cf. Hans Peter Krüger, "Eine Krake im Kampf mit sich selbst," *Frankfurter Allgemeine Zeitung*, June 13, 1991; Lothar Probst, "German Pasts, Germany's Future: Intellectual Controversies since Reunification," *German Politics and Society*, no. 30 (Fall 1993): 29–30; and Claus Leggewie and Horst Meier, "Zum Auftakt ein Schlußstrich?" in Cora Stephan, ed., *Wir Kollaborateure* (Reinbek bei Hamburg: Rowohlt, 1992), p. 55. The last two authors do not strictly view the GDR as an *Unrechtsstaat*.

6. Eckhard Jesse, "'Entnazifizierung' und 'Entstasifizierung' als politisches Problem," in Josef Isensee, ed., *Vergangenheitsbewältigung durch Recht* (Berlin: Duncker und Humblot, 1992), p. 35. For similar views, see Karl Dietrich Bracher, "Die Unterdrücker zur Rechenschaft ziehen," *Universitas*, 11 (1991): 1025–1028; and Hoffmann, *Stunden Null?*, pp. 247, 276.

7. Radbruch's words are cited in Uwe Wesel, *Ein Staat vor Gericht: Der Honecker Prozeß* (Frankfurt am Main: Eichborn, 1994), p. 38.

8. To cite the chancellor himself. See "Interview with Helmut Kohl," *Statements and Speeches*, 15, no. 12, August 13, 1992, p. 2. Also, see Karl Wilhelm Fricke, "Honecker unter Anklage," *Deutschland Archiv*, no. 10 (October 1992): 1009–1010.

9. To quote Kohl again: "We can't have it both ways. We can't have a bloody revolution and at the same time celebrate a peaceful revolution. If we have a system of government based on the rule of law, then the law applies to every citizen of this country, even if the citizen happens to be Erich Honecker." In "Interview," p. 2, cited in note 8 above.

10. See Donald Kommers, "Basic Rights and Constitutional Review," in C. Schweizer, D. Karsten, R. Spencer, R. Cole, D. Kommers, and A. Nicholls, eds., *Politics and Government in the Federal Republic of Germany, Basic Documents* (Coventry: Berg, 1984), p. 84.

11. See Article 315 of *Vertrag zwischen der Bundesrepublik Deutschland und der Deutschen Demokratischen Republik über die Herstellung der Einheit Deutschlands* (Bonn: Presse- und Informationsamt, 1990), p. 925. There were exceptions to this general rule. For example, the FRG reserved the right to apply West German law to offenses committed in the GDR when its own penal code was more lenient than the East German code. On the Unification Treaty, see Peter Quint, "The Constitutional Law of German Unification," *Maryland Law Review*, 50, no. 3 (1991): 475–631; and Paul Schwartz, "Constitutional Change and Constitutional Legitimation: The Example of German Unification," *Houston Law Review* 31, no. 4 (Winter 1994): 1027–1104.

12. This is not to say that German courts were *necessarily* bound to exclude suprapositive norms from their decisions but only that, in this particular case, both jurists and politicians reasoned that it was most appropriate to emphasize the positive law. On the tension between these norms within the Basic Law, see Donald Kommers, *The Constitutional Jurisprudence of the Federal Republic of Germany* (Durham: Duke University Press, 1989), p. 43.

13. Klaus Kinkel, "Wiedervereinigung und Strafrecht," *Juristen Zeitung* 47, no. 10 (May 22, 1992): 487.

14. Ibid., p. 487. I am aware that many German legal terms, such as *Totschlag*, cannot be perfectly rendered in English translation. However, in deciding upon translations, I have sought to use conventional terms that suit the general purposes of this essay.

15. On the sequencing of the trials, see Wesel, *Ein Staat vor Gericht*, p. 33. On the borderguard trials, Joachim Hruschke, "Die Todesschüsse an der Berliner Mauer vor Gericht," *Juristen Zeitung*, no. 13 (1992): 665–670; Jörg Polakiewicz, "Verfassungs- und völkerrechtliche Aspekte der strafrechtlichen Ahndung des Schußwaffeneinsatzes an der innerdeutschen Grenze," *Europäische Grundrechte Zeitschrift* 19, no. 9–10 (June 5, 1992): 177–190; Antje Petersen, "The First Berlin Border Guard Trial," *Occasional Paper* no. 15 (Bloomington, Ind.: Indiana Center on Global Change and World Peace, December 1992), pp. 1–39; Kif Augustine Adams, "What is Just? The Rule of Law and Natural Law in the Trials of Former East German Border Guards," *Stanford Journal of International Law*, no. 29 (1993): 271–314; Herwig Roggemann, "Zur Strafbarkeit der Mauerschützen," *Deutsch-deutsche Rechts-Zeitschrift*, no. 1 (1993): 10–19.

16. Cited in Petersen, "The First Berlin Border Guard Trial," pp. 24–25.

17. See Seidel's ruling, Landgericht Berlin ([523] 2 Js 48/90 [9/91]) of January 20, 1992, pp. 136–140. Seidel noted that in citing Radbruch, he was drawing an implicit parallel with the Nazi regime whose crimes, he admitted, were more extensive than those of the GDR. "Nonetheless," he added, "the court has no misgivings about following this legal approach in this case, for the protection of human life enjoys general validity and cannot be dependent upon a specific number of killings."

18. Ibid., p. 156.

19. Ibid., pp. 156–163.

20. For forceful critiques of Seidel's reasoning, see Wesel, *Ein Staat vor Gericht*, pp. 33–43; Adams, "What is Just?," pp. 298–300; and Petersen, "The First Berlin Border Guard Trial," p. 38. In March 1993, Germany's high appeals court, the Bundesgerichtshof, showed its reservations with the ruling. The court lifted the decision against one of the defendants and suspended the sentence against the other. Most significant for our purposes, the court explicitly based its judgment upon preexisting GDR law. See the ruling of March 25, 1993 (5 StR 418/92).

21. See the ruling of the Landgericht Berlin ([518] 2 Js 63/90 KLs [57/91]) of February 5, 1992, pp. 50–52.

22. Ibid., pp. 60, 63, 66–67.

23. In two respects, the court differed slightly with Tepperwein's reasoning. It took issue with a claim that it was unlawful for border guards to use "automatic fire" in preventing escape attempts. It also appealed to international law in judging East German border fortifications incompatible with the GDR's participation in the International Convention on Civil and Political Rights. Yet for our purposes, the high court's ruling was most significant in upholding Tepperwein's use of East German law. For the court's decision (5 StR 370/92), see *Neue Juristische Wochenschrift*, no. 2 (1993): 141–149. In contrast to my emphasis on domestic law, this trial and related proceedings have been analyzed from the standpoint of international law in an informative essay by Gunnar Schuster, "The Criminal Prosecution of Former GDR Officials" (unpublished).

24. The German term is *mittelbare Mittäterschaft*.

25. *Anklageschrift, Staatsanwaltschaft bei dem Kammergericht Berlin*, pp. 770–771. I am grateful to the Berlin Prosecutor General's Office for providing me with the normally confidential sections of the indictment dealing with the "legal justification" (*rechtliche Würdigung*) of the case.

26. For historical evidence supporting this position, see Peter Möbius and Helmut Trotnow, "Das Mauer-Komplott: Honecker verschärft die Teilung von Tag zu Tag," *Die Zeit*, August 16, 1991, p. 13; and Wolfgang Leonhard, "Erich Honecker und die Berliner Mauer," *Kursbuch*, no. 111 (February 1993): 125–131.

27. See the short form of the indictment, reprinted in Peter Richter, *Kurzer Prozeß* (Berlin: Elefanten Press, 1993), pp. 145–151. (This version of the indictment was released on November 30, 1992. The court reduced to twelve the number of charges against the defendants to simplify the proceedings.) For historical evidence supporting the court's reasoning, see Werner Filmer and Heribert Schwan, *Opfer der Mauer: Die geheimen Protokolle des Todes* (Munich: C. Bertelsmann, 1991), pp. 373–394.

28. For differing accounts of the trial, see Jacqueline Hénard, *Geschichte vor Gericht* (Berlin: Corso bei Siedler, 1993), pp. 57–74; Richter, *Kurzer Prozeß*, pp. 15–17; Erich Selbmann, *Der Prozeß* (Berlin: Spotless, 1993), pp. 6–70; Wesel, *Ein Staat vor Gericht*, chapter 1, 2, 5, passim; Rosenberg, *The Haunted Land*, chapter 8; and "On With the Show," *The New Yorker* 68, no. 11

(January 11, 1993): 23–26. The last account was penned by the wife of one of Honecker's attorneys.

29. Honecker's statement before the court is reprinted in Richter, *Kurzer Prozeß*, pp. 159–175. Feigning modesty, Honecker advised the court (p. 167) that the indictment against him gave him no choice, "without being an historian, [but] to recapitulate the history that had led to the [construction of the] Wall."

30. See Kommers, "Basic Rights," p. 114.

31. All charges against Stoph were finally dropped for reasons of poor health in July 1993, followed by the dismissal of charges against Mielke for similar reasons a year later. Mielke was incarcerated, however, for his conviction in the other case. In February 1995, the Federal Constitutional Court rejected his request for an appeal of the conviction.

32. Honecker outlived this prediction by only half a year; he died in Chile on May 29, 1994.

33. See VerfGH Beschluß (55/92), reprinted in *Juristenzeitung*, no. 5 (1993), 259–261. The court based its decision squarely on Article 1 of the Basic Law. For a detailed treatment of the legal issues, see Klaus Lüderssen, *Der Staat geht unter—das Unrecht bleibt?* (Frankfurt am Main: Suhrkamp, 1992), pp. 98–105. For reasons beyond the purposes of this essay, some observers contended that the court exceeded its competence in coming to this judgment. Among the voluminous critical accounts, see D. Meurer, "Der Verfassungsgerichtshof und das Strafverfahren," *Juristische Rundschau*, no. 3 (March 1993): 89–95; R. Bartlsperger, "Einstellung des Strafverfahrens von Verfassungs wegen," *Deutsches Verwaltungsblatt* 108, no. 7 (April 1, 1993): 333–349; and J. Berkemann, "Ein Landesverfassungsgericht als Revisionsgericht," *Neue Zeitschrift für Verwaltungsrecht* 12, no. 5 (May 15, 1993): 409–419.

34. *Süddeutsche Zeitung*, January 14, 1993, and *Süddeutsche Zeitung*, January 16/17, 1994.

35. Keßler's and Streletz's defense arguments are reprinted in Richter, *Kurzer Prozeß*, pp. 207–214, 222–231.

36. Bräutigam's dismissal from the case was as odd as some of the proceedings. The judge was not removed for reasons of political bias, as one might have expected, but instead because he sought, bizarrely, to obtain Honecker's autograph for a court official.

37. For the main sections of the court's decision (Landgericht Berlin, Urteil vom 16.9.93—[527] 2 Js 26/90 Ks 10 [92]), see "Urteil gegen ehem. Mitglieder des Nationalen Verteidigungsrates der DDR," *Neue Justiz*, no. 5 (1994): 210–214.

38. Ibid., p. 213.

39. Ibid., p. 212. Also see *Süddeutsche Zeitung*, September 17, 1993; *The Week in Germany* (German Information Center), September 24, 1993; Peter Jochen Winters, "Ein Sieg der Gerechtigkeit," *Deutschland Archiv*, no. 10 (1993): 1121–1122.

40. United Press International report, September 16, 1993.

41. *The Week in Germany* (German Information Center), September 24, 1993.

42. For the court's decision, see the Bundesgerichtshof press release of July 26, 1994 (As: 5 StR 98/94).

43. See the ruling of November 3, 1992 (5 StR 370/92), cited in *Neue Juristische Wochenschrift*, no. 2 (1993): 146.

44. Otto Kirchheimer, *Political Justice: The Use of Legal Procedure for Political Ends* (Princeton: Princeton University Press, 1961), p. 336.

45. Neal Ascherson, in *The Independent*, August 2, 1992.

46. Jens Reich, "À la lanterne?" *Kursbuch*, no. 111 (February 1993): 11.

47. In one study, the Allensbach Institute found that 73 percent of the eastern Germans it interviewed were unconvinced that the law was applied equally to all Germans; 72 percent felt themselves personally not well protected. See *Frankfurter Allgemeine Zeitung*, March 8, 1995. On the continuing problems of reuniting the two German populations, see the epilogue to the paperback edition of my study, *Germany Divided: From the Wall to Reunification* (Princeton: Princeton University Press, 1994), pp. 229–243.

48. See "Interview mit Ernst Benda," *Deutschland Archiv* 25, no. 12 (1992): 1341.

49. See Ronald Dworkin, Introduction to *Nunca Más: The Report of the Argentine National Commission on the Disappeared* (New York: Farrar, Straus, and Giroux, 1986), pp. xvii-xxii. That these trials were carried to their conclusion is significant, regardless of the government's later decision to pardon those involved. On this subject, see chapter 4 in this volume by Acuña and Smulovitz.

50. Ibid., pp. xxiv.

51. For this distinction, see the interview with State Attorney Bernhard Jahntz, in Dietmar Jochum, *Das Politbüro auf der Anklagebank* (Berlin: Magnus Verlag, 1996), p. 365.

52. The indictment (25/2 Js 20/92) is printed in ibid., pp. 135-37.

53. For Schabowski's speech, see ibid., p. 292–293. Ironically, Schabowski was the individual who, in a rambling press conference on November 9, 1989, inadvertently announced the opening of the Berlin Wall.

54. On this elementary distinction, see Karl Jaspers, *The Question of German Guilt*, trans. E. B. Ashton (Westport, Conn.: Greenwood Press, 1978), pp. 31–32.

55. See, for example, the statement by the SED's last general secretary, Egon Krenz, in Jochum, *Das Politbüro*, op cit., p. 242.

56. Ibid., p. 354.

9

Retrospective Justice:
International Law and the South African Model

John Dugard

THE PHENOMENON of retrospective justice is not new. History is full of cases in which successor regimes have dealt with the crimes of their predecessors by administering justice retrospectively. While pre–World War II history provides precedents of both punishment and amnesty, it is of little help today. The reason for this is that the subject has acquired an international dimension as a result of the growth of international human rights jurisprudence, the recognition of international crimes, and the establishment of international tribunals in Nuremberg, Tokyo, and Rwanda[1] to try those guilty of crimes committed by the leaders of the previous regime.

Unfortunately, transitional societies are not always as sensitive as they might be to this international dimension. There are several recent instances in which a successor regime, preoccupied with the immediate problem of dealing with the crimes of its predecessor, has failed to give adequate attention to international law and has proceeded to punish or, conversely, to forgive in the context of national law alone. Inevitably, opponents of such political settlements invoke international norms. If the successor regime is brutal, it is accused of failing to comply with international human rights norms, particularly in the field of procedural justice. If it grants amnesty to its predecessors, it is accused of failing to prosecute international crimes.

South Africa provides an example of a society in which considerations of reconciliation are seen to be paramount. Already, the course it has chosen has been challenged by the families of victims of the apartheid security apparatus who demand justice in the form of prosecution or civil claims rather than disclosure followed by amnesty. In this essay I shall examine the applicability of international law to the South African situation; the course followed by South Africa; the possible international consequences of such a choice; and the prospects for success of the South African model. Of course, the experience of every transitional society is different, dependent upon its own history. But none is unique. So it is with South Africa. The course it has chosen to pursue in dealing with the crimes of the apartheid era has been modeled on the experience of other countries, particularly Chile and Argentina. In turn, we can expect that its example will become a precedent for other societies to follow or discard.

The Applicability of International Norms to South Africa

The apartheid order was a legal order. Most of the injustices perpetrated by successive apartheid governments between 1948 and 1990 were committed in the name of the law.[2] Millions were deprived of their South African citizenship in order to provide the Bantustan states with citizens;[3] millions were arrested and imprisoned for violating influx control laws which required Africans to produce identity documents ("passes") on demand by a police officer and prohibited their free movement; and millions were forcibly relocated in order to achieve territorial and residential segregation. Thousands were detained without trial under arbitrary security laws and imprisoned for opposing apartheid. Many of these were mercilessly interrogated in solitary confinement under laws that permitted such treatment. The entire population was classified along racial lines and racial "purity" was maintained by laws which prohibited social mixing, sexual relations, and marriage between different groups. Those classified as "nonwhite" were denied the franchise and given inferior education, health care, social welfare benefits, and housing.

Other injustices were committed by officers of the regime acting outside the law but with the apparent blessing of the authorities. Detainees were physically and mentally tortured by their custodians under security laws that were silent on the subject of torture but permitted the unsupervised interrogation of suspects held in solitary confinement for months, and sometimes years. Political activists, such as Steve Biko and Mathew Goniwe, were killed by members of the security forces acting under the ostensible authority of their commanders. Others simply "disappeared" after their arrest. In the last years of apartheid, many were killed by members of a mysterious agency known as the "Third Force," generally believed to have been members of the security forces charged with the task of destroying the African National Congress (ANC). All these cases involved the perpetration of the common-law crimes of murder, culpable homicide, assault, and kidnapping. However, prosecutions were not forthcoming, given the authorities' explicit or implied role in sanctioning them.

The first category of injustices—the movement of populations and the detentions—were not crimes under national law. Indeed they were prescribed by national law. They were, however, contrary to international human rights norms contained in the International Covenant on Civil and Political Rights, the International Convention on the Elimination of All Forms of Racial Discrimination, the Convention against Torture and Other Cruel, Inhuman or Degrading Treatment or Punishment, and customary international human rights law. In addition, they were crimes under international law. The Convention against Torture obliges signatory states to prosecute acts defined as torture,[4] and it has been argued that the International Covenant on Civil and Political Rights requires states to investigate complaints of serious violations of physical integrity and to prosecute those responsible.[5] More important, the implementation of the policy of apartheid was condemned as "criminal" by the General Assembly of the United Nations in many resolutions[6] and labeled as a species of crimes against humanity in violation of international law by the 1973 International Convention on the Suppression and Punishment of the Crime of Apartheid, which by the end of apartheid in 1990 had been ratified by eighty-nine states. This Convention criminalized the entire legal order of apartheid in declaring that the crime of apartheid "shall apply to the following inhuman acts committed for the purpose of establishing and maintaining domination by one racial group of persons over any other racial group of persons and systematically oppressing them":[7]

(a) Denial to a member or members of a racial group or groups of the right to life and liberty of person:
   (i) By murder of members of a racial group or groups;
   (ii) By the infliction upon the members of a racial group or groups of serious bodily or mental harm by the infringement of their freedom or dignity, or by subjecting them to torture or to cruel, inhuman or degrading treatment or punishment;
   (iii) By arbitrary arrest and illegal imprisonment of the members of a racial group or groups;
(b) Deliberate imposition on a racial group or groups of living conditions calculated to cause its or their physical destruction in whole or in part;
(c) Any legislative measures and other measures calculated to prevent a racial group or groups from participation in the political, social, economic and cultural life of the country and the deliberate creation of conditions preventing the full development of such a group or groups, in particular by denying to members of a racial group or groups basic human rights and freedoms, including the right to work, the right to form recognised trade unions, the right to education, the right to leave and to return to their country, the right to freedom of opinion and expression, and the right to freedom of peaceful assembly and association;
(d) Any measures, including legislative measures, designed to divide the population along racial lines by the creation of separate reserves and ghettos for the members of a racial group or groups, the prohibition of mixed marriages among members of various racial groups, the expropriation of landed property belonging to a racial group or groups or to members thereof;
(e) Exploitation of the labour of the members of a racial group or groups, in particular by submitting them to forced labour;
(f) Persecution of organisations and persons, by depriving them of fundamental rights and freedoms, because they oppose *apartheid*.

International criminal responsibility is attached "irrespective of the motive involved, to individuals, members of organisations and institutions and representatives of the state" guilty of committing the crime of apartheid.[8] Offenders are to be tried by the courts of any state party "which may acquire jurisdiction over the person of the accused" or by an international criminal court.[9]

Although acts committed in pursuance of the policy of apartheid and under the laws of apartheid were criminal under several international conventions, it is doubtful whether the norms contained in these conventions were binding on South Africa at the time they were committed. Before 1994, when apartheid was brought to an end constitutionally,[10] South Africa was a party to only one treaty dealing with human rights, namely the Charter of the United Nations, which in Articles 55 and 56 requires member states to promote "universal respect for, and observance of, human rights and fundamental freedoms for all without distinction as to race, sex, language or religion." Since then, South Africa has signed but not ratified the International Covenant on Civil and Political Rights, the International Covenant on Economic, Social and Cultural Rights, the International Convention on the Elimination of All Forms of Racial Discrimination, and the Convention against Torture.

Whether customary international law criminalized the practices of apartheid during the apartheid era is unclear. Suggestions that apartheid constituted an international crime under the customary-law rules governing genocide, torture, and crimes against humanity require consideration because, if established, this would eliminate the argument that any attempt to punish the functionaries of the apartheid state for crimes of apartheid would violate the prohibition on retroactive punishment contained in several human rights instruments. Article 15(1) of the International Covenant on Civil and Political Rights, for example, provides that "[n]o one shall be held guilty of any criminal offense on account of any act or omission which did not constitute a criminal offense, under national or *international law*, at the time when it was committed."

The argument that apartheid violated a customary-law rule prohibiting genocide is difficult to sustain. In the first instance, it is by no means certain that the Genocide Convention of 1948 has itself become part of customary international law. Even if it has, it is doubtful whether it can be seriously argued that apartheid was committed "with intent to *destroy*, in whole or in part, an ethnical [or] racial . . . group" as required by Article 1 of the Genocide Convention.

That apartheid was intended to subordinate "nonwhite" racial groups in South Africa to the interests of the white group is clear. That many died and suffered in the course of the implementation of apartheid is clear. But, it is unlikely that the National Party, with whites outnumbered by ten to one, ever intended to *destroy* the African, Indian or "coloured" groups in South Africa. Certainly, there were no instances of deliberate mass killings or "ethnic cleansings" of the kind associated with the Nazis, Khmer Rouge, or Bosnian Serbs.

Torture is today recognized as a crime under customary international law. Treaties, national legislation, and judicial decisions[11] provide adequate evidence of *usus* and *opinio juris* to warrant such a conclusion. Although the law of apartheid did not authorize physical torture, it is highly arguable that laws[12] permitting custodial interrogation of detainees for long periods of time, without access to lawyers, family, private medical doctors, or anyone to whom the detainee might complain, implicitly authorized mental torture and in practice permitted physical torture.[13] That the South African authorities were unconcerned about mental torture, at least, was confirmed to the satisfaction of the present writer in a meeting with the Minister of Justice, Jimmy Kruger, and his two most senior police officers, Prinsloo and Geldenhuys, in 1977, when the minister and his police officers denied that mental cruelty constituted torture.

Today, it is beyond serious dispute that customary international law recognizes crimes against humanity.[14] It is also clear that "crimes against humanity do not require a connection to international armed conflict."[15] Although the precise content of this class of crimes is unsettled, it is accepted that systematic "persecutions on political, racial, and religious grounds" qualify as crimes against humanity.[16] Moreover, in the *Barbie* case, the French Cour de Cassation went further and defined crimes against humanity as "Inhumane acts and persecution committed in a systematic manner in the name of a state practicing a policy of ideological supremacy, not only against persons by reason of their membership in a racial or religious community, but also against the opponents of that policy, whatever the form of their opposition."[17] These definitions, and the fact that apartheid has been labeled as a crime against humanity by resolutions of the General Assembly, the 1973 International Convention on the Suppression and Punishment of the Crime of Apartheid, and the 1968 Convention on the Non-Applicability of Statutory Limitations to War Crimes and Crimes against Humanity, have led to widespread agreement that the practices of apartheid constituted crimes against humanity.[18] Certainly, it is difficult to resist the conclusion that forced population removals and the systematic persecution of members of the ANC and Pan Africanist Congress (PAC) fall under this rubric.

The first category of injustices linked with apartheid as systematic racial oppression qualified only as international crimes, by reason of the legislative approval of apartheid in domestic law. In contrast, the second category of injustices referred to above—namely, murder, torture, and "disappearances"—constituted crimes under both international law and South African domestic law.

For forty years, apartheid featured on the agenda of the United Nations. More than any other issue, it contributed to the weakening of claims to exclusive domestic jurisdiction under Article 2(7) of the United Nations Charter. Apartheid was regarded by all states—except the South African government itself—as a matter of international concern. Moreover, a majority of states viewed apartheid not only as a violation of international human rights norms but also as an international crime. In these circumstances, it is understandable that international norms, rules, and expectations should have played a role in the strategies employed by the democratic successor to the apartheid regime to deal with the principal perpetrators of the injustices of apartheid.

South Africa's Response to the Crimes of Apartheid

Although apartheid was an international crime, there was no suggestion from the United Nations after the peaceful transition from apartheid to democracy between 1990 and 1994 that those responsible for the worst features of apartheid should be brought to international justice. By 1994, the South African situation was no longer seen as a threat or potential threat to international peace, and it would have been impossible to justify the establishment of an international criminal tribunal along the lines of those established for the former Yugoslavia and Rwanda under Chapter VII of the United Nations

Charter.[19] The new South African government could have decided to prosecute members of the former regime for the atrocities of apartheid, in the way that collaborators were prosecuted in France, Belgium, and the Netherlands after World War II;[20] Nazis were prosecuted before German courts in the aftermath of the war;[21] the Greek colonels and their officials were prosecuted after 1974,[22] as we have seen in chapter 2 of this volume; and the officials of the Mengistu regime are currently being prosecuted in Ethiopia. Yet, political factors made such a choice impossible, particularly since the National Party participated actively in the transition from apartheid to democracy and was to be rewarded with places in a government of national unity to rule South Africa under an interim constitution. Although some observers reminded the African National Congress of its commitment to prosecution during the time it waged war against the apartheid state, such appeals were not taken seriously. Consequently, the legal difficulties that would have followed from such a decision, particularly the fact that it would have been necessary to invalidate apartheid legislation by retroactive legislation to allow such prosecutions, were not considered.

Politically there seemed to be only two options open to the negotiators of the new political order: unconditional amnesty, understandably favored by the National Party, or conditional amnesty.[23] The latter option was chosen. South Africa's interim constitution, to apply from 1994 to 1997, was drafted by the representatives of the country's twenty-six major political groupings at the World Trade Centre in Kempton Park on the outskirts of Johannesburg. After months of heated negotiations, they agreed upon a constitutional blueprint that was to be given final endorsement by the South African Parliament, through which the National Party had ruled for forty-five years. This draft constitution contained no provision for amnesty. However, in the period between the document's approval at Kempton Park and its adoption by Parliament at the end of 1993, the ANC and the National Party hammered out a postscript to the draft constitution behind closed doors on the subject of amnesty. This postscript, generally termed the "postamble" to the constitution, which appears in the interim constitution, commits post-apartheid

South Africa to a policy of reconciliation, to "a need for understanding but not for vengeance." In pursuance of this goal it provides:

> In order to advance such reconciliation and reconstruction, amnesty shall be granted in respect of acts, omissions and offences associated with political objectives and committed in the course of conflicts of the past. To this end, Parliament, under this Constitution, shall adopt a law determining a firm cut-off date, which shall be a date after 8 October 1990 and before 6 December 1993, and providing for the mechanisms, criteria and procedures, including tribunals, if any, through which such amnesty will be dealt with at any time after the law has been passed.

In 1995, Parliament enacted the Promotion of National Unity and Reconciliation Act 34 of 1995 which gives effect to this policy of conditional amnesty. Its preamble identifies the principal goals and procedures to be followed: reconciliation, amnesty, reparation, and the search for truth. On the search for truth, it declares that "it is deemed necessary to establish the truth in relation to past events as well as the motives for and circumstances in which gross violation of human rights have occurred, and to make the findings known in order to prevent a repetition of such acts in future."

The Act also provides for the creation of a Truth and Reconciliation Commission of seventeen members, appointed by the President in consultation with the Cabinet, to establish a complete picture of "the gross violations of human rights" committed between March 1960 (the time of the massacre at Sharpeville) and 1993 by means of hearings and investigations, to facilitate the granting of amnesty, to recommend reparation to the victims of human rights abuses, and to prepare a report containing recommendations of measures to prevent the future violations of human rights.[24] A commission broadly representative of the peoples of South Africa, presided over by Desmond Tutu, Nobel Peace Laureate and Archbishop of Cape Town, was appointed early in 1996 and has begun the task of conducting public hearings into human rights violations. This commission is assisted by a Committee on Human Rights Violations, responsible for investigating "gross violations of human rights,"[25] a

mittee on Amnesty,[26] a Committee on Reparation and Rehabili-
on,[27] and an investigative unit.[28]

The Committee on Amnesty, consisting of three judges and two
commissioners, occupies a pivotal place in the process. It considers
applications for amnesty and may grant amnesty if it is satisfied that
the applicant has committed an act constituting "a gross violation of
human rights,"[29] if he or she has made a full disclosure of all relevant
facts, and if the act to which the application relates is "an act associated with a political objective committed in the course of conflicts of
the past."[30] The criteria for deciding whether an act is one "associated
with a political objective" are drawn from the principles generally
used in extradition law for determining whether an offense is political in character. Among other factors, the criteria include the motive
of the offender; the context in which the act took place and whether it
was committed "in the course of or as part of a political uprising, dis-
turbance or event"; the gravity of the act; the objective of the act and
whether it was "primarily directed at a political opponent or State
property or personnel or against private property or individuals";
and the relationship between the act and the political objective pursued, and "in particular the directness and proximity of the relationship and the proportionality of the act to the objective pursued."[31] A
person granted amnesty shall not be criminally or civilly liable for
the act in question.[32]

There are two unusual features of the South African truth and reconciliation process. First, it is not confined to acts committed in fur-
therance of the apartheid state. Members of liberation movements,
notably the ANC and the PAC, together with officers of the apartheid
regime, fall within the terms of reference of the commission.[33] Secondly, the commission is not empowered to investigate the injustices
of apartheid itself.

The "gross violations of human rights" investigated by the commission[34] and the Committee on Amnesty[35] are confined to "the
killing, abduction, torture or severe ill-treatment of any person."
Clearly, the phrase "severe ill-treatment of any person" is to be narrowly interpreted to mean physical ill-treatment as this accords with
the categories of crimes that precede it. Thus "gross human rights violations" are limited to acts that were crimes under the apartheid legal

order, such as murder, culpable homicide, kidnapping, and assault. There is no attempt to bring within the ambit of the inquiry acts that constituted a crime under international law but were not criminal under the law of apartheid. As we have seen, many of the lawfully prescribed practices of apartheid relating to systematic discrimination and persecution on racial grounds but not involving physical violence to the person, might be categorized as crimes against humanity under customary international law or as crimes of apartheid under the 1973 Convention on the Suppression and Punishment of the Crimes of Apartheid.

Two factors explain the decision to limit the commission's scope of inquiry in this way. The first was the desire to avoid the suggestion that South Africa was engaged in a form of victor's justice directed exclusively at the vanquished. Hence, "gross violations of human rights" are carefully defined to embrace the crimes of both officers of the apartheid regime and members of the liberation movements. Second, the new government was determined to demonstrate its commitment to legality and to the rule of law by avoiding any attempt to invalidate the offensive laws of apartheid retroactively.

On May 8, 1996, the South African Constitutional Assembly gave its approval to a "final" constitution to replace the interim constitution of 1993. This constitution, whose compliance with thirty-four principles contained in the interim constitution is still to be certified by the Constitutional Court,[36] will come into effect in 1997. It includes a schedule providing that all the provisions relating to amnesty contained in the 1993 interim constitution are deemed to be part of the new constitution.[37]

The International-Law Implications
of South Africa's Amnesty Process

Clearly, the truth and reconciliation process chosen by South Africa is out of line with international law, for it envisages the granting of amnesty to persons guilty of serious crimes under international law. The "gross violations of human rights" in respect of which amnesty is to be granted include the *international* crimes of torture and crimes against humanity. Furthermore, it appears that crimes against humanity and crimes under the Convention on the Suppression and Punishment of the Crime of Apartheid that fall outside the jurisdiction of the Truth and Reconciliation Commission are to go unpunished. This feature of both the 1993 and the 1996 constitutions contrasts with other provisions in these constitutions which seek to ensure that international law will be respected by the legislature, the executive, and the courts, particularly in the field of human rights.[38]

In theory, this conflict between national legislation and international law could create serious difficulties for South Africa. First, it could be argued that the new South African government, as successor to the National Party government, is responsible for the internationally wrongful acts of its predecessor and that it could only escape international responsibility by prosecuting those responsible for such acts. This would accord with the principles that "the new regime takes the place of the former regime in all matters affecting the international rights and obligations of the state"[39] and that the successor government is obliged to investigate international human rights violations and to prosecute those responsible.[40] Both the judgment of the American Court of Human Rights in the Velásquez Rodríguez case,[41] involving a successor regime in Honduras, and the decision of the Inter-American Commission of Human Rights in cases involving successor regimes in Uruguay and Argentina,[42] support this conclusion. Secondly, it is also theoretically possible that apartheid's criminals might still face prosecution before the domestic courts of foreign states. For example, signatories to the Convention on the Suppression and Punishment of the Crime of Apartheid that have enacted domestic legislation to implement the Convention might decide to prosecute officials of the apartheid regime, as might other countries, such as Canada,[43] with domestic legislation for the prosecution of crimes against humanity.

In practice, neither development is probable. States are as unlikely to demand that South Africa comply with its international responsibility to prosecute apartheid's criminals as they are to prosecute apartheid's criminals who come within their jurisdiction. Understandably, the international community's joy and relief that apartheid has been abandoned and peacefully replaced with a democratically elected government is so great that it is prepared to accept without question the new South African administration's procedure for dealing with the past. Moreover, there are no international remedies under international human rights conventions to which aggrieved individuals may resort—as in the case of Velásquez Rodríguez or the complaints against Uruguay and Argentina—to satisfy their demands for justice in the face of South Africa's amnesty program.

However, the great unlikelihood that South Africa's scheme for dealing with the past will be challenged internationally does not mean that the conflict between international law and national decision is without importance. Such conflicts shape domestic perceptions of justice and fuel discontent among those dissatisfied with the granting of amnesty. In this way, they may also affect the perceived success of the exercise in reconciliation.

The interim constitution of 1993 took no account of international crimes. The 1996 constitution does, however, qualify the prohibition on retrospectivity in the case of international crimes by providing that everyone has the right "not to be convicted for an act or omission that was not an offence under either national *or international law* at the time it was committed or omitted" (section 35 [3][1]). This clause would seem to open the way for the prosecution for crimes against humanity of those not granted amnesty under the 1993 constitution and the Promotion of National Unity and Reconciliation Act. In particular, it might be used to prosecute persons guilty of racial persecution qualifying as a crime against humanity but not falling under the Promotion of National Unity and Reconciliation Act because it did not involve physical violence to those persecuted. Prosecutions of this kind are unlikely in light of the declared policy of the ANC and because they would raise a conflict between the prescriptions of the apartheid legal order and international law. Such prosecutions might, however, serve to achieve an integration of international norms and the process of truth and reconciliation.

The South African Model: Prospects for National Success

During the days of the ANC's armed struggle against apartheid, the precedent of Nuremberg featured prominently in its rhetoric.

Apartheid's criminals, it was hoped, would be tried for crimes against humanity before specially constituted tribunals, comprising international judges and South Africans untainted by apartheid. Lists were compiled of the main offenders, particularly those responsible for the torture of detainees. This vision was, of course, premised on the victory of the ANC over the apartheid regime in the armed struggle.

This did not happen. Neither side won the war. The National Party abandoned apartheid under pressure from within and without, and the ANC, aware that the fall of the Soviet empire made the continued armed struggle pointless, agreed to a negotiated settlement. Thus, the political compact that emerged from the negotiations between 1990 and 1993 was a compromise between the two major forces in South African society, the ANC and the National Party, backed by the armed forces and police. In these circumstances, large-scale prosecutions of those responsible for apartheid were impossible. The National Party would simply have withdrawn from the political compromise. The choice was therefore between forgetting the past completely—total amnesty—and qualified or conditional amnesty. Decision-makers turned to Chile and Argentina for guidance, for in both these societies the new regime had sought to deal with the past, in the presence of a powerful and undefeated army, by means of truth and reconciliation. Nuremberg was fast forgotten.

From the outset, voices were raised against this choice. For example, the families of those who had died at the hands of the security police led the opposition to a truth commission as a substitute for prosecution. Strangely, however, no voices were raised in favor of prosecution of the functionaries of apartheid, those responsible for race classification, population removals, the enforcement of the pass laws, the administration of Bantustan states, and other violations.

The Truth and Reconciliation Commission's work will continue until the end of 1997. Public hearings have been held in many parts of the country at which the victims of apartheid and their families have recounted the horror of those days in moving language. Those who suffered at the hands of the liberation movements have also testified before the commission. In contrast, although the Committee on Amnesty has begun work, it has yet to address the "hard cases" presented by gross human rights violations perpetrated by leaders of the security forces. Of course, it would be premature to judge the likely outcome of the process. But we can at least consider the advantages and disadvantages of the choices South Africa has already made.

Advantages

The exposure of the past and qualified amnesty are part of a broad process of reconciliation in democratic South Africa. Institutionally, this process finds form in the government of national unity,[44] the inclusion of members of the apartheid regime in bodies such as the Human Rights Commission[45] and the Truth and Reconciliation Commission itself, and the continued employment of high-ranking officials of the previous government. Politically, it is a policy that has been pursued with great vigor and success, in word and deed, by President Mandela and his government. It is a process that won the hearts of millions throughout the world and served as a hope and inspiration to many.

From a legal perspective, this process also has much to recommend it. It has removed the specter of victor's justice by discounting Nuremberg and by subjecting both the functionaries of apartheid and the members of the national liberation movements to the same treatment in granting amnesty. It has maintained respect for the principle of legality by not invalidating the apartheid legal order with retroactive effect. And it has saved the present South African judiciary, mainly appointed by the apartheid regime, from the awkward task of trying officers for crimes committed under a legal order of which they were once a part.

Additionally, persons who committed "gross violations of human rights" with a "political objective," under the definition of the Promotion of National Unity and Reconciliation Act, are not unconditionally exonerated from prosecution. Moreover, those who fail to apply for amnesty or to make a full disclosure of their crimes will not be granted amnesty and may be prosecuted instead. In fact, several important prosecutions have been initiated against high-ranking officials of the former security forces. Thus, the possibility of obtaining justice through the ordinary courts has not been fully excluded, despite the acquittal of the former Minister of Defence, Magnus Malan, and several of his generals in August 1996.

Disadvantages

The emphasis on truth and reconciliation minimizes the memory of apartheid. Dictators have frequently committed egregious human rights violations in the pursuit of power or in the implementation of a political ideology premised on the perceived advancement of a people's welfare. Yet modern history provides few examples of the systematic suppression of human rights in the name of an ideology premised on racial superiority. Nazism and apartheid are the twentieth century's prime examples of such systems. Indeed, the likening of apartheid to Nazism was a frequent refrain during the heyday of apartheid. Is it fair therefore to follow the precedents of Chile and Argentina in such a case? Or to treat the functionaries of apartheid and members of the liberation movements as equals for the purpose of amnesty? Or to forgive the architects of apartheid and to welcome them into the political fold as prodigal politicians? Or to allow them to continue to hold public office in the new order? Does not the very nature of apartheid require a more severe condemnation than conditional amnesty for those guilty of crimes of violence and complete immunity for those functionaries responsible for the atrocities of apartheid itself? Questions of this kind are asked by opponents of the chosen course, and they have not received a satisfactory answer.

Reconciliation serves the broad interests of society and state. But it is not clear that it takes adequate account of the interests of the victims of apartheid. This explains why the families of Steve Biko, Griffiths and Victoria Mxenge, and others challenged the constitutionality of amnesty before South Africa's post-apartheid Constitutional Court in May 1996.[46] Although the court held that the "postamble" to the 1993 constitution providing for amnesty took precedence over a clause in its Bill of Rights guaranteeing access to a court of law for the settlement of disputes and that the amnesty law did not violate the obligation to prosecute offenders for "grave breaches" under the Geneva Conventions on the law of armed conflict, it failed to consider the question whether the law was compatible with customary international law rules for the punishment of crimes against humanity. Like the family of Velásquez Rodríguez[47] and those families who brought complaints against the amnesty laws of Uruguay and Argentina,[48] the applicants in this case found the "truth" to be inadequate and instead sought redress in the form of judicial condemnation by a national court. However, unlike the citizens of Honduras, Uruguay, and Argentina, who enjoyed remedies under international human rights conventions, they have no recourse to international justice.

As we have found, South Africa's chosen course takes little account of international-law norms. This permits opponents of truth and reconciliation to appeal to international justice and to measure the failures of South African justice against the norms of international law. During the apartheid years the victims of the system frequently appealed to international norms as a "higher law" by which the laws of apartheid were to be judged. This resulted in the delegitimation of law and its institutions in South Africa.[49] Now, we might ask: Is the conflict between international and national norms in South Africa over amnesty likely to result in a similar delegitimation of the law?

Both the interim constitution of 1993 and the constitution of 1996 contain a Bill of Rights founded on respect for human dignity, equality, and liberty. Does the toleration of the great injustices of apartheid weaken the moral foundation of the Bill of Rights? Does such toleration serve as a deterrent to others who may in future embark on a course of racism and human rights violations? Are the values of human dignity, equality, and liberty best served by a policy of conditional amnesty that allows those who committed great crimes to go free?

Restoration of fidelity to the law is essential in a society which has been subjected to inhumanity in the name of the law. In one of the great jurisprudential exchanges of our time, H. L. A. Hart and Lon Fuller debated how this might best be achieved in postwar Germany.[50] For Hart, it was necessary to recognize the validity of such laws until they were repudiated by retrospective legislation. For Fuller, it was important that such "lawless laws" not be recognized by law, and that such nonrecognition be confirmed by judicial decision or legislative fiat. Post-apartheid society faces a similar dilemma. No one will deny that reconciliation and stability are values indispensable to the construction of a democratic society. But it is equally important that the memory of apartheid not be merely swept under the carpet of history, for this will undermine the moral foundation of the new order. The laws of apartheid, repealed with prospective effect in the transition years, must be denounced for what they were—expressions of power that failed to comply with the inner morality of the law.[51] South Africa's chosen truth and reconciliation process fails to accomplish this objective. It focuses solely upon those officers of the apartheid state who committed crimes of violence contrary to South African law, without, however, addressing the laws of apartheid or the functionaries who enforced them. By avoiding any denunciation of the laws of apartheid, presumably to avoid charges of retroactive legislation, it thereby fails to restore fidelity to the law.

The South African Model: An International Example?

South Africa's transition from racist authoritarianism to nonracial democracy has been a miracle. Its constitution displays an unsurpassed respect for international human rights norms. Its president has set new standards in toleration and forgiveness. In many respects, South Africa is a model to which other states, particularly those in transition, may aspire. Yet its amnesty process is open to question.

The fact that a society so determined to bring its conduct into line with international law and expectations, after years of international lawlessness, has failed to construct a process for amnesty that complies with international norms, serves to highlight the complexity of this challenge. Every case is different and calls for different constraints and compromises. Yet, drawing upon the experience of countries on different continents and reflecting the evolving norms of international law, there are certain international standards that should guide and shape the efforts of successor regimes to deal with predecessors who have shown no regard for the standards of modern civilization.

Retrospective justice is a difficult exercise. Reconciliation is essential for the building of a new nation. Without knowledge—that is, truth—about the past, this cannot be achieved. But justice, universal justice which transcends the requirements of political expediency, is an essential component of reconciliation. And this requires condemnation of the past as well. In South Africa, it is doubtful whether a just reconciliation can ever be achieved without the retrospective invalidation of the laws of apartheid and the condemnation of those who conceived and maintained this ideology through the instrument of the state. The exposure of the sufferings of bygone years in public hearings before a sympathetic commission, the investigation of atrocities committed by those who have applied for amnesty with little real remorse, and the selective prosecutions of some who committed crimes of violence in pursuance of apartheid, will not heal the mental wounds of the millions whose human dignity was denied for over forty years.

Perhaps the flaw of the South African model of dealing with the past is that it was founded on political compromise and not upon those principles that have emerged from the experience of other nations. An ideal approach to retrospective justice would be one which starts from principle and from the shared wisdom of the past and then proceeds to compromise where political needs dictate. Principle, however, of which the rules of international law form a part, must provide the foundation for a just reconciliation.

NOTES

1. Yugoslavia does not belong to this category as the tribunal established to prosecute those guilty of crimes in the former Yugoslavia aims to try those associated with existing regimes and not former regimes.

2. On these laws, see John Dugard, *Human Rights and the South African Legal Order* (Princeton: Princeton University Press, 1978); John Dugard, ed., *The Last Years of Apartheid: Civil Liberties in South Africa* (New York: Ford Foundation and Foreign Policy Association, 1992).

3. For this aspect of apartheid, see John Dugard, *Recognition and the United Nations* (Cambridge, England: Grotius Publications, 1987), pp. 98–108.

4. Article 4(1).

5. Diane F. Orentlicher, "Settling Accounts: The Duty to Prosecute Human Rights Violations of a Prior Regime," *Yale Law Journal* 100 (1991): 2571; Naomi Roht-Arriaza, ed., *Impunity and Human Rights in International Law and Practice* (New York: Oxford University Press, 1995), chapters 3 and 4.

6. The first resolution of this kind was Resolution 2202A(XXI) of December 16, 1966. Also, see Resolution 2627(XXV) of 1970 and 39/72A of 1984.

7. Article 2.

8. Article 3.

9. Article 5.

10. By the Constitution of the Republic of South Africa, Act 200 of 1993.

11. For example, *Filartiga v Pena Irala* 630 F2d (1980).

12. Section 6 of the Terrorism Act 83 of 1967; section 29 of the Internal Security Act 74 of 1982.

13. The 1984 Convention against Torture defines "torture" as follows: "the term 'torture' means any act by which severe pain or suffering, whether physical or mental, is intentionally inflicted on a person for such purposes as obtaining from him or a third person information or a confession, punishing him for an act he or a third person has committed or is suspected of having committed, or intimidating or coercing him or a third person, or for any reason based on discrimination of any kind, when such pain or suffering is inflicted by or at the instigation of or with the consent or acquiescence of a public official or other person acting in an official capacity. It does not include pain or suffering arising only from, inherent in or incidental to lawful sanctions."

14. See M. Cherif Bassiouni, *Crimes against Humanity in International Criminal Law* (Dordrecht, the Netherlands: Martinus Nijhoff Publishers, 1992).

15. *Prosecutor v Dusko Tadic* (International Criminal Tribunal for the Former Yugoslavia), in *International Legal Materials* 35 (1996): 72.

16. See the definition of crimes against humanity in the Statute of the International Tribunal for the Territory of the Former Yugoslavia, Article 5.

17. *Fédération Nationale des Déporte et Internes Resistants et Patriotes et al v Barbie, 78 International Law Reports*, p. 125.

18. Bassiouni, *Crimes Against Humanity*, pp. at 334–337; Roger Clark, "The Crime of Apartheid," in *International Criminal Law*, ed. M. Cherif Bassiouni (New York: Transnational Publishers, 1986), 1: 299.

19. See the judgment of the International Criminal Tribunal for the Former Yugoslavia on this subject in the *Tadic* case, note 15 above, pp. 42–48.

20. Luc Huyse, "Justice After Transition: On the Choices Successor Elites Make in Dealing with the Past," *Law and Social Inquiry* 20 (1995): 51.

21. Fritz Weinschenk, "The Nazis Before German Courts: The West German War Crimes Trials," *International Lawyer* 10 (1976): 515.

22. *Torture in Greece: The First Torturers' Trial 1975* (London: Amnesty International, 1977).

23. For an account of the political negotiations that preceded the decision on amnesty, see Lynn Berat, "South Africa: Negotiating Change?" in *Impunity and Human Rights*, ed. Roht-Arriaza, p. 267.

24. Section 3.

25. Sections 3(3)(a), 4, 12–15.

26. Sections 3(3)(b) and 16–22.

27. Sections 3(3)(c) and 23–27.

28. Sections 3(3)(d) and 28.
29. Sections 20(1), 19(3)(b)(iii).
30. Section 20(1).
31. Section 20(3).
32. Section 20(7)(a).
33. Section 4(a)(iv).
34. Sections 3(1)(a), 4(a), 14.
35. Section 19(3)(b)(iii).
36. Section 71(2) of the interim constitution.
37. Schedule 6, section 22.
38. See John Dugard, "The Influence of International Human Rights Law on the South African Constitution," *Current Legal Problems* 49 (1995): 305.
39. *Oppenheim's International Law*, ed. Robert Jennings and Arthur Watts (Harlow, Essex, England: Longman, 1992), 1: 234–235.
40. See Orentlicher, "Settling Accounts," p. 2595; Kader Asmal, "Victims, Survivors, and Citizens—Human Rights Reparations and Reconciliation," *South African Journal on Human Rights* 8 (1992): 491.
41. Judgment of July 29, 1988, Series C no. 4, reported in 95 *International Law Reports*, p. 259. In this case, the Inter-American Court of Human Rights declared that "the state has a legal duty to take reasonable steps to prevent human rights violations and to use the means at its disposal to carry out a serious investigation of violations committed within its jurisdiction, to identify those responsible, to impose the appropriate punishment and to ensure the victim adequate compensation" (para 174). It added: "According to the principle of the continuity of the state in international law, responsibility exists both independently of changes of government over a period of time and continuously from the time of the act that creates responsibility to the time when the act is declared illegal. The foregoing is also valid in the area of human rights although, from an ethical or political point of view, the attitude of the new government may be much more respectful of those rights than that of the government in power when the violations occurred" (para 184).
42. Inter-American Commission on Human Rights, Reports nos. 28/92 and 29/92 (October 2, 1992). Discussed by Robert K. Goldman, "Uruguay: Amnesty Law in Violation of Human Rights Convention," *Review of the International Commission of Jurists* (1992), p. 37.
43. For a discussion of the Canadian legislation on crimes against humanity, see *R v Finta*, 82 *International Law Reports*, p. 424.
44. The National Party withdrew from the Government of National Unity in June 1996. The Inkatha Freedom Party, however, remained part of the government together with the African National Congress.
45. Established in terms of section 115 of the interim constitution.
46. *The Azanian Peoples Organization (AZAPO), Biko, Mxenge and Ribeiro v The Government of the Republic of South Africa*, Case CCT 17/96. Judgment delivered on July 25, 1996.
47. See note 41 above.

48. See note 42 above.

49. On this subject, see John Dugard, "The Conflict between International Law and South African Law: Another Divisive Factor in South African Society," *South African Journal on Human Rights* 2 (1986): 1.

50. H. L. A. Hart, "Positivism and the Separation of Law and Morals," *Harvard Law Review* 71 (1958): 593 ff; Lon Fuller, "Positivism and Fidelity to Law—A Reply to Professor Hart," ibid., 630 ff.

51. For more on this subject, see Lon Fuller, *The Morality of Law* (New Haven, Conn.: Yale University Press, 1964).

Index

as means to incorporate military in new government, 116–17
offered to Greek junta members, 49
Parliamentary Resolution D, interpretation by Greek courts, 42–43, 44–45
PASOK (Panhellenic Socialist Movement), 28, 33
Pattakos, S., trial of, 41, 45, 48, 51
Pawlak, Waldemar, 198, 200, 201
PC (Center Alliance) (Poland), 192, 196
People's Poland (Polish People's Republic): memories and legacies of, 186–87, 190, 194–95, 200; view as period of Soviet occupation, 211–12, 221. *See also* Poland
Permanent Organization for Human Rights (Bolivia). *See* APDH
Peronist political party (Argentina): bid for presidency in 1983, 102–3; reaction to leniency ploys, 107; relationship to military, 97, 101
Pilsudski's coup, 206, 213
Pinochet, Augusto, threats to country's new democracy, 9, 10, 24 n.17, 132–33, 151 n.14
Plevrakes, E., 35
Podemski, Stanislaw, 216
Poland: accountability measures taken by, 155, 178–79; current regime as "The Third Republic," 195; electoral politics and attempts to prosecute former rulers, xi; electoral victories of postcommunists, 170–71, 177, 196, 198, 199–200; factional beliefs on how to handle the past, 190–91; independentists in, 190–91, 196, 230 n.11; lack of new constitution, 180–81; policy of nonaccountability, 2; prewar crimes against humanity, 206, 213, 222, 224; reaction to martial law of Jaruzelski regime, 187, 196–97, 205–17; "real socialism" period, 207, 208; redefining of through

symbolic uses of law and lustration, 194–205; Stalinist period, 207, 217–18, 220; use of roundtable in transition of power, 179. *See also* People's Poland
police
    Chile: implication in human rights violations, 128, 146–47; role in investigations of human rights violations, 127, 141
    DINA activities in Chile, 143, 150 n.6
    files of and lustration in Hungary, 156, 171–78
    Greece, removal from power and trials, 38–39, 46–48
    Poland: connections to by potential candidates for public offices, 197; and the Oleksy affair, 203–4
Polish United Workers' Party. *See* PUWP
"Political Dialogue" (1979), instituted by Argentina's military, 100
political parties: under Argentina's junta, 97, 102; revised communist parties as new contenders, 170–71, 177, 196, 198, 199–200; right-wing activities in Poland, 198, 200, 206. *See also individual parties by name*
Popieluszko, Jerzy, 224
Prinsloo, 274
Promotion of National Unity and Reconciliation Act of 1995 (South Africa), 277, 281, 283
Przemky, Grzegorz, 224–25
Przeworski, Adam, 117
PS (Socialist Party) (Bolivia), 68, 71
PSL (Agrarian Party) (Poland), 196, 198, 199, 200
PUWP (Polish United Workers' Party), 189, 196–97, 230 nn.10, 11, 231 n.29; demands that former members be barred from politics, 192; role during possible Soviet intervention, 209–10; satellite parties of, 196, 198